CROSSTALK

American Politics and Political Economy

A series edited by Benjamin I. Page

CROSSTALK

Citizens, Candidates, and the Media in a Presidential Campaign

Marion R. Just

Ann N. Crigler

Dean E. Alger

Timothy E. Cook

Montague Kern

Darrell M. West

The University of Chicago Press
Chicago and London

The University of Chicago Press, Chicago 60637
The University of Chicago Press, Ltd., London
© 1996 by The University of Chicago
All rights reserved. Published 1996
Printed in the United States of America
05 04 03 02 01 00 99 98 97   5 4 3 2

ISBN (cloth): 0-226-42020-5
ISBN (paper): 0-226-42021-3

Library of Congress Cataloging-in-Publication Data

Crosstalk : citizens, candidates, and the media in
    presidential campaign / Marion R. Just . . . [et al.].
            p.   cm.—(American politics and political
        economy)
    Includes bibliographical references and index.
    ISBN 0-226-42020-5.—ISBN 0-226-42021-3
    (pbk.)
    1. Presidents—United States—Election—
1992.   2. Electioneering—United States.
3. Voting—United States.   4. Mass media—
Political aspects—United States.   5. Mass
media and public opinion—United States.   I. Just,
Marion R.   II. Series.
JK256   19920
324.9730928—dc20   95-42190
                                        CIP

Contents

Illustrations

Figures

Acknowledgments

The discussions for this book began in May 1991 in a hotel coffee shop, when all six of us were attending the annual meeting of the International Communication Association in Chicago. At that time, the 1992 election looked like an open-and-shut case. George Bush was riding high in the polls, and there were so many Democrats saying they would *not* run for president that we wondered whether there would even be a contest. Nonetheless, our interests and shared concerns convinced us to collaborate on a project about the election that would allow us to explore our particular interests—ads and ad watches, media coverage, and how people think about politics. Of course, what began as a fairly small and contained project grew larger as the 1992 election became one of the most unpredictable and fascinating presidential races in recent history. Some five years after that first kaffeeklatsch, we have many to thank for help along the way.

Our deepest debt is to the generosity of various funding agencies whose generous support literally made this research possible: the National Science Foundation (grant 9122729), the MacArthur Foundation, the Ford Foundation, the Joyce Foundation, the Carnegie Corporation, and the Twentieth Century Fund.

We could not have carried out a project of this scale without the Shorenstein Center on Press, Politics and Public Policy at the Kennedy School of Government at Harvard, where our project was based for three years. The Center gave fellowships to three of our team (Dean Alger, Ann Crigler, and Montague Kern), provided us with office space, helped us find additional support, archived videotapes, and, not least, housed a small flotilla of research assistants who coded the news, ads, and interview programs and entered the data. The faculty and staff of the Shorenstein Center were a great joy to work with, and we thank them for their encouragement, patience, and advice. We are especially grateful to Marvin Kalb and Gary Orren, who were involved in the project from the beginning. Ellen Hume was of enormous help to us in raising funds for our research. Special thanks to Nancy Palmer, who was a source of advice and support and kept us in office space throughout the project. Edie Holway organized many conferences in connection with our research and coordinated the Center fellowships. Jennifer Quinlan and Brenda Laribee managed the finances so we could concentrate on other things. Additional encouragement and support were provided by Pippa Norris, Fred Schauer, Julie Felt, and Michele Johnson.

We are grateful to Wellesley College, which has also supported this research in numerous ways. We thank in particular Joan Gallagher for grant supervision, and Anne Meixsell and Susan Lindsey in the Political Science Department. At the University of Southern California we are grateful for the support of Michael Preston and Veronica Pete. Richard Hixson offered support at Rutgers University. Nancy Bellows at Williams College took up the slack for a distracted department chair.

Marion Just and Ann Crigler directed the project, including the data design, coordination, collection, and analysis. Ann Crigler led the research in Los Angeles, Marion Just in Boston, Montague Kern in Winston-Salem, and Dean Alger in Moorhead. The responsibility for supervising the data analysis and writing up the results were shared among us: Dean Alger, Montague Kern, and Darrell West for the ads and ad buys; Tim Cook and Ann Crigler for the in-depth interviews; Marion Just for the content analysis of the network, local television, and newspaper news and candidate interview programs; Montague Kern for the ad watches and the focus groups; and Darrell West for the public opinion surveys. Marion Just and Tim Cook undertook the final revisions of the text. All six of us, however, take full responsibility for the book as a whole.

Many people assisted in carrying out the research. Joanna DeLucia, Amy Wyeth, and later Dhawn Martin guided the Boston research staff in a variety of tasks, including videotaping, transcribing, newspaper clipping, coding, and entering data. Our thanks to Molly Ackerman, Anthony J. Adams, Lynn Akashi, Stephen Andaloro, Sonali Banerjee, Amy Blitz, Sarah Chellis, Marie Cloutier, Carol Conaway, Jennifer Dickey, John Domesick, Serene Fang, Michael Goldberg, Tom Just, Suzanne Neil, Dennis O'Connor, Deborah McClure Pastner, Nelson Reyneri, Michael Rinzler, Carla Sapsford, Nicole Silverman, Matthew Skelly, Robert Taliercio, Linda Tropp, Nadine Witkin, Zhengren Jennifer Yan, Tsui Shen Yeung, Diana Yin, and Lisa-Joy Zgorski. Newspaper clipping was carried out by the coding staff along with Mary Adele and John Crigler and Pat and Richard Warner, who served above and beyond the call of duty.

Our Los Angeles staff included Christie Carson, Dulaine Coleman, Francene Engel, Judson Lance Jeffries, Jolene Kiolbassa, Linda Lopez,

Christina McCall, Daria Novak, Bryan Scott Reece, Richard Willett, and Melissa Wye. In Moorhead we relied on the research assistance of Cynthia Miller, Timothy Nokken, and Amy Ann Peterson, as well as energetic student volunteers: Paul Dosch, Alan Estevez, Bridget Fordorer, Mindy Grantham, Carter Headrick, Coleen Rowe, Diana Tillman, Stacey Tjon, and Don Weber. Our Winston-Salem staff included Jane Ballus, Catherine McCaskill, Michael Robinson, and Kenneth Ward, and our research assistants at Rutgers University were Iris Hong Xie, Nina Weerakkody, and Paige Edley. Jolene Kiolbassa directed the videotaping in Los Angeles. William Van Hoy was in charge in Winston-Salem. All of the videotapes are archived at the Shorenstein Center.

For their help in recruiting subjects and conducting focus groups, we would like to thank Fieldwork Boston, Bellomy Research in Winston-Salem, Robyn Letters, and the South Pasadena Library. The in-depth interviews were conducted (in Boston) by Carol Conaway, Tim Cook, and Cicely Stetson; (in Los Angeles) by Ann Crigler, Dulaine Coleman, Jolene Kiolbassa, Richard Willett, and Bryan Reece; (in Moorhead) by Dean Alger and Cynthia Miller; and (in Winston-Salem) by Montague Kern and Frank Levering. Many of the in-depth interviews were transcribed by Peggy Bryant and Donna Chenail of Williams College. Jim Allison of the Williams College Center for Computing designed a program for handling the considerations data, which were entered by Sue Allison and Shirley Bushika.

The surveys were conducted by the John Hazen White, Sr., Public Opinion Laboratory at Brown University. Special thanks go to the A. Alfred Taubman Center for Public Policy and American Institutions at Brown, in particular to Jack Combs and Matthew Woods.

From an early stage of the research, we relied in particular on two graduate students and scholars in their own right: Tami Buhr and Russell Stevens. Tami Buhr was indefatigable in carrying out the data analysis. Her professional advice, good humor, and intellectual insights have immeasurably enhanced our research. Russell Stevens devoted long hours to the analysis of the candidate interviews, which were the subject of his own thesis at the Kennedy School of Government and his forthcoming book with Marvin Kalb, director of the Shorenstein Center.

The content data analysis was carried out using the computer facilities of Wellesley College and with the advice and support of Larry Baldwin, research advisor. His unflappability in the face of crises was invaluable.

We are most grateful to belong to a community of scholars who kindly provided suggestions, information, and critiques at crucial moments in the process of researching and writing this book. Tom Patterson was extremely generous from the start with advice and recommendations based on his indispensable 1976 election study, as was Doris Graber who kindly shared her original research materials with us. Michael Pfau and Allan Loudon were a great help in suggesting approaches to studying political advertising. Gary King gave us valuable statistical advice. We also thank others who were carrying out parallel projects on the 1992 election for keeping us posted on their work (and sometimes commiserating with us), most notably Paul Beck, Bruce Buchanan, Russ Dalton, Kathleen Jamieson, Kathleen Kendall, Matt Kerbel, Holli Semetko, and John Zaller. Numerous journalists and political consultants gave freely of their advice and expertise to this project. We thank in particular Andy Bowers of National Public Radio, Tim Russert of NBC, Renee Loth of the *Boston Globe*, Kathleen Frankovic of CBS, and Elizabeth Kolbert and Adam Clymer of the *New York Times*. Robin Roberts spent a great deal of time helping us to decipher and obtain ad buy data.

Once the election was over, and we turned to analyzing the data, George Marcus gave us invaluable advice. Papers presented at meetings were helpfully critiqued by Kathleen Jamieson, Tom Patterson, Henry Kenski, Lee Sigelman, and David Paletz, among others. Early chapter drafts were read by Richard Perloff and Kathleen Kendall. At a conference to discuss our preliminary findings in December 1994, organized by the Shorenstein Center and financed by the Carnegie Corporation, we also received helpful feedback, critiques, and suggestions from audience members as well as from the other participants: Patrick Devlin, Bill Gamson, Renee Loth, Dotty Lynch, Russ Neuman, Pippa Norris, Tom Patterson, Kirby Perkins, and especially Michael Delli Carpini.

We are grateful to John Tryneski of the University of Chicago Press, who has been an interested and supportive editor, and whose advice we have relied on throughout the process. Two outside reviewers for the University of Chicago Press also gave detailed suggestions that have improved the book considerably.

With gratitude we dedicate this book to our friends and loved ones who tolerated the long hours we spent on this research, who provided feedback and intellectual companionship, and who supported us throughout a long and arduous project: Hal, Sara, Marjorie, and Tom Just; Mary Adele and John Crigler, Ginny David, Isabel and William Guenette; Mike Milburn, Deborah Kelley-Milburn, and their family; Jack Yeager; Charlie, Chris, Alex, and Deane Kern; and Annie Schmitt.

We knew this research was off to a good start when we received the following description of the presidential campaign from a randomly selected interviewee in Los Angeles:

> *The presidential campaign is a process whereby people who wish to compete in the arena to become president of the United States have to become known to the people who are going to elect the president, the voters, and they need to establish an image with the voters through media coverage, through the expenditure of campaign finances, to become known by the public as an individual and to give themselves some exposure in terms of their awareness of issues which are important to the public, and their ability to deal effectively with those problems. And they need to develop a status whereby they can convince the voters that they are better qualified and better suited for the job of president than any other candidate. And so it's a process of money raising, and back slapping, and hand shaking, and media coverage that is organized, and essentially organized under a two-party system, Republicans and Democrats, who basically represent major political and philosophical parts of the spectrum from which the public has to choose. That's kind of a nutshell.*

ONE

Studying Campaign Discourse

ONE

Constructing the Campaign

Elections constitute critical moments in democracy, when citizens have an opportunity to talk back to political elites. Winners, losers, and pundits agree that "the people have spoken." But what did they say? What did the election mean? Did the people want less government or more action? Were the people worried about the economy or more fearful of social change? Did they punish the loser's record or embrace the winner's proposals? Or did the people simply vote for the candidate they liked best? The tally of votes only settles the question of who will hold office; it does not tell us what the election meant. The meaning of the election is forged in the discourse of the campaign.

This book is about one such campaign. It explores what the candidates said, what the media presented, and what the citizens talked about in the 1992 presidential election in the United States. We focus on what these three sets of participants said among themselves and to each other—the crosstalk of the campaign.

Our study of the campaign begins at the beginning—even before the election is underway—and follows the citizens, the candidates, and the media through the nominating stage of the election, through the summer party conventions, and into the fall campaign. Viewing the election over time highlights the interactions of campaign discourse—how the citizens, candidates, and media anticipate each other in the way they present issues and construct images, and how the participants interpret and revise their constructions in the light of what others say and do during the campaign.

Other important election studies have maintained that one set of participants is the *most* influential in the campaign—either the mass media (e.g., Patterson 1980, 1993) or the candidates and their handlers (e.g., Jamieson 1992a). Our focus is on the interactions. We see citizens, candidates, and media as able to provide crucial resources for the others in a campaign. Candidates can give speeches, broadcast advertisements, and stage media events that can give journalists something to cover and can provide citizens with insights into the candidates' persons, priorities, issue stances, and future promise. The media can print or broadcast news that enables candidate messages to reach a large audience, along with interpretations that can help citizens to understand what the campaign is all about. And, finally, citizens can express particular concerns by participating in polls, focus groups, and talk shows and by constituting critical audiences for campaign messages—favoring some by their attention and critiquing others by their lack of interest.

Of course, these participants may withhold resources from each other as well. After the 1988 election, a great deal of dissatisfaction was expressed with the process. In numerous election postmortems, candidates and their handlers decried their nine-second soundbites on the news, while journalists vented their frustration with inaccessible candidates and manipulative staged events. The public voiced displeasure with "dirty" campaigns and "gotcha" journalism—and polls showed declining public trust in both politicians and the press. The experience of 1988 demonstrated the campaign's ability to turn people off politics and even to delegitimize the process. For those reasons, we are concerned about the nature and usefulness of campaign crosstalk both among and between the various participants in the campaign.

"Crosstalk" as it is used in current journalistic lingo refers to the ad lib banter between television reporters and news anchors. But an older, dictionary, definition refers to crosstalk as a kind of feedback—with a double meaning that captures both the prospect for useful interaction on one hand and also the possibility of noise or interference on the other. We use "crosstalk" to point out that the campaign can sometimes enlighten (as in cross-fertilization) and sometimes frustrate (as in cross-purposes)—and that the interactions are always dynamic and unpredictable in the real world of elections.

This book makes several arguments about the crosstalk of the campaign: first, that the campaign matters—both to the immediate outcome of the election and to the long-term vitality of a democratic system; second, that the projection and development of candidate constructs are central to much of the discourse of campaigns—political ads, news coverage, and citizen conversations; third, that citizens take part in campaign crosstalk, communicating their concerns both directly and indirectly, and interpreting messages from a variety of sources; and last, that how people discuss the campaign, the issues, and the candidates depends on the information environment in which they operate. Let us take each of these points in turn.

Campaigns Matter

The notion that campaigns matter is certainly evident to candidates and journalists. After all, their activities for one (and, more often, two) years prior to the general election show how important they believe the campaign is to voters—and they spend millions of dollars to prove it. But over half a century of academic research on elections has tended to doubt whether campaigns have an impact—or if they do, whether the effect is democratic.

Indeed, when it comes to presidential elections, some scholars even wonder whether the campaign itself is "irrelevant" (Frankovic 1985; Gelman and King 1993). Election forecasters implicitly suggest that the outcome could have been predicted months in advance on the basis of facts and figures such as the distribution of partisans, the state of the economy, and the popularity of the incumbent president.[1] For other scholars, if campaigns make a difference, it is merely in mobilizing or demobilizing the electorate by reminding citizens of their predispositions and finding ways to connect political tendencies with the vote (Lazarsfeld, Berelson, and Gaudet 1944; Finkel 1993; Gelman and King 1993).

We argue that such an understanding of presidential campaigns is impoverished. First of all, presidential election forecasts have high margins of error (Greene 1993) and are quite useless in predicting the outcome of multicandidate races such as primaries or the three-way race of 1992. Moreover, the most accurate forecasts of the November elections in the United States are based on trial heats from August (Campbell 1993), when the country has already experienced several months of campaigning.

Even if campaigns served merely to "enlighten" voter preferences based on "fundamental variables" (Gelman and King 1993), the weights people put on various aspects of their values and interests shift during the campaign. We argue that the campaign is not merely a program of political reinforcement, but that concerns are "primed" by the campaign and used by voters in making decisions.[2] Our contention echoes E. E. Schattschneider's assertion that the most important part of the fight is deciding what it is about.

Beyond the substantial impact that campaigns have on who governs and with what agenda, campaigns can serve an important legitimating function in the democratic process. The discourse of the campaign is the wellspring of the victor's "popular mandate," as well as the yardstick of subsequent presidential performance ("read my lips"). In that sense, the quality of the campaign may be judged by the ability of citizens to enter into the discourse on their own terms. If the campaign takes public concerns seriously and provides forums for political discussion, it can help to reveal to individuals their power as citizens. Alternatively, if the campaign merely distracts or ignores the public and frustrates communication, the campaign may undermine the citizens' sense of their own power in the system and reinforce political cynicism.[3] This study of the 1992 presidential election shows that when the public is highly focused in the message it sends to candidates, and information is plentiful and accessible, a campaign can function as a long-running dialogue in which the candidates, the media, and the public inform and respond to one another and engage in meaningful crosstalk.

Candidates play the most obtrusive role—they are the object of campaign news and the citizen's decision. Like the media, candidates both respond to and influence the public. Campaigns give candidates a chance to convey a sense of who they are and what they stand for, but the model of candidate self-presentation is not a speech but a conversation. Especially in the American context, where election campaigns last nine or ten months, candidates have an extended opportunity to change, refine, or reorder policy proposals, claims, and self-presentations in the light of the electorate's response to their messages. Candidate communication also reflects an ongoing dialogue among the competitors, who attack, ignore, or debate with each other in an effort to improve their relative images with the voters. The campaign is the platform on which all of the candidates—known and unknown—formally present themselves in the context of a particular electoral decision and in relation to specific competitors. In their campaign discourse, candidates try to stamp their own meaning on the election campaign.

Candidates, however, have to contend not only with each other but with the coverage they receive in the mass media. In their reporting of the campaign, journalists raise topics, analyze and interpret candidate messages, evaluate strategies, and construct their own narratives about candidates and the campaign. Reporters continually balance their professional mission to evaluate the candidates and their policies against the need to make the news interesting to the audience. Both journalists and politicians try to anticipate, albeit not always accurately, what the public wants. During the course of the campaign, the news media may be forced to adjust their coverage if their stories are attracting audience disapproval, or if they are squeezed by competition to provide a different product. Thus, the news not only results from a collective negotiation between politician and journalists (Arterton 1984) but reflects their interaction with the public.

The public itself participates in several ways. First, people actively and, often, creatively interpret the messages that they receive directly from candidates (e.g., advertising, interviews, and debates) and through the media (e.g., news and other programming on radio and television and in newspapers and magazines) in light of their experience and knowledge about politics and specific candidates, as well as their personal and political concerns. The public's reaction can encourage or discourage both forms and topics of communication. Candidates and the news media conduct polls and focus groups to see which traits, issues, and themes resonate with the public. Critics argue that these techniques can be used as much to manipulate the citizenry as to make the candidates and media responsive. Beginning in 1992, however, citizens took a more direct role in campaign crosstalk, through call-in interview programs, town meetings, and the "citizens" debate—prodding candidates and journalists toward a more substantive engagement with the issues.

Candidate Constructs

Both political consultants and journalists focus campaign attention on candidates. But academics have generally ranked other factors as more important in the voting decision—especially partisanship, issue preferences that cut across party lines, and evaluations of the incumbent's performance—while assessments of the candidates are acknowledged somewhat reluctantly.[4]

One reason that scholars look elsewhere is that party orientation, issue preferences, and retrospective judgments fit more easily into analytical categories, and square more neatly with democratic theory, than candidate assessments. Theories of democracy can accommodate voting that is motivated by political ideology or issues, since these are criteria of future policy, or by a desire to hold the incumbent to account, since this involves approving or disapproving previous policies. Merely liking or disliking a candidate has been difficult to justify as a *good* reason for the vote. For example, in their classic work, *The American Voter*, Campbell et al. (1960, 26) could hardly hide their disappointment that, after he had served four years as president, Eisenhower's popularity with the electorate was based, not on what he accomplished in government, but on the person he was: "It was the response to personal qualities—to his sincerity, his integrity, and sense of duty, his virtue as a family man, his religious devotion, and his sheer likableness—that rose substantially in the second campaign. These frequencies leave the strong impression that in 1956 Eisenhower was honored not so much for his performance as president as for the quality of his person."

Scholars have not been able to ignore the sheer weight of candidate factors in voting. An analysis of the elections of 1952–72 found that the most commonly cited reason for voting one way or the other for president was "the personal traits and characteristics of the candidate" (Nie, Verba, and Petrocik 1976). Individuals will almost invariably vote for the presidential candidate with the higher score on the "feeling thermometer" or the candidate with the more positive associations (Brody and Page 1973; Kelley and Mirer 1974). Some have argued that with the waning role of political parties in the United States, candidate-centered elections are becoming the norm (Wattenberg 1990).

Clearly, the problem for researchers has been, not to demonstrate the empirical importance of candidate constructs, but to justify voters' preoccupation with candidates in the democratic process. After all, if the vote merely endorses how well a candidate recites the Pledge of Allegiance or smiles at the camera, then people are unlikely to find satisfaction in what policies the president does, or does not, pursue.

Accumulating evidence, however, suggests that candidate images are not simply emotional reactions to celebrated personalities. Richard Fenno (1978), in his classic study of members of Congress, noted how legislators presume that, for voters, words are less reliable gauges of past and future actions than their sense of the representative as a person. Consequently, while visiting their districts, legislators seek, through both actions and words, to "give off" a sense of being well qualified, of identifying with their constituents, and of empathizing with their situations—all factors that Fenno judged to be political criteria. Likewise, Samuel Popkin's (1991) "investment theory" of voting suggests that citizens are looking for good predictors of what candidates will do in the future. If campaign promises are presumed to be just hot air, and if retrospective evaluations are deemed imperfect indicators of future behavior, then voters may feel more confident investing in candidates based on how they campaign and what kind of *persons* they are.

If candidate images were devoid of political content, then the more politically sophisticated citizens should be least inclined to use personal criteria in voting decisions; scholars, however, have found just the opposite. One reason for the ubiquity of candidate constructs is that candidate images are intertwined with the more defensible factors in voting. As

Morris Fiorina argued (in explaining why he did *not* include candidate constructs in his model of voting): "Candidates are the vehicles by which issues are brought before the electorate, and at least some of them (incumbents) are the object of retrospective evaluations. Thus, candidates [are] bound up in the continual interplay of past, present, and future evaluations" (1981, 148–49).

In this book we will show that candidate evaluations are charged with political meaning. Our premise is that during their long exposure to the presidential campaign—lasting nine or ten months in the United States— even the most inattentive people pick up bits and pieces of information about the candidates. Most citizens can extract from the barrage of campaign messages a sense of the priorities, records, and character of the candidates, and they can match these values with their own sets of concerns. Voters use candidates' issue positions to make assessments of their personal qualities, and vice versa—just as candidates' ads "dovetail" issue appeals with statements about their character (Kern 1989) and the news mixes messages about candidate policy positions with their personality traits. The "considerations" citizens bring to bear about candidates become increasingly consistent with each other and with their vote preferences. Although the bottom line for many citizens is their relative assessment of the candidates' character, that assessment is informed by political information and political judgments.

Active Citizens

We do not dispute the well-established finding that citizens in the United States rarely go out of their way to search out information and scrutinize the issues. To be sure, in an era when the amount of time devoted to work has steadily increased and slack time has correspondingly shrunk (Schor 1991), we cannot expect citizens to devote much time and energy to politics. Nonetheless, when people *do* attend to politics, we contend that they do so in active and often creative ways. Ever since Lane's famous *Political Ideology* (1962), scholars have demonstrated the capacities of citizens to make sense of their everyday worlds, to find connections to larger political phenomena, and even to grapple with rudimentary versions of the essential questions of political theory (Hochschild 1981).[5]

This study focuses, not on what people fail to do, but instead on what they can accomplish politically in their day-to-day environments. How can people make reasonable political choices when so few have much interest or give much attention to public affairs?[6]

The answer is that the political information environment can be structured in such a way as to facilitate the ability of citizens to decide. Previously, scholars of public choice (e.g., Lupia 1994) have suggested that voters do not need full and perfect information as long as they can find a reliable source to guide them. Political psychologists have focused on the role of political elites in setting the public agenda and suggesting appropriate policy responses—making it easier for people to engage in informed self-governance.[7]

We emphasize the role of the information environment in a high-visibility election campaign. Citizens can make reasonable political judgments because political information is all around them. As Fiorina has recently posited: "Citizens often receive information in the course of doing other things. There is no question of information costs, no question of deciding to gather information as opposed to doing something else. Just as exposed portions of skin get tanned by the sun when people walk around out of doors, so people become informed as they go about their daily business" (1990, 338).

Political information is especially prevalent—possibly unavoidable—in a presidential campaign that is, by the standards of most democracies, unusually long. Not only is the presidential campaign prominently featured in the news for months on end, it usually involves two or more well-funded and relatively evenly balanced campaigns. Thus the challenge for citizens is, not to find information, but instead how to "tame the information tide" (Graber 1984).

In this study we will show that people do not merely pick and choose in this wealth of information but actively *consider* what they encounter and figure out whether it makes sense. People interpret information using their abilities to judge the qualities and capabilities of other persons and what they know from their personal experience about these particular politicians, parties, and issues; how politics works and what politicians are like in general; and the world and its problems. Their "considerations" can run the gamut from rigorous hypothesis testing to simply wondering whether some new piece of information could be true.[8] Individuals will come to different conclusions from the same evidence, based on their prior beliefs and experiences; they are not blank slates. But at times, when new evidence does not fit the old framework, it causes a shift in the way individuals view the candidates, the parties, or the issues.

In the chapters below, we see how citizens use the information freely available in their environments to figure out what kind of persons the candidates are, what kind of presidents they are likely to make, and which candidate will make the best "investment" for the future. We will show

how, over the course of the campaign, considerations become increasingly consistent and point toward a vote decision. As with other recent works in political psychology, we do not see the process of considerations as exclusively cognitive. We recognize that some considerations are deeply emotional and most bear some affective coloration. People may reason back and forth from their gut feelings to the data at hand, sometimes filling in logical reasons for impressions they have already formed (Sniderman, Brody, and Tetlock 1991). In our view, it is at least as important to hear what people have to say about their political judgments as it is to explain what information led to the considerations in the first place.

Political Information Environments

While the presidential campaign may barrage citizens with information, some kinds of information may be especially accessible or obtrusive. The degree to which citizens can be active participants in the campaign may be either powerfully encouraged or discouraged by the particular "political information environments" in which they find themselves.[9]

Not only do resources differ, but people vary in the way they approach the campaign. Some are interested in the political process and approach the campaign discourse ready-armed with commitments to party, ideology, or issue agendas, or with firm convictions about the success or failure of the incumbent. These people might be presumed to need very little information, if all they have to know is which candidate is the Democrat or the Republican, the liberal or the conservative, the prolife or the prochoice proponent. Other people, however, have no fixed ideological or partisan guide to electoral choice. For these citizens, the information function of the campaign could be more critical. We find, however, that most citizens are not comfortable with the idea of simply voting for party, ideology, or issue and that regardless of their *need* for information, citizens want to have a sense that the person they support has the background, qualifications, character, and personality traits to perform well as president.

When we interviewed citizens around the country in January 1992, the only candidate most could identify was the incumbent president, George Bush, although a few were aware of another candidate "with the gray hair." By election day, after months of news coverage, advertising, appearances on interview programs, and debates, the overwhelming majority of citizens could identify the candidates and could talk about a range of considerations about them—their personal backgrounds, issue positions, chances for election, leadership experience, and abilities.

People develop constructs of the candidates from the information they encounter. Because communities vary in the amount or quality of information available and because people vary in their abilities to take advantage of the information available, our study looks at different kinds of people in different information environments. We investigate both large and small media markets, and communities with both high and low competition in the statewide primaries and the general election phases of the campaign. In general, we find that the richer the information environment, the greater the variety and number of considerations people are able to bring to bear in their voting decisions.

In any particular environment some information stands out. The candidates concentrate on information that puts them in the most favorable light, and the news media carry more of certain kinds of stories. What obtrudes in the information environment may "prime" citizens to use one set of criteria more than another in making their voting decisions. Therefore, our study focuses on what the candidates and the news media emphasize in their communications to particular audiences.

Candidates' messages in ads, debates, and speeches address the considerations that citizens value highly in making a decision. Reagan's spinmeister, Michael Deaver (1989), for instance, has described how polling about Reagan in 1983 revealed low evaluations of him on the dimension of "caring." After a barrage of pseudoevents, which showed Reagan dedicating schools and nursing homes, and an intense advertising campaign featuring nurses and grandmothers, Reagan's "caring" ratings went up. Alternatively, candidates may focus on considerations that reflect negatively on their opponents. The most famous recent example is how George Bush in the 1988 presidential campaign featured ads that increased the weight that people gave to the crime issue, as well as the proportion of people claiming that his opponent, Michael Dukakis, was "soft on crime" (Hershey 1989). The most successful political ads present the candidate in a good light and the opponent in a bad light (Kern 1989). For example, in the 1992 campaign, Pat Buchanan's "read my lips" ad attacked President Bush for raising taxes and at the same time identified Buchanan as the candidate who would never raise taxes. For the most part, ads are designed to speak to specific, and often comparative, candidate considerations in an attention-getting and memorable form.

The news media also play a role in the valuation of candidate considerations. Patterson (1980) documents how the news emphasis on the "horse race" provokes citizens to talk about and judge the candidates by the qualities of their campaigns. Often, the personal aspects of a candidate's life become the focus of news. Many campaign stories are built around narratives in which candidates are the individual protagonists. Investigative journalists sort through the candidates' pasts to reveal personal and, occasionally, scandalous information that might bear on their electability or future performance. Sometimes, as allegations surface, candidates issue rejoinders, and other politicians and journalists raise new evidence or question the damage to the campaign, the results can become what Sabato (1991) has dubbed a "feeding frenzy." In short, the news, like the ads, presents candidates as persons, but with a greater emphasis on horse race and scandal.

If the news points obtrusively to a particular consideration about a candidate, and if all of the media present candidates the same way, then one could argue that the considerations the electorate brings to bear in assessing the candidates are constrained by a common, reinforcing media vision (Entman 1989). In 1992, we found substantial homogeneity in the selection of news. The issue of the economy, for example, dominated campaign news in every outlet we examined. Likewise, in spite of differing interpretations, what journalists found newsworthy about the candidates was similar from one news outlet to the next.

While journalists may agree on what makes news, we find that citizens are not mere sponges for views expressed in the press. Even when they take up the most obtrusive messages of the campaign, people are capable of weighing and counterarguing their meaning. For one thing, there is considerable public skepticism about the veracity and credibility of the news media, which bolsters resistance to messages perceived as biased. Second, people make sense of the news in the context of their own personal and political knowledge and experience, much of which is not derived from the news media. Finally, while there was substantial convergence on the news agenda, the news outlets in every community offered some variety in the tone of their coverage, and the candidate advertising provided widely divergent perspectives on the campaign. As a result, citizens are not trapped by a single media interpretation of events and actively process what they see and hear.

A Constructionist Perspective

Our approach to the electoral process emphasizes the construction of meaning over the course of the campaign. The process of construction involves not only elites, such as candidates and journalists, but also the citizens themselves. Indeed, far from being out of the loop, citizens were placed in new positions of power in the 1992 presidential campaign. Candidates used countless polls and focus groups to decide what their messages should be. More directly, the rise of the interview programs gave new prominence to average citizens questioning candidates directly and resisting the efforts of candidates and journalists to shift the discussion to issues other than the economy. In 1992, citizens even hijacked one of the presidential debates and forced journalists to abandon their usual emphasis on the game in favor of more substantive questions. The campaign of 1992 may well have been unusual, given the remarkable consensus that the state of the economy was the central issue of the race. Still, our evidence does suggest that when citizens are aroused and in consensus on what the key issues are, they can play an important role in shaping the campaign discourse.

Using a constructionist perspective, the electoral process is presented here as a dynamic struggle among the actors to influence the priorities of others engaged in the process. Each player gets more information about the others as the campaign progresses, and the actions of each are modified in light of new information from other participants. Throughout the campaign process, candidates adopt strategies that resonate with citizen priorities and do not bring down the wrath of the media; journalists try to report campaign news that will excite the audience, maintain access to the candidates, and impress their peers in the news business. And citizens, for their part, actively construct meaning about the candidates and the campaign by interpreting information in light of what they already know and value. People, in short, are neither pawns of the politicians nor dupes of the news media but can be active participants in constructing the campaign.

In the next chapter we show how a multimethod research design captures the essence of the constructionist orientation. Chapter 2 provides more details about the social psychological theories, especially about the concept of considerations and the role of the political information environment, that led us to conduct surveys, focus groups, in-depth interviews, and content analyses of news and ads in four diverse communities. In the next several chapters we explore the discourse of the three principal participants in the 1992 presidential campaign—the citizens, the candidates, and the media—from the beginning of the nominating phase of the campaign to election day.

Chapter 3 lays out the citizens' agenda. Both public opinion surveys and in-depth interviews with citizens in January of the campaign year establish the remarkable consensus on the economy as the greatest concern of citizens in all four communities. We show how this consensus, far from being fragmented by the course of the campaign, became more concentrated as the year went on. Moreover, early campaign interviews reveal a deep distrust—of both politics and of the news media—which colored the campaign. By looking at what the people had to say before the campaign began in earnest, we are able to demonstrate how the candidates and the media were responsive to the public in the course of the campaign.

Chapter 4 discusses how the candidates presented themselves to the citizens. We focus our attention on televised advertisements, which constitute the largest expenditure of any presidential campaign and are recognized as one of the most effective ways for candidates to present themselves on their own terms to a wide audience. Our analysis of the ads and the strategies candidates used to buy advertising time highlights the dynamic interaction among the competitors and between the candidates and the shifting campaign environment. The analysis shows how Bush challengers Clinton and Perot successfully responded to the citizens' priorities and dovetailed their messages around what was wrong with the economy and how they had the ability to fix it—a strategy largely denied to the incumbent.

Chapter 5 focuses on the news environment in which voters decide. We show that citizens in each of our four sites have substantially different amounts of news available to them because of the wide variation in campaign coverage between different newspapers and different local television affiliates. We examine the general news consensus that concentrates so much on candidate personal qualities and chances for election, as well as on particular aspects of each of the candidates—Bush's policies, Clinton's campaign style, and Perot's chances and unusual nonparty organization. We also show how the news media—network news, local television news, and newspapers—diverge in the substance and tone of their coverage of the candidates. In particular, we find a more negative tone of coverage in newspapers primarily because they lead other media in offering stories initiated by journalists, while local television, with meager resources for independent investigation, is the most neutral to the candidates overall.

In chapter 6, the examination of the information environment turns to two innovations of the 1992 campaign: ad watches and candidate interviews. Ad watches evolved from the aftermath of the 1988 campaign, when journalists berated themselves for passing along and reinforcing what they perceived as George Bush's deceptive messages. Ad watches gave journalists an opportunity to analyze the claims made in, as well as the strategies behind, candidates' ads.

Interview programs, in turn, became increasingly prominent during the 1992 campaign, as candidates sought new ways to reach the electorate with less journalist interference and in longer formats. Although Ross Perot received most of the credit for introducing this campaign modality, the 1992 candidate interview programs began in January with the Clintons' interview on "60 Minutes" in which they defended their marriage in the wake of Gennifer Flowers's allegation of a past affair. Candidate interviews gained so much credence that even George Bush, who began the year openly condemning such formats as "unpresidential," appeared on a number of programs in the summer and fall.

We study these new formats primarily to see what kind of resources they provide for citizens. Evidence from focus groups and in-depth interviews suggests that citizens appreciate and can use ad watches that analyze the veracity of candidates' claims but have little use for ad watches that talk about "effectiveness" in strategic terms. As for interview programs, we find that this innovation is much applauded by the public as a way to bypass reporters and experts and concentrate more fully on the candidates' messages and their interactions with the public.

Chapters 7 to 9 examine how citizens understand the campaign and what considerations they use to evaluate the candidates. The chapters draw on evidence from public opinion surveys, focus groups, and in-depth interviews. The converging evidence shows citizens attending to, ignoring, and interpreting messages from candidates and the media in light of their own personal experiences and perspectives. Moreover, as the campaign continued, citizens gathered more and more considerations. Partisanship became important only at the end of the campaign, as people assembled assessments of the candidates that matched their stated voting preferences. Comparing our four sites, however, it becomes clear that richer information environments produce richer discussion by citizens. Similarly, our focus groups show how certain kinds of news and ads produce relatively lackluster discussion while others provoke engagement and insight. These chapters provide important evidence that while citizens can be active participants in the campaign discourse, their ability to participate is enhanced by the quantity and quality of the political information environment.

In the concluding chapter, we propose a new approach to election analysis in which campaigns matter because of the interactions of the participants in constructing candidate images and the meaning of the campaign. We show how early candidate self-presentations and media coverage stimulate new considerations, but that by the end of the campaign, citizens are able to ignore, transform, or reinterpret candidate and media messages. We argue that in the course of the campaign, candidate character takes on an overarching political meaning involving issue positions, experience, and leadership ability. By viewing the campaign crosstalk as a dynamic process of assessment and construction, we point to both the active role of citizens and the critical nature of the information environment in which they decide.

TWO

The Design of the Study

A constructionist account of the campaign necessitates an ambitious research design. Our approach to the 1992 election is richly textured, longitudinal, and multifaceted. We chose to study four contrasting communities in different regions of the United States: Los Angeles, Boston, Winston-Salem (North Carolina), and Moorhead (Minnesota). We studied the candidates' communications by analyzing their television advertisements and finding out which ads were most often aired nationally and in each of the four locales. In each media market, we analyzed the campaign news in the metropolitan newspapers and the most highly rated local television news broadcasts, in addition to the nightly news shows of the four major networks. Finally, we sought out the views of the public in these communities through in-depth interviews, focus groups, and public opinion surveys, beginning in January and ending on election day in November.

We employed all of these perspective and methods because we believe that only by looking at the communications of citizens, candidates, and the media could we evaluate the crosstalk of the campaign. Our research is designed around four propositions—that campaigns matter, that candidate constructs are key to the discourse, that citizens play an active role in shaping the campaign, and that their information environment is important to their participation, the richness of their assessments of the candidates, the way they vote, and their satisfaction with the electoral process. This chapter sets forth the methods we used to address these issues and the rationale for our methodology.

The Whole Campaign

Far too many studies—particularly those that refer to the "irrelevance" of the campaign—only begin around Labor Day of election year. But by that time, the presidential nominees have been chosen after long, often bruising, and highly publicized primary campaigns and reintroduced to the American people through stage-managed party conventions. Candidates enter the fall campaign as known quantities. It is little wonder, then, that political scientists have given the brief, fall campaign short shrift.

By contrast, we began our study considerably earlier, with baseline in-depth interviews in late January and media monitoring beginning on February 1, 1992. Our focus is on the long-term development of public images of the three ultimate competitors in November: George Bush, Bill Clinton, and Ross Perot. Each of them posed a surprising threat to conventional wisdom. George Bush had been the most popular president in history one year and the next year received the lowest percentage of the popular vote of any incumbent president running for reelection since William Howard Taft. Bill Clinton first appeared on the public's radar screen as the result of allegations of infidelity, draft dodging, and pot smoking that might have been expected to destroy his candidacy, but survived the primaries to win the party nomination and ultimately the election. Ross Perot, for his part, was able to establish himself as a candidate to reckon with apparently, not in spite of, but because of his billions, his nonpolitician status, and his unconventional campaign. If we had only begun to study the development of impressions of these candidates in September, we would have missed the crucial nominating battles and media innovations that had already gone into the public's construction of the candidates during the fall campaign.

Candidate Considerations

Our approach to candidate constructs originated as a response to current debates in political psychology, dominated by a split between scholars using experiments to set forth an "on-line" model of candidate assessment and others who contend that the process is more haphazard and fragmentary.

We will argue here that when making sense of the candidates, citizens bring a variety of "considerations" to bear. This term was first popularized by Kelley and Mirer (1974) and later defined by Kelley as "prima facie reasons for choosing in one way or another" (1983, 10). Kelley and Mirer set forth what they grandly called "the Rule," a simple model to explain voters' decisions. As they saw it, voters, having determined what they like and dislike about the candidates, add those factors up and vote for the candidate for whom there are "the greatest net number of favorable attitudes." In the case of a tie, they argued, voters rely on partisanship—unless they have no party identification, in which case they abstain.

Although the Rule empirically explains almost all votes, the implicit psychological model on which Kelley and Mirer relied is problematic. It has become a commonplace of social psychology that people cannot accurately recall the reasons that led them to make a judgment in the first place.[1] Milton Lodge, Kathleen McGraw, and Patrick Stroh at SUNY–Stony Brook conducted a series of experiments, demonstrating how this process works in electoral decision making.[2] In the Stony Brook model, citizens process candidate information "on line" rather than using a "memory-based" system (see Hastie and Park 1986). In on-line processing, citizens note information as it comes in, form impressions, and then discard the bits and pieces of information on which their judgments were based. If people are asked after the fact how they justify their choices, they invent reasons that are more similar to new rationalizations rather than cite the original information they encountered. By showing the difference between the original information given and the post hoc reasons people offer, the Stony Brook researchers demonstrate the explanatory power of on-line processing over memory-based models in accounting for candidate assessments.

If Lodge and colleagues are correct, then the likes and dislikes about candidates that people give to survey researchers are merely rationalizations of already arrived at choices—in which case the preference for a candidate explains the considerations rather than the other way around. By casting doubt on Kelley and Mirer's decision rule, the Stony Brook researchers echo the arguments of Brody and Page (1972; see also Page and Brody 1972) about the problems of causality and rationalization in studying voting decisions. Brody and Page pointed out that a similarity between a citizen and the citizen's preferred candidates' issue positions may or may not mean that the citizen chose the candidates because of their issue stances. Instead, citizens may change their viewpoints on issues to match more closely the views of their preferred candidates (see also Wattenberg 1991) or could rationalize their choices by believing that their preferred candidates mirror their own issue stances, whether or not that is the case (Berelson, Lazarsfeld, and McPhee 1952, chap. 10). The Stony Brook model offers an intriguing alternative to the rationalization dilemma. If citizens process information on line, we would expect them to emphasize summary judgments of the candidates, to avoid mentioning considerations that are at odds with their vote choices, and to express more socially acceptable (e.g., more politically relevant and less personal information) considerations about the candidates over the course of the campaign.

The on-line model has its detractors, most notably, John Zaller. In his ambitious book *The Nature and Origins of Mass Opinion,* Zaller (1992) criticizes the on-line model as having essentially the same drawbacks as conventional theories of attitudes. Philip Converse (1964) first argued that it is difficult to detect underlying attitude dimensions because responses to specific public opinion survey questions show so much variation over time. Attempts to locate stable attitudes about political objects have been further stymied by evidence that responses are very sensitive to slight changes in question wording and question order (e.g., see Schuman and Presser 1981) and may be "primed" by particular information that is close at hand (Iyengar and Kinder 1987).

In the face of evidence of unstable attitudes, Zaller hypothesizes that few people have the time or energy to store attitudes in their heads and that, therefore, a survey response is not so much an expression of an existing attitude as an attempt to try to figure out the answer to an unexpected question. He argues that a particular answer reflects considerations that are salient to the individual at the time of the survey, whether that salience is provoked by question wording, recent news events, or other momentary events that push that consideration to the "top of the head." [3] For "consideration," Zaller adapted Kelley's definition to denote "any reason that might induce an individual to decide a political issue one way or the other. . . . [It is] a compound of cognition and affect— that is, a belief concerning an object and an evaluation of the belief" (1992, 40).

So, in contrast to the Stony Brook model's suggestion that people take the time to continually update their constructs, Zaller sees citizens as possessing a wide range of considerations, not always sorted out in consistent or structured ways, which can be invoked in different ways in different contexts. While the valence of these considerations might vary a great deal, they each have a central tendency, which can be specified by increasing the number of observations across individuals or over time. Indeed, when aggregated over a large sample, these central tendencies can converge so that public opinion at large and within groups is remarkably stable in the aggregate, in spite of high individual instability (Page and Shapiro 1992).

Yet Zaller's model, despite his claims to the contrary, may not work as well for candidate constructs in campaigns as it does for survey responses about public policy choices, which is his main focus. We might expect these to differ for several different reasons. For one thing, people are rarely called upon to register their viewpoints on public policies in the same way that they are asked to choose a particular candidate on election day.[4] During a campaign, citizens can be expected to be more attentive to new information and to update running tallies on the candidates for the simple reason that they know they will have to cast a vote. Second, candidate constructs may be different from policy opinions because citizens are assessing persons rather than issues—something that may more easily tap skills developed in everyday life, where people constantly size up others on the basis of their competence, intelligence, warmth, power, compatibility, and ideas.[5]

In this debate between the Stony Brook on-line processing model and Zaller's central tendency of considerations, the two sides have depended on very different kinds of evidence. Zaller relies on surveys, where the phenomenon of "nonattitudes" can seemingly create considerations when none existed before. Lodge et al. base their on-line model on experimental evidence. How well these experiments reflect real-world voting decisions is problematic.[6] In particular, subjects might see experiments as "tests," especially when the experiments involve unknown, fictitious candidates. Therefore, subjects may have less incentive to remember the issues that went into their candidate constructs.

By looking at methods other than surveys and experiments—most notably, focus groups and in-depth interviews—we hope to be able to cast new light on this ongoing debate. We turn to the theoretical contributions of Hastie and Park (1986). They note how the results of on-line and memory-based research can be reconciled if we ascertain the conditions that provoke individuals to connect their memory more fully with their judgments. And, as Hastie and Pennington (1988) have since pointed out, the dichotomy between "memory-based" and "on-line" may be a false one. Instead, people may well use an "inference-memory–based" process, initially making isolated inferences about persons at the time of encountering information without making an overall judgment. Only when they have to make a decision do people then use those inferences to make a judgment. Hastie and Pennington's example is decision making in a jury, where jurors collect information and infer the credibility of witnesses and evidence, but do not bring these together to a tentative judgment until the judge has given them the instructions. In that sense, "inferences are made some time after the observations and do not rely on 'raw' memory but rather on previously made inferences" (Hastie and Pennington 1988, 7).

By requiring a decision at a specific time, and by giving jurors the expectation that they will have to account for their choices, jury decisions may parallel the process of citizens' decision making during a campaign. Citizens do not have to store in memory the bits and bites but may instead infer information about the candidates (e.g., Clinton is friendly; Perot is quick to anger; Bush is tired) that they recall from memory when they have to vote. As with Sniderman et al.'s (1991) concept of "reasoning chains," citizens may go right from general information to judgment, and then fill in the gaps, reasoning both backward and forward.

While our methods test models of information processing and decision making at the individual level, we also take a social view of campaign discourse. We agree with recent critiques of voting research (e.g., Sniderman 1993) that political scientists have focused too much on the causes of individual voting choices and too little on the meaning of elections as collective processes. We pick up a cue from Zaller and accept that survey responses reflect what a person is willing to say to a relative stranger during a political campaign. Instead of dismissing the reasons that people give for favoring a particular candidate as mere "rationalizations," we note that citizens often have to publicly justify their private decisions. Information is important not only as a way to create opinions where none exist but also as a way to justify otherwise unspecified feelings about the candidates. Since individuals do not usually face a reinforcing political environment (see Beck 1991), they may anticipate negative reactions to their viewpoints. And if individuals find it difficult publicly to rationalize a choice, they may feel impelled to reassess their preferences.

Such "rationalization" is important for democratic theory as well. As Pitkin (1967) has noted in her theory of representation, explaining what one has done is an important way to maintain accountability. Although some choices may be difficult to explain, what cannot be defended to others may be called into question by oneself. By finding reasons for one's choice and communicating them to one's fellow citizens, the process of assessing considerations can be seen as an important part of democratic deliberation.

This does not mean that all citizens are carefully sifting and weighing evidence. In fact, our use of the term "consideration" covers instead a wide variety of ways in which citizens can consider information. The dictionary tells us, "*consider* often indicates no more than think about but may suggest a conscious direction of thought." Thus, "to consider" can range all the way from noting and ignoring information, through wondering about its implications, to hypothesis testing in which the old theory is judged against new information. All these various ways of considering share the sense that citizens need reasons that can be accessed and publicly stated for them to be able to vote.

We studied candidate considerations in several ways: through public opinion surveys, assessing which considerations about the candidates were most prevalent and what kinds of people favored which considerations; through the focus groups, in which individuals justified their evaluation of information to other people and talked about the candidates among themselves; and especially through one- to two-hour in-depth interviews, in which every mention of a candidate was evaluated as a consideration. By seeing how candidate considerations evolved over the four waves of interviews over the course of a year, we were able to ascertain whether these considerations reflected ongoing individual concerns, or "top of the news" rationalizations, or some mix of the two. All three methods together help us to evaluate the reasons citizens give for choosing candidates and how they view the process of campaigns and elections.

Citizens Speak

Debates have raged for decades over the question of the capability of individuals to be democratic citizens. This theoretical debate has been complicated by the tendency for different methodologies to elicit different conclusions. For instance, at the same time that Campbell et al. (1960) were using election surveys in 1952 and 1956 to advance a highly skeptical account of the citizenry in *The American Voter*, Robert Lane was using in-depth interviews to evoke the rich and complex worldviews of working-class men that he admiringly described in *Political Ideology* (1962).

In designing our study, we were aware that every method that attempts to find out what is on citizens' minds is somewhat artificial. While in-depth interviews are probably closest to allowing an individual to "think out loud," a citizen rarely finds the opportunity to monopolize the attention of an interested interviewer in the everyday world. Similarly, focus groups do not replicate real-world situations, given that there are few moments when individuals can sit down, watch political ads and news, and shoot the breeze with total strangers. Surveys, of course, require people to respond to questions in a very particular order and only from a prescribed list of answers.

Consequently, to guard against the possibility that our results could be methodological artifacts, we used a range of methods to study how citizens made sense of the campaign: in-depth interviews, focus groups, and public opinion surveys. By approaching the public in different ways at the same time in the campaign calendar, we can compare the results from one method to those from another. Presumably, the more that the findings confirm one another, the stronger our confidence can be in them.

In-Depth Interviews

We conducted a series of four in-depth interviews with panels of citizens in our four sites. In each site, we conducted an interview at the end of January 1992, followed by a second interview a few days before the primary election in that state; the third wave took place at the end of September, and the fourth wave took place the weekend before the election (see table 2.1).

In each location, we chose 15 individuals from the community, building the sample to be representative in terms of political interest, partisanship, income, education, and ethnicity (see appendix A). We were successful in retaining the great majority of these interviewees through four waves: 14 interviewees completed the four waves in Los Angeles, 12 in Moorhead, 12 in Boston, and 10 in Winston-Salem, for a total of 48 individuals and 192 interviews.

In recruiting interviewees, we told them only that we were interested in talking with them about politics. Interviewees were compensated for each interview and received a small bonus when they successfully completed all four waves. We conducted these interviews in semiformal but nonacademic settings: two in consumer research facilities (Fieldworks in Waltham, Mass., and Bellomy Research in Winston-Salem) and two in public libraries (in South Pasadena, Calif., and in Moorhead). The interviews were tape-recorded and transcribed verbatim. In addition, we spoke with panel members by telephone between waves to coincide with other

Table 2.1 Data Collection Schedule

Local and Network News Taping[a]	Local Surveys	In-Depth Interviews	Focus Groups	Newspaper Clipping
		Jan. 20–28		
Feb. 1–Nov. 6				Feb. 1–Nov. 6 (every-third-day sample)
	Preprimary Each site[b]	Preprimary Each site	Postprimary Each site	
	Sept. 28–Oct. 4 Each site[c]	Sept. 28–Oct. 4 Each site	Sept. 28–Oct. 4 Each site	
	Oct. 23–Nov. 1 Each site[d]	Oct. 23–Nov. 1 Each site	Oct. 23–Nov. 1 Each site	

[a]Local television news station was the leading station in each site. In Boston and Los Angeles, the two leading stations were taped. The four networks were ABC, CBS, CNN, and NBC.
[b]Los Angeles, Boston, and Winston-Salem. Statewide Minnesota poll was used in Moorhead.
[c]Los Angeles, Boston, and Winston-Salem. Statewide Minnesota poll was used in Moorhead.
[d]Los Angeles, Boston, Winston-Salem, and Moorhead.

states' primaries and the conventions. The telephone interviews were briefer and focused on the candidates and the campaign.

In each of the interviews, we asked the respondents to speak freely about the candidates, the campaign, and the issues. We began by asking a typical opening "horizon question" about what the interviewee thought was the most important problem facing the country. We then turned to general nondirective questions about the campaign and the candidates. For instance, rather than rely on the standard "like/dislike" questions from the National Election Studies (NES), which essentially invite people to search for reasons to support or oppose a particular candidate, we asked simply, "How would you describe the candidates?"[7] We completed the interviews by asking more specific queries about particular forms of campaign communication (e.g., ads, ad watches, candidate interview programs, and debates). Following the interview, we asked each interviewee to fill out a closed-ended questionnaire that included questions about his or her demographic characteristics, partisanship, media attention, and candidate preferences.

During the one- to two-hour interviews, we did not discourage apparent tangents so that we could see how individuals connected ideas. We specifically avoided directed probes. Instead, interviewers simply followed up on comments made by the interviewee (e.g., "Tell me more" or "How do you feel about that?"). By keeping the probes vague, we encouraged the interviewees to make connections between ideas on their own, rather than having interviewers supply the connections.[8] As a result, in-depth interviews offered individuals an opportunity to talk about political phenomena in their own language, which may differ from the neat, preset categories of survey responses. As Hochschild argues, "In opinion polling, the *researcher infers* the links between variables; in intensive interviewing, the researcher induces the *respondent* to *create* the links between variables as he or she sees them" (1981, 24; emphasis in original). Our aim was to collect a rich base of information about the considerations people brought to bear about the candidates, unrestricted by a priori categories. By asking some of the same questions each time, we were able to obtain a clear sense of how initial constructs about the candidates changed over time and whether the considerations and assessments of the candidates were stable or changing. Quite likely, by reinterviewing the same people over the course of the year, we may have provoked some individuals to be more attentive to and engaged in the campaign than they otherwise might have been. Even so, the in-depth interviews suggest considerable variability between subjects in their willingness to follow the campaign and their ability to talk about politics.

Analysis of the interviews involved listening to what people said and discerning the connections that they made through seeming detours, dead ends, and contradictions. We are mindful, however, that open-ended responses have problems of validity just as closed-ended responses do (Foddy 1993, chap. 10). Interviews, like surveys, entail a joint construction of meaning between interviewer and interviewee (Mishler 1986). Consequently, we cannot assume that these interviews necessarily provide a more accurate insight into the thought processes of subjects than other methods. As with other methods, these interviews should be seen as "speech events," representing what one person will say to a relative stranger.[9]

Our interpretation of the in-depth interviews was primarily qualitative. In one instance, however, we did use quantitative measures with preestablished categories to evaluate the considerations that interviewees brought to bear when discussing candidates.[10] Other quantitative coding (e.g., most important problem) used inductive categories derived from the respondents themselves. Otherwise, the interviews were generally analyzed qualitatively, by an iterative process of reading, rereading, and distilling the transcripts, identifying commonalities across respondents and variations from one to the next (McCracken 1988).

The in-depth interviews enable us to delve into rich and often unique individual understandings of and feelings about the presidential election, the candidates, and the media. They have, however, several disadvantages. First of all, their unstructured discursiveness makes it difficult to compare across interviewees, while their numbers make it hard to generalize to the community as a whole on the basis of characteristics such as partisanship or media habits. Furthermore, we found it difficult to tell what sources of information interviewees brought to bear on the campaign. Individuals frequently did not volunteer where information came from or would vaguely say, "I heard it on the news," or "I saw that on TV."

Consequently, in order to more precisely gauge the impact of ads and news, we also conducted focus groups in which participants viewed and discussed videotapes of specific ads and television news stories from the campaign. Though this approach is not experimental, the ensuing discussion gives us excellent insight into how people can use the resources provided to them by ads and news in social interaction. In order to check the results from in-depth interviews and focus groups against a cross section of the four communities, we conducted surveys in three of our four sites in the spring, and in all four sites in the fall.[11] The surveys asked respondents to recall their news habits and whether they remembered seeing ads by particular candidates. This triangulation of methods allows us to correlate aspects of the information environment (both across and within sites) with particular political responses.

Focus Groups

Focus groups were conducted at three points during the primary and general election phases. In order to assess how citizens used media, participants were exposed to brief video segments of campaign media and given an opportunity to discuss what they saw (see Kern and Just 1995).

Participants in the focus groups were recruited by market research firms in each area. Twelve to 14 participants were recruited, and the actual groups ranged in size from 10 to 12 persons. The small-group nature of these discussions allowed us to examine the potential for interpersonal communication in the construction of political meaning (see Delli Carpini and Williams 1994; Lederman 1990; Gamson 1993). Subjects were restricted to American citizens who were at least 18 years of age. Aiming to target those who might be most open to campaign messages, we recruited individuals who did not have strong partisan or ideological loyalties.

We used two different strategies in constituting the focus groups. In the spring, we held two focus groups in each location—one for men and one for women, in order to maximize social interaction. The focus groups were scheduled just prior to the primary in each state. In the fall, in order to achieve the most varied ad and debate exposure, we held two focus groups in each location—one at the end of September and the second at the end of October. The fall focus groups targeted undecided citizens and involved both men and women. Altogether we conducted 16 focus groups over the course of the campaign.

Before starting the focus group discussion, each person was asked to fill out a brief demographic questionnaire.[12] To help put the participants at ease in the group discussion, participants were asked to describe themselves to the group and then to indicate what they thought was the most important issue facing the country today. Then the groups were shown several video segments, each of which was followed by group discussion. The stimuli varied over the course of the campaign. During the primaries, clips were taken from news, ads, and ad watches aired on the community's local stations. For the general election, we used the same video exposure across locales: the September stimuli consisted of clips from network news, candidate interview programs, and ads, while the October clips were taken from ads, ad watches, debate and commentary, and political humor.

In order to prevent the group discussion from overwhelming individual responses, people were asked to write down their impressions of the stimulus and the candidates after seeing each segment but before the discussion actually had commenced. This was designed to deal with the well-known problem of "groupthink" (Janis 1972) and to encourage participants to contribute their own ideas to the discussion (Kern and Just 1995). When the participants were finished writing down their impressions, a discussion leader began the talk by asking some general questions: "Was there anything in these news stories [ads, etc.] that stood out in your mind?" "After seeing these news stories [ads, etc.], what do you think of the candidates?" The focus groups were both audiotaped and videotaped with the permission of all participants. The audiotapes were transcribed verbatim, with the videotapes used to identify participants in the audio discussion. From the transcripts, all topics of conversation between two or more participants were analyzed to identify the personal experiences, political knowledge, and media sources that individuals brought into the conversation. Analysis also focused on the references people made to the verbal, visual, or both verbal and visual messages in the media stimuli. Since the focus group method is of particular value in showing social interaction about politics, the excerpts from focus groups that we cite in the book exemplify dimensions of conversational exchanges in response to the particular stimuli shown to the group. Examination of the topics of conversation in focus groups throughout the election campaign shows what kinds of media stimulate what types of conversation and illustrates the way people evaluate, use, and reject information when constructing arguments about politics.

Public Opinion Surveys

The surveys allowed us to probe the sources of citizen reactions to news and ads, and to validate and generalize about the qualitative material gathered from in-depth interviews and focus groups. During the nominating process, local surveys were conducted in three of our sites: with 590 adults in the greater Boston metropolitan area from March 2 to 9; with 600 adults in Forsyth County (Winston-Salem), North Carolina, from April 30 to May 3; and with 484 adults in Los Angeles County from May 18 to 31.[13]

Two sets of general election surveys took place in each site, one near the end of September and another at the end of October. These surveys were conducted from September 28 to October 4 ($N = 615$) and October 25 to 30 ($N = 622$) in Boston; September 28 to October 4 ($N = 600$) and October 26 to 31 ($N = 601$) in Los Angeles; September 28 to 29 ($N = 616$) and October 23 to 27 ($N = 609$) in Winston-Salem; and October 2 to 6 ($N = 830$) statewide in Minnesota, and October 25 to November 1 ($N = 604$) in Moorhead.[14] Cross-sectional rather than panel surveys were used in order to avoid the problems of sample mortality and respondent sensitization to the campaign that we were facing with the in-depth interviews.

These surveys were timed to coincide with the in-depth interviews and focus groups in each area. Our goal was to have parallel analyses in each community using comparable questions about the campaign. We repeated a number of survey questions at different points during the campaign to investigate the processes of agenda building and candidate image formation. The surveys asked citizens specific questions about the most important problem facing the country and about the candidates, the media, and the campaign. Specific questions addressed the candidates' name recognition and electability.[15]

We paid particular attention to considerations that have been identified by previous survey research as important, such as the candidates' perceived leadership abilities, their honesty and degree of caring, their ability to manage the economy, and a series of emotional reactions (e.g., "makes me proud" and "makes me worried"). We also asked a number questions about the perceived issue positions of the candidates, overall assessments of the competitors, and the respondents' vote preferences.

We were particularly interested in gauging the association between the candidates' chances and perceptions about their qualities and the media resources people said they employed in the campaign. Respondents were asked: "How many days in the last week have you seen presidential campaign ads on television for [each candidate]? Five days or more, three or four days, one or two days, or not at any time." We asked three similar questions about news exposure: "How many days in the last week have you seen [local television news, national television news, or newspapers]?"[16]

Political Information Environments

It was crucial to the research to examine several communities, given that a nationally based study would make it virtually impossible to correlate a citizen's actual information environment with the decision process. This project integrates the analysis of particular information environments with the considerations people in that environment bring to bear on the vote. In this respect, it is similar to Patterson's (1980) and Graber's (1984) studies of the 1976 election. Patterson undertook a comparative study of media and public opinion in Erie, Pennsylvania, and Los Angeles. Using a detailed content analysis of television and newspapers as well as panel surveys of citizens at several points during the presidential campaign, he was able to demonstrate the media's ability to set the agenda and influence citizen impressions of candidate images. Graber investigated how people process the news, by conducting a content analysis of Chicago news and in-depth interviews with 21 Chicago residents. Each person's impressions were probed in hours of interviews, which were compared against diaries in which the interviewees recorded their media use. This led to a revealing analysis of how people ignore, process, and reinterpret news coverage of political events.

The choice of locations was a crucial decision in this study. Throughout the United States, the mix of citizens varies widely—some locales have more educated or wealthy people than others, some have greater racial and ethnic diversity, and so forth. On the political dimension, communities differ in terms of political culture or partisan mix. Finally, some places have more news outlets than others, with larger media markets generally regarded as better able to support a greater quantity and quality of news. Consequently, we were careful to choose areas that differed from each other along these dimensions in the four major geographical areas of the country.

The four locations we chose to study were Los Angeles in the West, Boston in the Northeast, Winston-Salem in the South, and Moorhead, Minnesota (the twin city of Fargo, N.D.) in the Midwest. As one can see from the census information for the metropolitan areas, in table 2.2, these communities provide us with a good variety: Boston and Los Angeles have higher per capita incomes than Winston-Salem or Fargo/Moorhead; Los Angeles and Winston-Salem have higher percentages of people of color than Boston or Fargo/Moorhead; Boston and Fargo/Moorhead have higher percentages of educated people than the country as a whole, Winston-Salem a lower percentage, and Los Angeles differs on both ends of the scale, with higher percentages of both college graduates and those with less than a high school education than is the case nationally.

Politically, too, these locales are quite distinct. First of all, the primaries in each state were held at different times during the campaign, evenly spaced across the spring: Massachusetts in March, Minnesota in April, North Carolina in May, and California in June.[17] This schedule provided us with an extraordinarily convenient opportunity to examine the nominating campaign as it unfolded, by timing in-depth interviews, focus groups, and surveys to coincide with the primary in each state. These communities also represented a range of political leanings. Boston is the capital of Massachusetts, one of the most consistently Democratic

Table 2.2 Demographics of the Metropolitan Areas (1990 U.S. census)

Metropolitan Area Media Market (ADI rank)	Percentage Nonwhite	Percentage Hispanic	Percentage Less Than 12 Years Education	Percentage College Graduates	Median Per Capita Income	November 1992 Clinton/Bush Vote Percentages
Los Angeles/Long Beach Los Angeles (2nd)	33.2	37.8	30.0	22.3	16,444	52.7/29.2
Boston/Lawrence/Salem Boston (6th)	11.9	4.5	17.4	30.8	18,672	48.1/29.5
Greensboro/Winston-Salem/Highpoint Winston Salem (48th)	12.6	.8	28.0	19.2	14,588	39.9/45.9
Fargo/Moorhead Fargo (108th)	2.8	1.2	14.9	25.0	12,447	36.5/45.7
United States	19.7	9.0	24.8	20.3	14,420	43.3/37.7

Source: Courtenay M. Slater and George E. Hall, eds., *1993 Country and City Extra: Annual Metro, City, and County Data Book* (Lanham, Md.: Bernan, 1993).

states in recent presidential elections. Los Angeles has leaned Democratic, while California as a whole prior to 1992 tended to go Republican in presidential elections. Winston-Salem has become, along with the rest of the state of North Carolina, increasingly Republican. And Moorhead is almost evenly divided between Democrats and Republicans (its congressional district has been perhaps the most competitive in the nation) in an otherwise Democratic state. As we anticipated, the final vote tallies in the fall awarded the Los Angeles and Boston metropolitan areas to Clinton, while Bush carried the Winston-Salem and Fargo/Moorhead metropolitan areas.

"New" News and Old News

In order to understand how people use information to develop images of the candidates, we conducted content analyses of national and local campaign news. Previous studies have shown that the news tends to be homogeneous because of the common professional norms of journalists and the routines of news organizations (Sigal 1973; Gans 1979; Hofstetter 1976; Patterson 1980). Researchers came to the conclusion that consumer differences had comparatively little impact on the news product. Instead, news content was assumed to vary primarily as a result of the resources organizations brought to bear on reporting and by the news sources available in different locales. Altheide (1976), for example, found that national and local television news shared a common news perspective, but local news relied upon a narrower circle of sources, emphasized the local angle in news reporting, and utilized more modest resources in reporting. Differences in content between different media outlets have been deemed matters of degree rather than of kind—reinforced by the tendency of all journalists to turn to newspapers of record, such as the *New York Times,* or to the wire services for ideas about what is newsworthy.

This conclusion about the homogeneity of news, however, has not been thoroughly tested recently, even though there has been a plethora of changes within the communication industry that have substantially increased the variety of news content available to the average citizen. The decline of the networks' audience share from 90 percent in the 1970s to under 60 percent today, the increasing penetration of cable television into the marketplace, and the takeovers in the 1980s of ABC, CBS, and NBC by profit-oriented firms have lowered the barrier that used to shield news professionals from the economic bottom line. In addition, the national networks are now competing against local stations, which have expanded their news programs from 30 minutes to one, or even two, hours. Indeed, local television news is the only news outlet that has not significantly lost audience in the past 10 to 20 years, as has happened to newspapers and network news (see McManus 1994, chap. 1).

Our interest in news homogeneity is related to our concern for the citizen's interaction with the information environment. If the media present a consensual view of the campaign, a greater burden is put on individuals to challenge the prevailing view. If there is diversity in the media, then people have a greater opportunity to select, compare, modify, and interpret messages in order to make sense of the campaign. Since we argue that the constructions of the media are crucial to image formation during the campaign, it is important to explore the diversity of resources available in the news environment. Network news, national newspapers, and the wire services have been the main focus of previous scholarly attention; our innovation is to examine the neglected medium of local television news, alongside national networks and local newspapers.

In 1992 it became clear to everyone, however, that the information environment extended far beyond the traditional evening news programs. The number of newsmagazine programs in prime time had increased significantly. The candidates attempted to circumvent the national press corps by targeting local television stations and the talk show circuit. Consequently, as the year progressed, we added to the analysis a "new news" component—candidate interview programs—television programs or segments of programs in which candidates had an opportunity to interact at length with the program's host, with journalists, and sometimes with a studio or call-in audience.

The specific media outlets we studied covered a broad range. In each of the four communities in our study, the principal metropolitan daily newspaper(s) were monitored: the *Los Angeles Times, Boston Globe, Boston Herald, Winston-Salem Journal,* and *Fargo Forum,* along with the most watched early-evening local television news broadcast(s): KABC and KNBC in Los Angeles, WCVB and WBZ in Boston, WXII in Winston-Salem, and WDAY in Fargo/Moorhead. A random sample of 35 candidate interviews on national broadcasts was also analyzed along with the network evening newscasts on ABC, CBS, CNN, and NBC (CNN's hour-long "Primetime News" was selected as the closest approximation to the other networks' half-hour evening news shows).

For television news, monitoring began on February 1 and continued daily through November 8, 1992. Newspapers were sampled every third day in the same period. All news stories that concerned the campaign, the candidates, the president, or the vice-president, no matter where they were located in the newscast or newspaper, were analyzed. Newspaper items included news stories, news analysis, cartoons, editorials, and columns, whether in-house, syndicated, or wire service. The candidate interview sample was drawn from a listing of network interview programs aired throughout the campaign, including the morning news programs, the daytime and late-night talk shows, newsmagazine shows, Sunday news programs, and "Larry King Live."

Similar categories were used to examine each of the media formats: story length, main focus of the story (e.g., the candidate(s), the campaign process, presidential action, or issues), candidates and issues mentioned, sources quoted in the story, campaign themes (such as trust, change, or family values), and characteristics associated with the candidate, including personal attributes, aspects of the campaign organization, strategies, chances in the race, and issue positions. Personal attributes were further broken down to cover leadership, professional experience, ability as campaigner, personality, personal background, and scandal. For each story or interview, coders assessed the overall positive or negative tone of the story toward the candidate(s) mentioned, using a five- point scale. Verbal and visual tone were measured separately. Verbal tone refers to the audio channel of television and the text of newspaper stories. Visual tone applies to television video and the pictures or graphic material that accompany the text of newspaper stories. Measurements were made for number and length of candidate quotes (soundbites) as well as the number of seconds the candidate was on screen.

In addition, some categories of analysis were designed to capture the unique aspects of each media format. News was evaluated in terms of the "news peg"—why was the story news (was it initiated by journalists, was it a result of campaign events or candidate or presidential actions, or was it a reaction to some external event such as the Los Angeles riots)? Special attention was given to news stories that critiqued candidate advertising (often called "ad watches"). These stories were analyzed in relation to the content of the critique (how much of the ad was shown, who made the critique, and what was evaluated). We also considered whether local news stories contained a "local angle" (e.g., candidate visits, native son, or local reporter on the campaign trail).

Interview program segments were specially analyzed in terms of questions (who asked what) and candidate answers. Given the length of some of the shows (running to two hours in some cases), random samples of question/answer segments were drawn for those interviews that contained more than 10 questions. In addition to assessing the interview in terms of its positive or negative tone toward the candidate, interview questions were coded for level of confrontation (e.g., focusing on scandal or embarrassing discrepancies) using a 5-point scale running from "not at all" to "highly confrontational."

In addition to coding whole news stories and interview program segments, we also conducted a more detailed and intensive analysis on a sample of stories from each of the media we studied. A random sample of 20 stories was drawn from the entire campaign period from each of the following: each network, the leading local television station, and the leading metropolitan newspaper in each of the four communities we studied. The 240 sampled news stories, along with all 35 of the sampled interview programs and the candidate ads were analyzed by message (a sentence or single idea). The aim of the message-level analysis was to explore the media discourse more precisely, and to gain a sense of the extent to which different aspects of a story, such as candidate issue positions, were emphasized.

The coding of the network news, some local news, and the interview programs and all of the message analysis was conducted by teams of trained coders in Boston. The remaining local news coding was carried out in three of the research sites (Los Angeles, Boston, and Moorhead). Intercoder reliability tests were made on each variable. Some variables that we hoped to use resulted in unacceptably low levels of intercoder reliability and were either eliminated or refined until reliability reached acceptable levels. For the variables we report here, intercoder reliability ranged from .86 to 1.0 using a simple correlation test.

The analysis was designed to explore how various national and local media outlets presented the campaign. The analysis shows how news professionals construct images of the candidates, which can be compared with the information the audience considers and incorporates into their own constructs of the candidates. In particular, the content analysis focuses on the attributes that citizens might weigh in considering the candidates. While much of campaign coverage might be expected to be similar across outlets (Patterson 1980), it is reasonable to suppose that community values, modality constraints (such as the size of the "news hole" or the reliance on visual information), as well as editorial decisions might influence the way the campaign is presented across media and markets. Presumably, the richer the media environment, the more likely some portion of it will resonate with the diverse members of the audience.

Candidate Messages: Political Spot Advertising

In addition to the news media, candidates have used four venues for communicating their messages directly to citizens: political advertising, party convention coverage, debates, and television interviews. These vary in the degree to which the candidate controls the content, with candidates exercising the greatest control over their ads and speeches and sharing control in debates and interviews.

Political advertising is designed to grab attention and to persuade the audience to construct favorable images of the sponsor or unfavorable images of the opponents. Previous research has shown that the repetition of messages, exciting visuals, and dramatic music make advertising information more likely to be remembered than news or even debates (Just, Crigler, and Wallach 1990).[18] We have concentrated our analysis of candidate messages on political advertisements, which represent the largest expenditure of contemporary presidential campaigns. Radio and television advertising costs have risen to about two-thirds of overall campaign spending. For example, in 1992, Bush and Clinton devoted about 60 percent of their 1992 general election budgets to campaign spots. Perot was less forthcoming about his ad expenditures, but estimates range from about 70 to 75 percent of his fall budget. This heavy emphasis on advertising led one candidate, Paul Tsongas, to describe ads as the "nuclear weapon" of the campaign business.

In an effort to understand whether and how citizens use advertising to construct images of the candidates, our analysis looks at candidate communications throughout the nominating, summer, and general election stages of the 1992 campaign. We are interested in a number of different questions relating to advertisements: How do candidates construct advertising messages in an effort to create particular impressions of themselves? How do the news media cover candidate advertisements? And how do advertisements play into citizens' considerations of the candidates?

Candidate advertisements were obtained by taping from broadcasts in each location as well as through tapes made by commercial vendors, such as Aristotle Industries. While previous research has given equal weight to all candidate ads, no matter how often or where they aired, our research specifies which messages candidates emphasized by tracking how much they spent on specific ads, both nationally and in the locales we studied. In the primary period, we obtained local ad buy data for Boston, covering all of the candidates who participated in the New Hampshire or Massachusetts primaries. In the general election, we compiled local ad buy data in each media market, for Bush, Clinton, and Perot from July 1 to November 2, 1992. We used station log books from KNBC in Los Angeles, WBZ in Boston, WXII in Winston-Salem, and WDAY in Fargo/Moorhead. National ad buy data for Bush and Clinton were obtained from Robin Roberts of National Media, Inc., one of the nation's premier ad buyers. Data on Perot's national ad buys were provided by Clay Mulford of the Perot campaign and David Lyon of the Temerlin McClain advertising agency, which handled the Perot account. The local ad buy data contain information on which specific candidate ads ran and when, and on the cost of each time slot. The cost figures are particularly useful as surrogates for audience size when we try to calculate which messages candidates sought to disseminate most widely. The national ad buy data contain all of the same information, but do not include the cost figures.

We examined the content of the ads to determine what messages candidates were stressing and what cues were provided to citizens. Some researchers have shown that ads may contain more information about the candidates' issue positions than network news programs (Patterson and McClure 1976; Kern 1989), while others have questioned how much issue information is actually present in candidate ads (Joslyn 1986; Boiney and Paletz 1991). The candidate ads were analyzed using codes that paralleled the news content analysis, so that comparisons could be drawn across information sources. In addition, each ad was classified as focusing on the candidate's character and accomplishments, the candidate's issues, character and issues combined, attacks on the opponent's issues, attacks on the opponent's character, and attacks on character and issues combined.

Ad Watches and News Coverage of Advertising

The 1992 campaign offers the occasion to evaluate a new kind of news coverage. We have in mind not only the coverage of advertisements as news events but the criticism of advertising techniques and claims. The style of coverage in the previous (1988) presidential campaign had been profoundly disturbing to citizens, political professionals, academic experts, and reporters themselves. Countless seminars, conferences, and white papers urged journalists to alter their approach, particularly as it related to campaign spots. Critics claimed that by not having challenged the 1988 Bush ads more effectively, and by including ads in news stories, reporters had inadvertently amplified Bush's message. The widely perceived failures of the press in 1988 led to calls for fundamental changes in media coverage of ads (Broder 1990; Jamieson 1992a; West 1993; Wicks and Kern 1993).

Beginning in 1990, some news media introduced "ad watch" features. These news stories review the content of prominent or newsworthy ads and discuss the accuracy of candidate claims and the effectiveness of the ad. News commentary and analysis of the ad can either reinforce or undermine the candidate's message. Since then, ad watches have become regular features in leading newspaper and television outlets around the country. The number of media outlets involved in ad watches increased substantially in 1992. In some cases, the only way some audiences were exposed to a candidate's ad was through the lens of an ad watch.

We examine the prominence and structure of ad watches and compare them to the news coverage of the candidates. As we will see, local television programs and newspapers in Boston and local newspapers in Los Angeles reviewed ads far more regularly than the outlets in Winston-Salem and Fargo/Moorhead. Variation among our four media markets allows us to compare how ads and ad watches were received by citizens.

We were fortunate in that, by the end of the campaign, these four locales varied in interesting ways in terms of the richness of the campaign information environment. During the nominating process, all of the major candidates advertised on Boston stations, which reached most of New Hampshire. Boston had more campaign news than any other locale. It is the only one of the communities we studied that has two competitive newspapers, as well as two award-winning local television news programs. In the fall, however, Boston moved from being "news- and ad-rich" to being news-rich and ad-poor, as only Bush made any ad buys in the market. The result was that the major source of advertising information came from the large number of ad watches, most notably those published in the *Boston Globe.*

Advertising campaigns were considerably less central during the primaries in the three other locations, but in the fall, Winston-Salem was ad-rich, with both Bush and Clinton targeting North Carolina as a major battleground state. As we shall show, however, Winston-Salem was news-poor with the local media carrying the fewest presidential election stories. Fargo/Moorhead was, in general, both ad- and news-poor throughout the campaign, but with an interesting twist. While Clinton bought no local time during the general election campaign, Bush and Perot did, particularly in the closing weeks of the campaign, when the North Dakota race tightened, producing in the ads a lopsided race where Bush and Perot ads went relatively unanswered by Clinton.

Los Angeles, finally, was ad-poor but (newspaper) news-rich. Although Los Angeles had the most competitive local news market—with fully seven VHF stations broadcasting news—its local television coverage, comparing the two most popular news programs in each site, was less extensive than Boston's. The *Los Angeles Times* is one of the leading newspapers in the country, and it provided thorough coverage of the campaign, but again less than Boston—presumably because of the timing of the primaries. Moreover, the candidates bought few ads in Los Angeles, given the high cost of airtime in a huge media market and the general expectation in the fall that Clinton had locked up California.

Such variations in the political and media contexts of citizens are important from the standpoint of a constructionist framework. One would expect that variations in audience demographics and political competitiveness would, in turn, influence patterns of political communications and understanding. For these reasons, these locales present a diverse laboratory for studying the links between campaign messages and citizen responses. By studying people in four locations at crucial points throughout the nominating and general election contests, it is possible to trace the consequences of advertising strategies as well as styles and amounts of news coverage. The differences we observe across communities help us refine our understanding of the use people make of information resources as they consider the candidates.

TWO

Citizen, Candidate, and Media Messages

THREE

The Citizens' Agenda

Campaigns begin and end with voters. The candidates want to know what people are concerned about in order to present their claims in the best light. Likewise, the media are attentive to the public mood in crafting a narrative of the campaign. As Schattschneider argues, "The spectators are as much a part of the over-all situation as the overt combatants . . . for, as likely as not, the audience determines the outcome of the fight" (1960, 2). Schattschneider, however, also noted that clever candidates might try to shift the debate away from issues that undercut them toward issues that maximize their support. The possibility of "displacement of conflicts" reminds us that the agenda for the campaign is not merely a reflection of the concerns people had at the outset. Instead, the campaign is *built* by the dynamic interactions of citizens, candidates, and news media.

The 1992 campaign presents an intriguing example in which all three sets of participants were involved in shaping the campaign discourse. The public's overwhelming perception that the economy was the major problem facing the country meant that the candidates and the media found it difficult to displace their attention onto other issues.[1] In addition, the public entered the campaign worried about a (previous) negative campaign involving mudslinging candidates and a scandalmongering press. Because of their strong issue focus and proscription of certain candidate and media behavior, the public's participation in the construction of the campaign had considerably more impact than in the recent past.

This chapter begins by asking what kind of campaign discourse the public wanted and expected at the outset of the campaign. Which issues did citizens want the candidates to address and how did they want the candidates and media to carry on the discourse? The first question concerns the issue agenda; the second concerns candidate and media behavior. To understand the public's issue agenda, we asked our survey respondents and in-depth interviewees, "What do you think is the most important problem facing the country today?" To understand the voters' conceptions of the campaign, we asked our interviewees, "How would you describe a presidential campaign?" These broad questions brought forth both descriptive and prescriptive responses.[2]

Clearly, the citizens' concerns at the beginning of the election campaign did not emerge from nowhere. The process of constructing an understanding of the Bush presidency involved interactions among the administration, the press, and the public over the preceding four-year period. Opinion polls as early as October 1991, prior to the election, showed increasing concern about the economy and negative ratings of Bush's economic performance.

Our interviews with citizens in four communities around the country in January 1992 illustrated this remarkable consensus about the issues facing the country. The responses stressed the economic recession and its impact on jobs and unemployment. As for the political process, the public focused just as strongly on a condemnation of the dishonesty and manipulation of contemporary campaigns. This dual public agenda persisted throughout the campaign and became more tightly interconnected, making it difficult for candidates and the news media to shift the discourse to other issues.

The Public's Issue Agenda over Time

Looking back over the past 25 years, it is apparent that concentration or dispersion of issue attention varies from election to election. For example, in 1972 the public's issue agenda was almost equally divided among economic, social, and foreign policy concerns. In 1976 one issue, the economy or "stagflation," was overwhelmingly identified as the key issue of the campaign. In 1980, inflation and America's position in the world, as captured by the Iran hostage crisis, were the two major preoccupations during the campaign. In the campaigns of 1984 (and 1988), by contrast, public concerns were very broadly diffused over a range of issues (Abramson, Aldrich, and Rohde 1986, 166).

By 1992, however, a consensus about economic concerns was evident. National opinion polls consistently recorded the public's focus on the economy and jobs. Throughout the campaign year, a clear majority of respondents to our surveys in all four communities cited the economy and unemployment as the most important problem facing the country. The only exceptions were the Winston-Salem and Los Angeles primary surveys, conducted during and shortly after the Los Angeles riots. In these two locations, a strong plurality of respondents still reported that the economy and jobs were of greatest importance (44 and 39 percent, respectively), although concern about race made a temporary appearance on the issue agenda. In our pooled general election surveys in September and October, the economy and jobs overwhelmed all other issue priorities—mentioned by between 56 and 70 percent of respondents in each community.

The breadth of concern about the economy was stunning. The view that the economy was the most important problem cut across a variety of groups, both Democratic and Republican, politically attentive and politically inattentive, high and low media users, men and women, high-income and low-income, black and white.[3]

The in-depth interviews reinforced and enriched the survey evidence of the centrality of the economy and jobs in the campaign. Figures 3.1 and 3.2 report the survey and interview results. The interview data combine responses from the four communities we studied, including only concerns that were mentioned by at least 10 percent of the interviewees at each wave.[4]

As was true of national and local polling throughout 1992, the vast majority of our interviewees—over 83 percent—cited jobs and unemployment in every wave of interviews during the campaign.[5] No other issue approached this level of concern. As Vince, a Boston interviewee, correctly predicted in January, "In today's economy you're probably going to get the same answers from everybody."

Why was the public so single-mindedly preoccupied with the economy across virtually all regions, social groups, and political orientations—particularly when, as a number of economists noted during the campaign, the downturn was less severe than previous recessions? One answer is that the public may have been responding to other indicators, such as the duration of hard times; one of our communities (Boston), for example, had been in recession for almost all four years of the Bush presidency. The depth of layoffs also contributed to public concern, as white-collar workers felt newly vulnerable, and as blue-collar workers felt even more pinched. But there are other answers, provided by our in-depth interviews, that speak both to the kinds of evidence people offered to support their concern and to the deeper anxieties that the economic recession provoked.

First, economic issues are highly "obtrusive." People had ample opportunities in their everyday worlds to see evidence of recession, whether in their own experiences, in those of friends and family members, or in their communities at large. Although we did not ask them to do so, our interviewees usually explained *why* they believed a problem was the "most

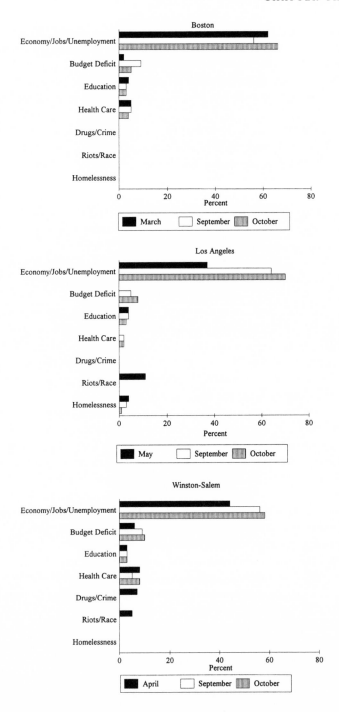

Figure 3.1   Most important problem in public opinion surveys.

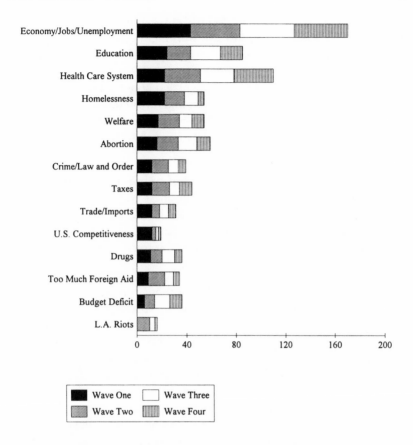

Figure 3.2   Issue concerns of in-depth interviewees. *Note:* Figure includes issues mentioned at least five times in one wave.

important." Their explanations provide insight into the data available to ordinary people and why they considered these data persuasive indicators of a policy problem.

Our interview panel drew predominantly on personal experiences rather than on media accounts to explain the primacy of jobs as a problem. Some people did talk about the rate of unemployment, the difficulties of selling American products abroad, and the like, but more often they referred to direct, immediate experiences with the economy.[6] Some reported that their friends were unemployed or that their children could not find jobs. Others feared they might become unemployed themselves. Thus, Jorge, an Angeleno, saw unemployment as an imminent possibility and said, "I'm afraid to go on vacation, you know, or leave my job, because I may not have one when I come back." Cathryn in Winston-Salem put it this way: "Thank God I'm still working, but it's so many people, hundreds of people that are out of work, and still being laid off, companies fold up. The company I work for may fold up the next day—you never can tell." People who had jobs worried about future prospects of shrunken wages, forced early retirement, and other consequences of businesses restructuring. Even those who owned businesses were worried. Lars drew on his experiences around Moorhead to support his concern about the economy:

> The number one issue right now, of course, is the economy. . . .
> It has started to even affect my business within the last week to
> ten days. See, we just don't have the traffic we, that we normally
> have. We can also tell that by the number of service calls we
> do. . . . We've always had it a little bit tough, but I can't remem-
> ber when we were quite this slow.

Other kinds of observations of the local environment reinforced the perception of hard times. Bostonians were especially vocal. Linda remarked in a January interview, "You think Woolworth's is not a big-time job, you know, and they're laying off and they're closing places, we're really hurting, we're really in a lot of trouble when a place like Woolworth's is having to close their doors after so many years of being here." Similarly, Vince commented in September: "I've gone by, just for instance, a mall one day. I knew this one store was opening and you could go in and fill out an application, and I was just stopped at the light and I was amazed. There was like 20 people standing on line just to get in to make out an application." Gloria explained, "I'm in the process of selling my house and I have found that prices have just gone down, down, and down in value drastically," and then noted that her company had made no new hires in months. Selma, in a spring interview, pointed out how people were cutting back by no longer inviting friends over to dinner and by renting videos instead of going to the movies.

Older interviewees drew comparisons to previous periods of economic prosperity and fretted about what they saw as the downward trajectory of the American economy. Ingrid, a Moorhead woman, wistfully recalled the New Deal and the pride that people had in their work and then contrasted that with her children's current employment and economic worries:

> I lived in Idaho for ten years and there were WPA's work every-
> where . . . and these people were proud of it and their families

were proud of the work they did. I really think they are going to have a hard time feeding people and keeping people working so this country does not come to a standstill. . . . My kids, I have a stepdaughter who is married. Her husband is now working minimum wage part-time in a bakery and they have a child. She is working for a law firm. She has two degrees in education, one in humanities and one in English as a teacher. . . . Well, she is working in an office. My son is an engineering grad from NDSU. He is working as a maintenance person in a candy factory in Boise, Idaho. . . . I don't know what is going to happen. It is really scary, it really is. My son can't pay back his loan to school. They are always calling, like, do you know where [he] is? He hasn't made a payment in such and such a time. Hey, he doesn't have a job. I mean for a while there he was completely unemployed. . . . I said, how do you expect people who are unemployed to pay.

Even when our interviewees did draw on media information to back up their economic concerns, they generally tended to place it in the context of what they themselves had witnessed. For instance, Maria recalled her state governor, Pete Wilson, on television talking about welfare and the economy. Her personal experiences, however, told her that Wilson was being unrealistic to think that welfare recipients could find jobs:

I was watching one night, I was watching the news when he said that, that these people on welfare are just on welfare so they wouldn't work. And he said that there are plenty of jobs out there that these women could, you know, could do babysitting jobs. . . . I think Pete Wilson doesn't realize that there's, I mean that the unemployment, there's just no jobs out there at all, whatsoever. . . . I've seen people, you know, hard workers who could, like I said, have degrees and can just not find a job. And they're not being picky, asking for a certain salary, they're, just, you know, lucky to get anything—that type of thing. . . . Things have gotten really bad. I see it now, because I'm a working adult.

Similarly, in the late fall Gloria, in Boston, rejected news coverage of an improving economy:

The job situation is horrendous. People just aren't making it. I don't see it getting any better. *I don't care what the papers say.* I

see people around me who aren't working or their hours have
been cut and still having a really bad time. (Emphasis added)

The economy resonated particularly strongly among our interviewees
because of deep-seated concerns about the decline of the United States as
a nation, as Ingrid's family stories suggested. Public opinion surveys
showed this to be a widespread and durable concern. The proportion of
Americans who believed that things in the country had "gotten pretty
seriously off on the wrong track" hovered around 80 percent throughout
the campaign, according to ABC News/*Washington Post* polls. In our interviews it was a rare individual, such as Herb in Boston or J. D. in
Winston-Salem, who said there was little to worry about given the good
shape that America was in compared to other countries around the globe.
Instead, our interviewees often linked economic worries to a broader pessimism about the passing of an "American way of life," and a rising cul-
tural crisis befalling the American family, with the strong sense that their
children would be worse off than they were. Rose, in Boston, put it this
way in September:

> Another thing that worries me is that—I know this isn't an
> original thought—is that this is the first generation where the
> children aren't doing better than the parents. You automatically
> expected your kids to do better. I did much better than my par-
> ents. The way I brought my children up, they have more
> education than I have. I expected them, I didn't know what they
> were going to do with their lives, but I expected them to do
> better than I did and they haven't. . . . Even staying at the same
> level is good. We have several children that are really nowhere
> near our level. I wonder how they're going to get there.

Similarly, Luis, from Los Angeles, remarked that even people "from other
parts of the world" could see that "America is a country in decline." Luis
believed that major economic change would need to be effected:

> Now, something drastic, something real has to be done not only
> to change that perception that they have, you know, but for our
> own well being . . . create jobs, create jobs, create jobs. Ah, jobs
> that will pay more than minimum wage.

Pedro reminisced about his arrival in the United States from Mexico many
years earlier, describing a vibrant country with many opportunities: "You
feeling like you come to the dream country. You feeling like you come to

the New World." Interestingly, this first-generation American identified immigration as the cause of decline in the United States:

> Now it's very, very different. I don't know what happen, but I think it's too much immigration, we got people from all over the world here.

In short, many of our interviewees worried that the recession was not a temporary downturn but reflected something deeply wrong with the nation and looked ahead anxiously at the potential for major disruption. Kelly, a young unemployed woman, expressed it this way at the end of the campaign:

> If Wall Street falls and we go into a depression and we're history as far as world-wide economics—what are we going to do? Where are we going to stand? When that happens I personally won't be affected too much. I'm already unemployed. It will just give me a chance to go back to the grass roots of things. We need to start over, but in doing so are we going to put ourselves into the position where we're going to have to worry about being taken over? . . . Sometimes it looks very overwhelming when you look at the whole picture.

Even those who saw themselves not to be much affected by the economy still pointed out potential problems on the horizon. Thus, Mike, a young prolife conservative, was cautiously optimistic in January about what the economy might portend but acknowledged both opportunities and problems for the future of the family:

> Maybe it's because of the economy, or whatever, putting people closer together. I think we're getting more into the family. It's tough for two. I know my wife has to work at night for us to even survive and pay rent. A house is not a realistic thing for us. So, maybe it's not a moral issue but I'd like to be able to own a house and that's not feasible.

The economy was also prominent because of its connection to status and race. Many of our white interviewees blamed the hard times at least in part on others' (whether racial and ethnic minorities in the United States or foreign beneficiaries) receiving more than what the interviewees considered a fair share. In that way, they linked racial and ethnocentric arguments to the decline of American values and the American standard of living. In turn, interviewees of color (African Americans in Winston-Salem, Los Angeles, and Boston, as well as Latinos in Los Angeles) expressed anxiety about increased racial tensions that they thought were provoked and worsened by the economic slump.

For instance, Tom blamed California's economic problems, in part, on immigrants from Mexico. "I feel like part of the reason why we have problems here in California is that we have no restriction on immigration through Mexico, which has essentially affected the ability of all people to get jobs." Herb, a Bostonian, noted how his daughter and son-in-law were moving to Georgia and said, "The economy, actually quotas. He can't get the job he really wants because of the quotas and they don't have any vacancies, so he might do better in Georgia. [Interviewer: The quotas meaning?] Racial, basically it's racial." Lillian, in Winston-Salem, began her January interview by pointing out, "I'm concerned about the billions of dollars . . . that could be better used to, for the economy," and continued with a theme she repeated throughout the campaign:

> I can't help it, but even the welfare program, I think we put too much money into that for the wrong reasons. I think there are people who are getting welfare that don't deserve it. I'm concerned about the—I won't necessarily say black, of course they're predominately black—they're having all these children, and apparently purely for monetary reasons. The more children they have, the more money they get. And they sit on their backsides and just don't do anything about their children.

Caren in Los Angeles viewed unequal education of different racial and ethnic groups as a root cause of economic problems:

> It's the minorities have not been educated, and they're coming from other countries, and they're working lower-class jobs, and going on welfare. And that hurts everybody, because that hurts the economy, too.

Interviewees often talked about wanting to get rid of what they saw as an unfair burden on themselves. In his first interview Paul, in Winston-Salem, put it this way: "I know there's problems with poverty, and I know there's problems with education, racism, all this other stuff, but the middle-class Americans can't continue to carry the load for everybody." This sense of having to cut back extended, not surprisingly, beyond American borders, as many interviewees noted how it was time to stop helping other countries and return the money to America where it was needed.[7] Germany and Japan, as economic competitors, came in for special scrutiny. Paul argued:

> I know we have to have a foreign policy, I know we can't have
> colonialism, and all these big isms that they talk about on TV,
> but it's time that we took care of our own for awhile. I mean,
> the world is such a big place, and all these other countries that
> we used to pay their way have become so powerful, and I think
> it's time to watch after our own for a little while.

In January, Sandra in Winston-Salem was more direct than most in saying:

> The United States won the war against the Japs. And the Japs is
> winning the war now, and they don't even have to drop the
> bomb. They are winning the war economically against the
> United States, and the United States is letting them.

African American and Latino interviewees were more likely than the
white interviewees to speak directly about racism and discrimination in
connection with the economy. Tracey, an African American from Los
Angeles, was concerned about "whites and minorities," adding:

> Well, racism is still strong. I mean, in 1992, I see, I see a lot of
> racism still. As far as jobs for minorities, I don't think that—a
> lot of times, it's not fair.

But Tracey then expressed resentment about the opportunities given to
Asian immigrants that were not as readily available to others:

> And as far as the recession about how the country allows other
> races to come over here and make a lot of money and they
> don't, you know, they're more apt to give an Asian person a
> loan to start a business than someone that is here that is a citi-
> zen. So that's, I think, that's a problem, too.

In a September interview, Selma, an African American in Boston, explicitly linked what she saw as a rise in racism to the decline of the economy:

> Possibly because the economy is so biased I think there is a lot
> of tension between whites and blacks around jobs. There's a
> strong feeling that many black or other minorities who have po-
> sitions don't belong there in the workforce that they got there
> through the back door and is taking my job. . . . There's a lot of
> rivalry and tension. I think that's why so many white people are
> so angry about affirmative action. I think it's because there
> aren't a pool of jobs. I think if there were plenty of jobs for
> people or at least the unemployment rate was a lot lower, I
> don't think there would be as much conflict.

A few white interviewees also spoke of their concerns about racism and anti-immigrant feelings (e.g., Cora in Moorhead and Saul in Boston), or at least their sense that minorities would be right to complain about discrimination (e.g., J. D. and Paul in Winston-Salem), but our interviewees of color were considerably more likely to directly point to these as continuing problems on their own, reinforced by the dismal state of the economy rather than the other way around.[8] Thus, Luis spoke very emotionally about racism against Latinos in the United States:

> Racism is a cancer, a cancer that is eating this country. And will continue to, to, to hurt it. . . . [We] got every race in the world here. You know, that's how this country started. Take the—not the Latins, take the Mexican American, we've been here all our lives. You know? And we are an invisible minority.

While the economy was the overarching concern of the campaign, there was a second tier of issue concerns, cited by between one-third and one-half of our overall sample in the January baseline interview: education, health care, homelessness, welfare, and abortion. But rather than add to a laundry list of disparate concerns, the interviewees often linked these second-tier issues to the economy and unemployment, especially as the campaign progressed: Sandra said in January, "I mean, everything rolls in together"; Carlton argued in September, "Right now we face an accumulation of different problems and we can put it together into one major problem"; and one of our most informed interviewees (Saul in Boston) resignedly said at the campaign's close, "Other things not tied to the economy—I'm afraid in my mind—it seems everything is tied to the economy somehow." Similarly, in Moorhead, Jane connected several issues:

> I suppose the deficit, and because of the deficit, we have, we've had so much unemployment. And I think that's the most important thing [pause] the unemployment. People losing jobs and uh, and then in turn, you know, the welfare system had to pay for those people and then that comes out of our tax money, and so our taxes go up and you know. Oh, I just see, there are just so many things that come from that, you know. Then we start closing schools, and, it's just, oh I guess the things, the problems come from unemployment, I guess.

Even issues that would seem to be more distant from the economy were linked. Some mentioned that crime would go down if the economy did not make it necessary for people to steal. And one interviewee (J. D. in a September interview) even speculated that outlawing abortion would aggravate the economy's problems: "There's so many people that have children in the world and they have no sense of responsibility to provide for their upkeep and all that, that's bound to put a strain on the economy. As if it isn't strained enough already."

The trajectory that these middle-range issues took is instructive. Concern about two issues, education and abortion, remained relatively constant over time or dipped only slightly near the primary or general election. Welfare fell from its moderate level to become a minor concern by the fall. What is most intriguing, though, are the dramatically different paths taken by health care and homelessness, which were equally cited in the first wave. Whereas health care gradually rose over time to become second only to jobs and unemployment as a central issue by the end of the campaign, homelessness gradually diminished until it was barely on the radar screen during the general election. The Harris poll showed identical trends nationwide.

The divergent paths taken by health care and homelessness suggest an important thesis about agenda building: the effects of the campaign are less in saying what is *on* the agenda than in saying what is *off* it. While the campaign probably contributed to a growing concern about the health care system, the campaign undercut the concern about homelessness. The most plausible explanation for these trajectories is that the candidates and the news media were talking a great deal about health care and very little about homelessness. The difference suggests that whatever immediately visible problems may exist in citizens' worlds, these may not be perceived as problems that should be remedied by government unless elite actors (whether the candidates or the media) debate them and suggest ways to solve them (see Gamson 1992).

After all, both health care and homelessness were equally obtrusive issues, the effects of which people readily saw in their immediate worlds. To be sure, health care was usually deemed a problem that our interviewees were directly experiencing, whereas few saw homelessness as an immediate problem for themselves. Many noted how their medical bills, their insurance premiums, or the cost of prescriptions had skyrocketed or how their insurance benefits had been cut back. But homelessness was also all around them. Note how, just before the Massachusetts primary, Linda linked homelessness, health care, and the economy:

> Homelessness, I look around. I'm from New York originally
> and I look at the abandoned buildings and places and they're
> just there wasting away and people using them illegally. . . . We

recently heard about a distant relative of mine whose husband
lost his job because he got sick. The wife was already sick. They
lost their home—just like that. I assume it took a period of
time, but again, these were people who thought they made it
and, you know, something like an illness can take it all away.

Another possibility is that homelessness became subsumed under the
economy—that is, it was a symptom of economic hard times rather than
a distinct problem. But while our interviewees did indeed link homelessness to the economy over time, they did the same for health care. Eddy,
in our preprimary interview in Boston, talked about both homelessness
and unemployment but then added, "Unemployment would probably
come before homelessness because one kind of washes the other. When
unemployment isn't as low, you obviously don't have as many people out
on the street and whatnot." But Mark from Moorhead also said:

> I know all this socialized medicine, too, and I think that is a
> really, really good idea, too. Because, personally, myself and all
> my friends and stuff, none of us can afford health insurance
> these days. We don't make enough money and we can't find a
> job that will allow us to make enough money to get health
> insurance.

Los Angeles resident Jorge argued that improved physical health would
produce a better workforce: "If we improved their physical [health], you
would think that there would be a higher class of people, their work,
better quality of work from Americans." Carlton concurred at the end of
the campaign: "The health issue is one along with unemployment. I still
don't think they've touched enough on that. If you're not healthy how can
you go to work?"

Because the public began the year with so much concern about the
economy in 1992, it was hard to establish new items on the agenda and
keep them there. The closest to a "new" issue was the deficit question,
which went from low to moderate levels, accompanying the rise of Ross
Perot, who concentrated on this issue. There were also momentary up-
surges of concern about particular issues during the campaign associated
with specific contemporary events. Thus, for instance, citing trade, imports, the lack of American competitiveness, and the threat of Japanese
products was concentrated most in January, following closely on George
Bush's disastrous trade trip to Japan. Likewise, the Los Angeles riots at
the end of April and in early May produced a short-lived concern about
the riots, urban problems, and gangs among Los Angeles interviewees, as

well as in Winston-Salem, which were the two places where we conducted interviews shortly after the civil disturbances.

Instead of the agenda becoming richer and more diverse as candidates developed their campaigns, however, the opposite occurred: the agenda became more concentrated and consensual. Over time there was greater agreement across individuals about the central problems and a declining tendency for competing issues to disperse the public's attention. To measure the dispersion of the issue agenda, we counted the total number of different issue concerns that were mentioned in each of our four communities during the campaign; the results are shown in figure 3.3. In general, the pattern shows the effect of agenda simplification. In our interviews the total number of issue concerns declined substantially between the two spring waves of interviews and the two fall waves. The data illustrate that the interviewees were much less likely to name a variety of problems as the campaign progressed—with one exception. Note that in Winston-Salem, the breadth of the public agenda remained fairly constant over time. As the lone "battleground" site, Winston-Salem became substantially more information-rich in the fall. This increased activity in the information environment was associated with virtually no reduction in the number of issue concerns in the later stages of the campaign. Instead, faced with large amounts of new information, and the competing agendas of the three candidates, people in Winston-Salem continued to have as rich a list of issue concerns as they reported in the spring. The maintenance of varied issue concerns in North Carolina is consistent with an interactive construction of the campaign agenda. Likewise, in communities where the candidate and media activity was relatively constant or declined, the number of issue concerns diminished over the course of the campaign. The result of the narrowing issue focus was that in this respect at least, the meaning of the campaign was clear. As Clinton's storefront headquarters in Little Rock proclaimed, "It's the economy, stupid!"

The Public's Concerns about Campaign Behavior

Just as there was a strong consensus from the opening of the 1992 campaign that the economy was the defining problem of the election, people also agreed about how candidates should campaign. They believed that previous political campaigns were marked by mudslinging, scandalmongering, avoidance of important issues, manipulation, and lying. People held both the media and, to a lesser extent, the candidates responsible for the character of campaign discourse. In such a climate it was difficult for

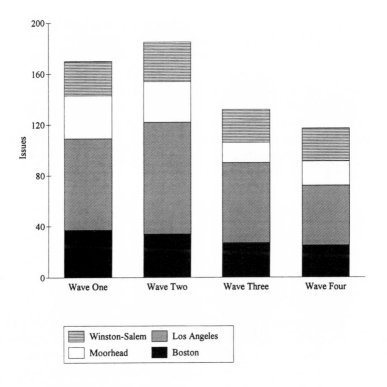

Figure 3.3   Number of different issue concerns of in-depth interviewees.

any candidate to attack an opponent without being seen as "wallowing in the mud." Indeed, the Republicans' anticipation of public disdain for negative campaigning apparently discouraged them from making the kind of assault on the opposition they had made so successfully in 1988 (Royer 1994). The public mood and preoccupation with a dominant set of policy issues even made it difficult for them to shift the agenda to matters of character or experience. Throughout the campaign, citizens praised and rewarded issue-based appeals and news and decried what they perceived as gratuitous character assassination.

Anticipation of a dirty campaign was prevalent during the nominating season. Our first wave of interviews was conducted in January, around the time of Gennifer Flowers's allegations about her extramarital affair with Bill Clinton. At this time, most of the interviewees had difficulty identifying the candidates except for President Bush, so that for some people these allegations were the first bits of information they encountered about Clinton. Interestingly, while many people talked about these allegations, they identified them as the opening salvos of another dirty election. As a result, our interviewees tended to discount this story as an example of negative campaigning rather than a defect of Clinton's character. Attaching scandals to negative campaigning, however, fed the general mistrust of candidates and the news media. For example, Frank, from Los Angeles, commented on the allegations of a Clinton affair without using the candidate's name. He expressed his concern that mudslinging deflected attention from substantive issues:

> It seems like, at least in past campaigns, somebody might bring something up, you know, some dirt thing, whether it be true or not. It doesn't seem like they have to prove anything, they just, you know, they can just say, this guy, you know, fools around on his wife, or whatever. . . . So then the guy's got to spend half his time defending himself on something that's not even true, instead of talking about the issues, that are you know, unemployment, whatever, the issues that pertain to everybody. And so, I don't know whether it's true or not, this tabloid thing.

Disgust with campaign practices was widespread. A majority of interviewees in each of our four communities expressed considerable skepticism. Thus, to take some of our Boston interviewees in January: Eddy said that candidates could "cop out" by "putting down their opponents instead of worrying about themselves." Kelly was newly discouraged, saying:

> Over the years my views have changed. It used to be everybody trying to be the best. Somebody competing to be the best. Now it's everybody saying things whether they mean them or not to get this job of prestige and money and a nice big white house, whether it affects them or not.

John said simply: "It's a bunch of crooks trying to get into an office where they can be even bigger crooks. Flat out."

Although, in January, interviewees who supported Dukakis in 1988 expressed the most doubts about the quality of the coming campaign, most of the interviewees who reported voting for Bush in 1988 complained as well. The concern was not limited to Boston—the home turf of Bush's opponent Michael Dukakis. We found a similar suspicion about the campaign-to-come prevalent in other locales. In Winston-Salem, for example, Sara laughed and said: "Well, it gets kinda nasty. With mudslinging. And I don't know, most of what you hear really won't come around." J. D. said, "A lot of ads on TV, they fight against one another, and a lot of them put out statements—anything to win a vote." And Diane condemned

> candidates judging each other or seeing who can put more dirt
> on the other one. That's basically what comes to mind, you see
> all these commercials, you know, one slamming another. I just
> think it's bad. That's what sticks in my mind, that it just starts a
> lot of negative campaigning.

Well before the first caucus or primary, when asked to describe the 1992 presidential campaign, Grace responded simply, "one word—mudslinging."

Nor was this criticism restricted to candidates. Instead, the news media, from the outset, were also seen to contribute to the trivialization and sensationalization of the campaign. Thus, our interview panels' impressions of the media and candidates were generally pessimistic and mistrusting. They expected to be lied to and presented with partial or untrue information. Lenny summed up many of the interviewees' suspicions about the news media coverage of politics:

> Well, you can't believe everything you hear or read or see on
> there either, so mean, it's so, it's so distorted that they show
> what they want to show or, you know, it depends upon who
> owns the station or stuff like that it's hard for the average per-
> son to find out what's really going on, it's really hard, really
> hard.

William wondered whether the news reporters might even have had a part to play in President Bush's illness in Japan:

> A little fainting on camera in Japan seems just a little bit too
> much coincidence for me. . . . That just seemed impossible, the
> camera was set right on him, I'm sure all the little reporters of
> that camera happened to. I'd like to trust them, but I think they
> tell me what they want me to hear.

Conclusion

In 1992, then, the public entered the campaign with a clear sense of the issues they wished to be addressed and an equally clear agenda for how they wished the candidates and the news media to do so. The concern about the economy started high and crossed not only party lines but most political and social divides. The economy became even more central over the course of the campaign, as people connected other problems to it; by the fall, there was a strong sense that if there were other problems, the state of the economy had made them worse.

In addition, no new issue concerns pushed their way onto the fall agenda without having been present from the beginning of the campaign, although candidate emphasis clearly had an impact on the priority given to the deficit and health care. This suggests that in 1992, public issue priorities contributed substantially to the campaign discourse. Public concern, however, is not enough to keep an item such as homelessness on the agenda if the candidates and media ignore it. Rather, the interactions of citizens, candidates, and media together build the campaign discourse. The issues raised by candidates and discussed in the news media are a resource for citizens as they try to make sense of the campaign. In their information environments people can find out what is on the candidates' agendas, what they think the problems are, what solutions they have to offer. Many of our interviewees went into the 1992 campaign with an issue agenda and deep suspicions about the candidates and the news media. In the next chapter we will examine how the candidates shaped their messages in light of their perceptions of the public mood and their own strategic goals.

FOUR

Candidate Advertising

What candidates say in their campaign messages reflects on important democratic issues. How accountable are incumbents for their records? How responsive are the candidates to the issues that the public cares about? Do candidate messages distinguish the competitors and provide useful choices for the electorate? This chapter examines candidate communications, focusing in particular on the dimensions of policy, performance, and personal qualities. These were the issues that people expressed the most concern about at the outset of the 1992 campaign and are also the issues that previous voting studies suggest are crucial elements of decision making. Here we explore not only what the candidates said, but also how they said it, and argue that people build candidate constructs from both the substance and the style of candidate communications.

Scholars have worried about whether candidate communications provide information for voters—whether they provide enough understanding of who the candidates are, what party and issue orientations they represent, and what personal qualities they will bring to the office. Evaluating candidate communications as a democratic resource should be guided, however, by the realization that what is uppermost in the candidate's mind is winning the election. Candidate communications are meant first and foremost to persuade, and only to that end, to provide information. In addition, the candidate's strategic position—incumbency status, record, number and nature of challengers, and so forth—constrains what the candidate can say.

Following a brief review of the previous research on candidate communication, the chapter describes the actual content of candidate communications in the 1992 election, especially the relative attention to issues and personal qualities. We also explore how and why candidates differed in constructing their messages, particularly regarding the issues of the economy and trust, and the impact that had on the tone of candidate discourse.

Theoretical Perspectives on Candidate Communications

The 1992 election was the fortieth anniversary of the first use of televised political ads.[1] Political spots are particularly attractive for candidates because, unlike news, they enable the candidate to completely control the content of the communication (the "ad watch" and other effects of news coverage on the ultimate public reception of ads are discussed in chap. 6). Especially when candidates feel ill treated by the news, as all three major candidates did in 1992, they have strong reason to rely on ads to get their messages across to voters. The fact that candidates for major office devote nearly two-thirds of their campaign budgets to the making and airing of television spots attests to their perceived significance.

Political ads are especially important in the nomination phase of a presidential campaign, which often involves a number of relatively unknown candidates competing against each other. News coverage of a large field of candidates is uneven and party cues are not available to help voters distinguish among the candidates. Since many citizens do not pay much attention to campaign news at this stage, advertising can get their attention and provide an important source of information. Indeed, ads are designed to reach people who may not be very involved with the campaign and who may be resistant to political messages. Bill Hillsman, creative head of the award-winning Wellstone for Senate ad effort, pointed out that a political ad is not just in competition for attention with the opponent's ad. Rather, it is "in competition with every other commercial on the air, such as the Pepsi ad that cost $475,000 to shoot" (Alger 1995). In 30 or 60 seconds, television ad makers try to communicate some attention-getting and memorable images and, usually, some information about the candidate's or opponent's political orientation, experience, or views in a way that resonates with the target public.

Underlying advertising messages is a theory of how voters can be persuaded. Using language, symbols, and narratives and visual, aural, and verbal cues, ads attempt to connect with the voters' issue concerns, emotions, ideal conceptions of candidates, and notions of politics and society. Research suggests that successful ads encourage voters to believe that the candidate shares their own concerns about issues, their feelings and aspirations.[2] Through the use of symbols associated with particular emotions and meanings, ads seek to transfer those emotions and meanings to the candidate or opponent. Many ads also use personal narratives to evoke experiences with which the viewer can identify (Kern 1989).

Candidates often appear in ads in order to communicate directly with voters. The medium of television is regarded as particularly effective in

forging personal connections between candidates and viewers. As
Jamieson and Campbell note: "The language of the television screen is
the language of close-ups. . . . Distance is related to intimacy. Television
simulates intimate relationships" (1983, 45). Particularly for those candidates who are comfortable on camera and whose appearance and manner
work well on television, the medium enables them to communicate in a
personal way with the viewer (Alger 1995; Graber 1984; Kern 1989).

Candidates not only use ads to build trust in themselves but use "negative" or "attack" ads to break or prevent the development of bonds of
trust between the public and the opposing candidate. As Kern (1989) and
Jamieson (1992a) have pointed out, there is substantial evidence, experimental and otherwise, that "when evaluating 'social stimuli,' negative information carries more weight than positive information" and "negative
information seems better able than positive to alter existing impressions
and is easier to recall" (Jamieson 1992a, 41). However, one must try to
distinguish between ads that attack the opposing candidate based primarily on policy issues and/or performance in office and those that primarily
attack the opponent personally. Research has found that the public tends
to recoil from ads that attack on the basis of personal qualities while they
see attacks on issue stands and record to be more legitimate. But Johnson-
Carter and Copeland report a difficulty in distinguishing personal attacks
from substantive ones: "ad hominem arguments deal directly with leadership style. In other words, they are arguments used to call into question
a given candidate's fitness for office" (1991, 37). Thus, in moderate form,
an attack on official performance will seem like a legitimate questioning of qualification for high office, but in a more extreme form, such
an attack can suggest that an opponent is fundamentally deficient in
moral character and is personally unfit for office. Given the increasing
melding of issue and character in ads, one would expect that candidates,
viewers, and even analysts have difficulty discerning when such a line is
crossed.

The classic typology of ads includes three basic categories: positive ads
for the sponsoring candidate, "true negative" or attack ads targeted at
the opponent, and comparative ads which provide at least some material
on both candidates for comparison (see, e.g., Newhagan and Reeves
1991, 198). This analysis expands those categories to make finer distinctions about "who" and "what" is the subject of the ad. The categories
include: (1) candidate's own character and accomplishments (typically
biographical ads), (2) candidate's issues, (3) candidate's character and issues, (4) attacks on opponent's character, (5) attacks on opponent's issues,

(6) attacks on both opponent's character and issues, (7) attacks on opponent's issues, while promoting one's own, and (8) attacks on opponent's character and issues, while promoting one's own.

Our analysis of candidate messages focuses on advertising, but other forms of candidate communication also reach large national audiences. Speeches are the oldest mode of candidate communication. On television, however, only brief "soundbites" reach the general public through most news outlets, with one important exception. Candidate acceptance speeches at national party conventions are the opening salvo of the general election campaign, where the nominees introduce themselves to the nation and articulate themes and symbols, political orientations, and policy stands that they will emphasize. Televised conventions give candidates an opportunity to present themselves to millions of viewers. Many recent candidates have shown a "bio film" at the conventions to illustrate their personal narratives with pictures and to help define themselves more distinctly as persons, individuals, and leaders (see Kendall 1995).

Debates provide a different mode of communication for candidates. Unlike ads or speeches, the subject matter in a debate is not completely under the candidate's control. Certainly, candidates do not slavishly respond within the narrow confines of the questions posed; they seize the opportunity to direct their answers toward their preferred themes, symbols, and proposals. Candidate debates also provide a unique chance for the public to see and hear the candidates "side by side" and make direct comparisons. Debates give the candidates their greatest television audience. They are watched by tens of millions of people and are treated by the media as major news events, thus reinforcing their salience. Moreover, the public actively anticipates the debates as a principal way to discover what the candidates are like (Royer 1994; Hellweg, Pfau, and Brydon 1992).

In the face of a range of candidate-controlled communication we have concentrated on ads for several reasons. First, ads stretch across the entire campaign, while other forms of communication are episodic. Second, political spots reach a large and varied audience since they are often sandwiched between prime-time network programs. Third, because ads represent a huge expenditure of candidates' resources, candidates design them to deliver their main messages in their briefest, most dramatic forms. Although we did not carry out a thorough analysis of the nationally broadcast convention speeches, the longer-format "infomercials," or the debates, our analysis refers to those forms of communication to clarify more fully the candidates' strategies.

Candidate Communications: Messages, Images, and Strategy

Our content analysis of the candidates' ads systematically explores which considerations the candidates tried to get people to remember—and which techniques they used to communicate these considerations.[3] For the nomination phase, ads were analyzed for Bush and Buchanan on the Republican side and Clinton, Brown, Harkin, Kerrey, and Tsongas on the Democratic side. In the general election, the content analysis focused on the three major candidates—Bush, Clinton, and Perot.[4] We obtained data on candidate "ad buys" from the three major networks[5] for the general election, as well as from the leading television station in the four media markets serving the four areas in our study: Los Angeles, Boston, Greensboro/Winston-Salem/Highpoint, and Fargo/Moorhead. By examining the ad buys we can see not only what the ads were about but also which ads the candidates emphasized to which audiences. The ad buys therefore reveal a crucial element of candidate image building that has not been explored previously. The convention speeches and long-form ads (infomercials) were examined to see the extent to which advertising messages were reinforced or augmented in these more discursive formats.

Our analysis of ad contents focuses on four broad categories. First is partisanship, which has long been recognized as a principal consideration in voters' electoral decisions, though its significance has decreased over the past three decades. Second is candidates' stands on policy questions and perceptions of blame and credit regarding important issues, especially economic performance. A third category is "candidate evaluation"—the perceptions people have of the candidates as persons and leaders, including formal qualifications for office and leadership capacity, honesty, integrity and trustworthiness, moral character and personality, and how much each candidate cares about and understands the concerns of average people. In 1992, a fourth element became central: a theme of political cynicism and distrust for "politics as usual."

Partisanship

Following trends established earlier (Wattenberg 1990), candidates in 1992 offered few partisan cues. For instance, we note three patterns in the candidates' ads: messages explicitly reinforcing partisan orientation were virtually nonexistent; explicit attacks on the opposition party were rare; and in the context of increased public suspicion of parties in the

1990s, Clinton criticized his *own* party and sought to present an image of himself as a Democratic agent for change. Criticisms of the opposition were largely directed at individual officeholders within the party, rather than at the party itself. But three Clinton ads in the nomination stage made critical mention of the Democratic as well as the Republican party ("Bill Clinton is the only one challenging the failed politics of both parties"), and three ads in the general election positioned Clinton and Gore as "new kinds of Democrats" and claimed "they've rejected the old tax and spend politics." Bush and Clinton ads gave few ideological cues other than some standard lines such as, "My opponent suggests an old answer: just go back to having government solve all our problems" (Bush), or doing away with unfair "tax breaks for the wealthy" (Clinton). Perot's spot ads made only one partisan attack, and that was on both parties.

As one would expect, references to party or ideology in the convention speeches were more numerous (Clinton mentioned the Democrats seven times and Bush made sixteen references to the Republican party). Clinton, the candidate who was "new" to the national scene, and who was portraying himself as a new and different kind of Democrat, offered less partisan discourse than the incumbent president. Even Bush, however, did not emphasize party. Although the national party conventions are the prime partisan event in presidential elections, the candidates' acceptance speeches are now intended for the whole viewing public at least as much as for the convention delegates. Thus, even in the conventions, there was only a modest amount of explicitly partisan rhetoric.

In the first debate, the candidates talked somewhat more about party and ideology than they did in their ads, though not in the second debate. In the standard setting and format of the first debate, Clinton made several critical references to the Republican party and numerous references to "trickle-down economics" and how "the rich" benefited disproportionately from Bush's and Reagan's policies. Bush made eight references to Democrats in the first debate. It appears that the confrontational format of the typical candidate debate brought out partisan discourse, whereas the second "citizens' debate" discouraged partisan talk.

The independent candidate Perot's nonbiographical long-form ads did not speak in party terms. Perot did emphasize, however, a theme related to Republican ideology, which reinforced Clinton's message: he argued that Republican policies of the previous 12 years had benefited the wealthy few and hurt the majority, especially the middle class. Perot's infomercials repeatedly referred to "trickle-down economics" and "voodoo economics." In the debates, Perot made only two party-related comments, both of which questioned the responsibility of the Democratic and Republican parties, in keeping with his main message that all politics in Washington had gone awry.

In sum, out of the thousands of mentions of issues, themes, symbols, and personal matters in the short and long ads, speeches, and debates, candidates raised few party-based considerations; instead, their appeals or attacks focused primarily on the individual candidates (and their predecessors). These communications were principally candidate centered (Wattenberg 1991), and they did not encourage electoral choice based on collective party responsibility.

Candidate Communication on Policy Issues

The democratic ideal is to provide people with a choice between candidates, with leadership capacity, specific policy stands, and general political philosophy central to that choice. At the heart of the electoral outcome is a "policy mandate" for action in government. In this election, did candidate communications emphasize policy? Did one candidate lead or dominate the discourse on policy matters? Did the candidates engage one another in a dialogue over policy directions, or did they talk past one another and make separate appeals to the public? This section analyzes the candidates' discourse on policy issues, beginning with economic and foreign policy.

We begin our analysis of ad content with an important caveat. While our results show a considerable number of ads and messages mentioning issues or even policy alternatives, the tally may not mean that significant issue information has been imparted—particularly if one employs Joslyn's standard that information should be "the basis of policy choice or [could be used] to hold a public official accountable for political actions" (1986, 147–48). In addition to Joslyn's problem of specificity (is the issue merely mentioned or is a substantial amount of information provided?) is the question of consistency or subtexts (are the visuals, sound, and symbols consistent with the text, or does a different message overwhelm the meaning of the text entirely?).

The Bush general election ad "What I Am Fighting For" illustrates the problem of specificity. In the ad, Bush mentions a series of issues:

> The world is in transition. The defining challenge of the '90s is
> to win the economic competition, to win the peace. We must be
> a military superpower, an economic superpower, and an export

superpower. In this election you'll hear two versions of how to
do this. Theirs is to look inwards, ours is to look forward. Pre-
pare our people to compete, to save and invest so we can win.
Here's what I'm fighting for: open markets, lower government
spending, tax relief, opportunities for small business, legal and
health reform, job training, and new schools, built on competition, ready for the 21st century.

Virtually every message in this ad mentions an issue. But there is little
information that distinguishes the positions of the candidates. Any one
of the three candidates could have delivered Bush's message word for
word. For example, Clinton made clear in one of the debates that the
United States should be an "economic superpower" and stressed exports
and open markets, as did Perot; Clinton and Perot both urged preparation
for international economic competition, including savings and investment, job training, and "opportunities for small business"; Clinton repeatedly urged "tax relief" for the middle class; even Bush's promise to
"lower government spending" was not unique, as Clinton ads rejected
"the old tax and spend" politics and Perot emphasized bringing down
the deficit.

Nowhere in his ad does Bush provide information about a particular
means to accomplish a policy objective. As is typical of presidential candidates (Page 1978), Bush's appeals involve agreed-upon values more than
policy promises. Similarly, the most heavily aired ads by Clinton in the
general election focused on Bush's performance in office, macroeconomic
policy, and some specific areas such as trade policy. These ads provided
some policy indications, but not in much detail. Perot's ads ran the gamut
from spot ads that were almost totally devoid of policy information to his
first two infomercials, which had an abundance of factual information
about economic and budget difficulties, as well as some solutions to the
deficit problem.

The second problem of message consistency in classifying policy ads is
exemplified by a Bush ad attacking Clinton's "Arkansas Record." The visuals consisted of a barren (some described it as post–nuclear war) black
and white landscape; and the sound track was an ominous, foreboding
rumble which accompanied specific attacks on the governor's record. The
ad raises a troubling question. Is this simply an ad criticizing the opponent's record, or is it a threatening, ungrounded attack? Many ads use
"sound and visuals [to] add a character dimension and affective style of
argumentation to an ad that does not use human symbols and is therefore
[on the surface, at least] concerned with issues, but only as one part of a

broader message" (Kern 1989, 98). Was "Arkansas Record" about tax increases, or did the vulture in a dead tree convey a different message altogether? With that cautionary note in mind, we turn to a comparison of issues emphasized in candidate advertising during the primary and general election campaigns.

Focus on the Economy Compared to Foreign Policy Issues
Our discussion of the policy messages in ads begins with the public's chief policy concern, the economy. We evaluated ads both as a whole and also at the individual message level in order to get at the emphasis within the ad. At the ad level, we coded attention to economic issues into two categories: the economy in general and jobs.[6] Comparing how the two principal candidates dealt with economic issues in the nomination and general election phases shows substantial differences, which can best be understood in light of the strategic demands on each candidate. In the nomination phase, where President Bush was challenged by fellow Republican Pat Buchanan in the economically devastated state of New Hampshire, 44 percent of the Bush ads mentioned jobs or unemployment (hereafter labeled "jobs") and 67 percent mentioned the economy generally. Running against Clinton in the general election, Bush ads made fewer references to the economy. Jobs were specifically mentioned in only 30 percent of Bush's ads, and the economy was mentioned in only 26 percent. If we look at the proportion of attention to economic issues in the ads, Bush's emphasis on the economy fell from 24 percent of his messages in the primary election ads to 14 percent in the general election ads. By contrast, from the primaries to the general election, Clinton increased his focus on the economy. In the primary season, 17 percent of his ad messages were about economic matters; but that figure increased to 26 percent of all messages in the general election. A majority of his primary ads noted that Clinton had a "plan" for the economy and discussed at least some aspects of it; several Clinton ads listed an 800 number to call for copies of the plan. In the general election, fully 71 percent of Clinton ads mentioned jobs, and 34 percent mentioned the economy and one focused exclusively on his economic plan. Taking the election as a whole, including both the nominating and general election phases, twice as many Clinton ads as Bush ads dealt with the economy.

Comparing the candidates' relative attention to the economy and the foreign policy–military area (Bush's forte) is instructive. In the primaries, 11 percent of all the president's ad messages were on foreign policy matters, as were 9 percent of the general election ads. Out of a total of 1,350 messages in Clinton's general election ads, a mere seven involved international issues. (Even that overstates the case, as six of the seven concerned Japanese trade policies and were as much about the economy as about foreign affairs!)

Over time Bush maintained a greater emphasis on foreign affairs and downplayed the economy while Clinton remained focused on the issue that most concerned the public. This was not only true of the ads. The candidates' speeches at their national party conventions manifest similar patterns. Clinton spent more than twice as much time discussing economic issues in his speech as Bush did. This pattern was reversed in the foreign policy realm, with Bush spending five and a half times as much of his speech on international affairs, compared to Clinton.[7] Likewise, in the debates, the basic distinction between economic and foreign policy agendas is evident, although the contrasting structures of the debates moderated the pattern. Clinton talked somewhat more about foreign policy in the first debate, in which journalists asked questions about presidential leadership in international affairs, and Bush put more emphasis on economic matters in the second debate, in which citizens zeroed in on their top priority. But even when discussing foreign affairs in the debates, Clinton managed repeatedly to turn attention back to economic matters. For example, in the first debate, when a journalist asked about America's national interest in the post–cold-war world, Clinton said, "We have to face the fact that economic security is a whole lot of national security."

The closing statements of the debates are especially revealing. The statements give candidates an opportunity to articulate the considerations they want voters to take into account in making electoral choices. The centerpiece of President Bush's closing statements was a focus on international crisis and the need for decisive leadership in foreign affairs. Clinton's closing statements were devoted almost entirely to economic matters. He pointed out that "we do not need four more years of an economic theory that doesn't work" and noted his economic plan for the future— including the fact that the plan had been endorsed by leading economists and business leaders, with a generous helping of Republicans among them. As those who studied the debates found, Clinton maintained a "tight focus on a single overall theme, the need for economic change" (Friedenberg 1994).

As for Perot, his policy emphases largely echoed Clinton's, and the way he presented them reinforced Clinton's messages—including the derogatory references to "trickle-down economics" and "voodoo economics." Perot's campaign lent further weight to the agenda that Clinton promoted as the focus of his campaign. Over 75 percent of Perot ads mentioned jobs, and 41 percent mentioned the economy generally. But in terms of proportion of attention, Clinton's focus on the economy was greater than Perot's—only 12.5 percent of Perot's spot-ad messages discussed economic matters, compared to 26 percent of Clinton's.

In his issue-oriented long-form ads,[8] Perot featured the economy but stressed government reform and the budget deficit as well. In the debates, Perot's discourse looks similar to Clinton's, but with marginally less focus on economic matters, as a result of his greater attention to government reform and deficit reduction.

Policy Emphasis in Ad Buys

To more fully understand the candidates' relative emphasis on the leading issues, it is important to know which ads they spent the most money on. Most previous studies of ads have investigated the content of each ad and have aggregated the totals to discern patterns among candidates. But the public, at whom the ads are aimed, is not exposed to each of the ads in equal measure; some ads are aired many times, some only a few. (In fact, some ads—found in research archives—were not aired at all; a presidential campaign's ad creators produce many ads, and the campaign managers use those they think are right for the strategic situation at the time.) The ad buys establish the issue emphasis that candidates actually communicated to the public and provide an inside look at the way the candidates sought to construct their images for the public.

The most frequently aired general election ad for Bush ("Agenda") was an attempt to convey the message that Bush did indeed have an economic plan (see appendix B). But as in other facets of campaigning, good strategy is not only how much, but when. "Agenda" only began airing a week and a half before election day—too late to establish the economic plan as a central feature of the Bush candidacy. Only one other national Bush ad even mentioned his economic plan (a once-aired, four-minute ad), and only one other ad dealt with the economy at all—and then only as one of a long list of issues. At the local level, in the media markets we studied, not one of the Bush ads dealt with economic matters; one focused on foreign affairs leadership, and the rest were attacks on Clinton's personal character or tax-raising propensities.

The Clinton ad-buy strategy, on the other hand, made the economy—and Bush's performance on it—the centerpiece of his message. Clinton's most frequently aired national ad ("Remember 2") was a 15-second ad that opened with video of Bush himself saying, "Read my lips, no new taxes." It asked people to remember that line, and then showed video of Bush in the 1988 election saying, "You'll be better off four years from now than you are today." The ad concluded, "Well, it's four years later.

How are you doing?" Clinton's second most frequently aired national ad focused entirely on his economic plan and numerous prestigious endorsements of it. All the other ads dealt with economic issues in varying degrees. Clinton ran ads in only one of the four local areas we studied, Winston-Salem, which was in one of the 20 states targeted by his campaign as key to an electoral college victory. Each of the five Clinton ads most frequently aired in that market dealt with the economic issue in various ways; the second most frequently aired ad used four video segments of Bush saying he did not think the country was in recession and that there was no need to extend unemployment benefits. It was a companion to "Remember 2" as a pure distillation of the questions about Bush's economic performance. The Clinton ads most frequently aired, and hence the messages he emphasized most, focused on the economy and sought to make the campaign into a referendum on the incumbent's performance on economic issues. In his ads, Clinton played "the blame game" (West 1993), but with his economic plan striking a positive note alongside his criticism of the incumbent.

Perot's ad buys put less emphasis on the economy than Clinton's. The ad Perot most frequently aired nationally (and in Los Angeles) was about the deficit issue, but it also mentioned jobs. All but one of his other national ads and those aired in Los Angeles and Fargo/Moorhead included very little discussion of the economy.[9]

Engaging in Dialogue on Policy Issues

Thus far the analysis shows that the common thread of candidate discourse during the campaign was the economy, but with varying degrees of emphasis. Did the discourse allow the voters to make useful comparisons among candidates or did the candidates talk past each other? As figures 4.1 and 4.2 show, in the general election Bush increased the range of issues mentioned in his ads compared with the primary campaign, while Clinton limited the number of issues he discussed going from the spring to the fall campaign. One candidate was diversifying his agenda, while the other was focusing more narrowly. The economy was the common topic of discourse between the two candidates.

One explanation for the difference in candidate agenda strategies was the nature—and number—of challengers that each candidate faced in the primaries. Bush's sole challenger, Buchanan, focused almost entirely on three issues: taxes, the economy, and morality. He did not even mention health care in his ads for the nomination stage, and neither did Bush. The first concern for Bush was the primary in New Hampshire, a state in deep economic trouble. Therefore, Bush had to focus on his one challenger and

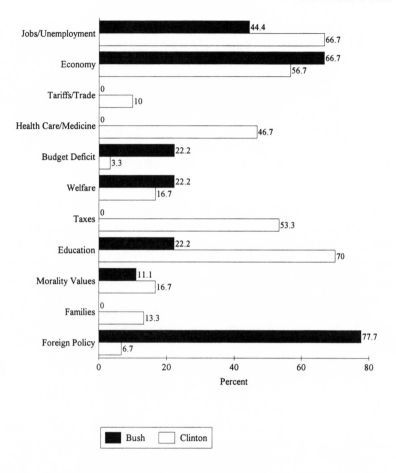

Figure 4.1 Policy issues mentioned in nomination campaign ads. *Note:* Figure includes issues mentioned in at least 10 percent of a candidate's ads in either the nomination or general election campaign.

on the economy. Clinton, on the other hand, faced four vigorous opponents for the nomination, who emphasized various concerns: the deficit, health care, and education, as well as economic matters. Clinton countered his primary opponents across a range of issues in the spring, but in the fall his campaign team focused on the economy. To be sure, Clinton's ads addressed one of Bush's themes: taxes. In fact, the percentage of Clinton ads mentioning taxes increased from spring to fall. Not surprisingly, the two candidates took up different aspects of the tax issue. Bush argued that taxes were too high and spending must be reduced; Clinton empha-

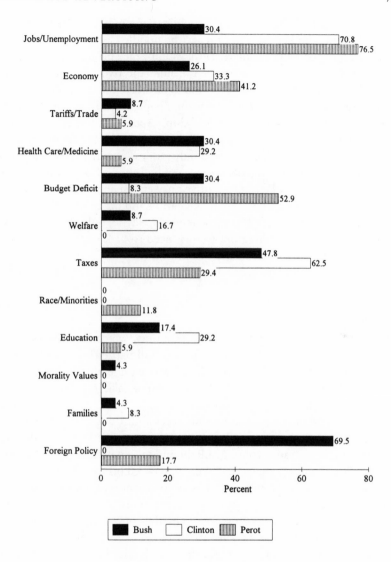

Figure 4.2   Policy issues mentioned in general election campaign ads. *Note:* Figure includes issues mentioned in at least 10 percent of a candidate's ads in either the nomination or general election campaign.

sized who had benefited from the Republican tax policy of the 1980s (the wealthy) and who needed a tax break (the middle class).

As an independent candidate, Perot did not face primary competition, and therefore his strategy developed around the two major candidates. His ad messages converged with and reinforced the Clinton focus on Bush's management of the economy for the previous four years and the need for change in economic leadership. Apart from that, Perot was largely singing his own tune. His other issues were the deficit and government reform, both of which received only modest attention from the other two candidates. In fact, the debates we studied showed Bush and Clinton striving to offer reasonably substantive answers on approaches to a range of issues, from work and welfare to education and the environment, while Perot repeatedly responded to those issues by saying only that "there are plans lying all over Washington, we just need to pick one and act on it." Then he would turn back to the deficit and the need to reform government. Only on economic issues did Perot really engage the other two candidates in dialogue.

The Politics of Blame

Bush was "dealt a bad hand" on the economy, which has always made presidential popularity and reelection an uphill battle (Brace and Hinckley 1992). But his playing of that hand was hampered by an uncertain focus on economic issues, which conveyed a lack of concern about people's economic woes. By contrast, the Clinton campaign reinforced Bush's responsibility for the economic recession, using increasingly simplified messages. The attack ads presented a picture of Bush as failing to understand the nation's economic plight and taking no meaningful action to remedy it. Clinton's messages then emphasized his own economic plan for the future and, by implication, his responsiveness to popular demands for a substantive discussion of economic solutions.

Bush's difficulties were compounded by the converging messages of all of the other candidates, who constituted a kind of "tag team" of criticism through various stages of the campaign. From the earliest primary through the general election, opponents focused on the magnitude of the economic problem and the need for a change in policy direction. The candidates who received the greatest amount of media attention during the early primaries were Buchanan, Clinton, and Tsongas—the candidates who focused most intensely on the economy. Then, later in the spring, the center of attention shifted to the independent candidate Perot, whose message further continued the focus on the economy. After Perot dropped out in July, Clinton's rebound carried the message of change in economic policy and leadership from the party convention through to election day.

Dovetailing the Message

Our public opinion surveys showed that some of the best-remembered ads in the 1992 campaign were the "read my lips" ads. The idea of using video of the president making his no-tax pledge actually originated with Pat Buchanan in the New Hampshire primary. Buchanan aired three ads which showed an excerpt of Bush's 1988 convention speech, saying, "read my lips, no new taxes." To dramatize the public's displeasure with that broken promise, Buchanan presented a group of New Hampshirites saying on film, "Read *our* lips . . . ." The Clinton campaign took the Buchanan idea and expanded it. More than one-third of Clinton's general election ads used video of Bush. Notably, the Clinton ad most frequently aired on the networks used video taken directly from a broadcast and, on the "read my lips" line, the camera zoomed in so close that the lines of resolution on the television screen were evident, a technique reminding viewers that Bush had promised them these things on their own TV screens.

The power of the video in anti-Bush ads suggests the importance of connecting the sight and sound of Bush making a promise that he subsequently broke with the message about Bush's lack of understanding and concern about the economy. As described by Kern (1989), such "dovetailing" is the blending of visuals and sound around a story or narrative that combines issues with messages on candidate character, personality, or leadership. By linking failed economic leadership with betrayal and callousness, the "read my lips" ads against Bush dovetailed sight and sound, character and policy.[10]

Perot's spot ads used two different techniques of video impact. The first series consisted of the "scrolling script" ads, and the second and subsequent series were "talking head" spots. The former simply printed the ad scripts and scrolled down the screen with muted visuals as a background. As we shall see, our focus groups were impressed by such "plain speaking" ads because of their contrast with the "slick" ads of the other candidates for office.

Bush and Clinton ads took the usual form of attack and counterattack. Because of the very absence of elaborate visual elements, Perot's ads—the simple scrolling script and somber narrator—dovetailed the visual element with the impression of a no-nonsense candidate who was addressing the issues rather than "bashing the other guy." As one focus group participant phrased it, Perot was "off to the side [in his ads] with a completely different look than the other guys." It is important to note that the first two of Perot's infomercials, which had 16.5 million viewers, also conveyed the impression of him as a serious, issue-oriented candidate through the use of his props, including charts, graphs, and a pointer. These long-form ads were positively received by participants in our focus groups and surveys.

Projecting Candidate Images

Television and the Candidates' Presentations of Self

Candidates can use the audio-visual power of television to project an image to the electorate. Graber's research on the 1976 elections noted how her subjects responded to candidates on television: "If physical appearance could be judged, [candidates] were described as having or lacking an 'honest look.' . . . Avoidance of eye contact in televised encounters was universally interpreted as a sign of dishonesty, whereas a straight look into the eye and firm, unhesitating responses were interpreted as evidence of honesty" (1984, 162). Other studies point to facial displays as especially crucial to candidate communication: "Psychologists have long recognized the face as the primary channel for effective communication. . . . Moreover, the communicative effects of facial expressions involve the vicarious instigation of an emotion in the viewer" (Lanzetta et al. 1985, 86).

Clinton and Perot used television in quite different ways to reinforce the images they were trying to project. The Clinton campaign had a candidate who was very good at communicating warmth and caring on television. Presumably, this is why Clinton appeared in the visuals of 86 percent of his general election ads, compared to 42 percent for Bush. A large number of Clinton's ads shot him close up, looking directly into the camera in a personal fashion, and with facial expressions and vocal inflection that sought to show passionate concern for people's problems.

Clinton's ability to connect with people through television was particularly important to the reconstruction of his image following the battering he took on "character issues" during the primaries. His campaign managers decided to show "him off in settings that would display his personal warmth" (Arterton 1993, 91). The campaign scheduled Clinton for as many interview programs as possible and bought 30 minutes of time on NBC in June for a town-hall–style question/answer session with a crowd of independently selected voters. The biographical video of Clinton aired at the Democratic national convention also sought to make a warm, human connection through television. Over one-third of Clinton's general election ads showed the candidate walking into crowds and being enthusi-astically received—an image that, as we will show, was recalled by many of our interviewees around the country.

Personal Narratives

The use of narrative is another key element of the candidates' presenta-tion of themselves. Stories about candidates can present their values and character, typically in settings and through experiences to which people can relate. Much as in the case of a jury trial, characterological coherence and consistency is vital to whether a story and its implications are be-lieved. In this respect Perot was especially successful. The personal story Perot created for himself resonated with the public because it was in ac-cord with a popular theme of American culture—the maverick as reluc-tant hero.

Perot constantly said he did not really want to "get in this thing" and he did not really care about being president in Washington, but the coun-try was in trouble and the people put him on the ballot, so he had better do it. He announced in the second debate that he "would serve only one term and return to Texas" and would not accept any salary. He also talked about how the system had become corrupt and how, as he said in his closing statement in the second debate, "if you want to do it, not just talk about it, and if you want a man of action, consider me." In classic "Mr. Smith Goes to Washington" style, with a bit of Texas bravado mixed in, he said in the first debate that if he was elected, "all those guys in $1,000 suits and alligator shoes, they'll be over in the Smithsonian—we'll get rid of them!" Perot completed the maverick hero presentation in the first debate in his closing statement, which stressed that he was "doing this" for the children, the veterans of the battlefield, and the elderly and "to re-create the American Dream for your children and grandchil-dren"—not for himself.

Clinton also effectively used personal storylines in his campaign com-munication. His campaign had discovered from their own focus groups in the spring that many people thought Clinton—the Yale Rhodes scholar—was from a wealthy, privileged background. To counteract that perception, Clinton used his convention speech to tell the story of his fa-therless childhood, his mother's sacrifices to build a better life, his grand-father's country store, where his grandfather's equal and fair treatment of blacks and whites alike "taught him more about equality than all the professors at Georgetown University" and so on. Responsibility was a key theme of the stories, along with hard work paying off, the importance of education, and hope for the future. The most thoroughly produced narrative was Clinton's biographical video made for the national convention, about "a place called Hope," which included 10 interlocking stories about the emergence of a leader from humble and difficult beginnings.

Bush also made use of narrative in his convention speech and in the debates, though less so than Clinton and Perot. Almost without exception, however, he drew his narratives from foreign affairs and his experience in the military. Such a pattern reinforced the policy messages Bush was making, with its greater emphasis on leadership in international affairs.

Bush may not have achieved a coherent "presentation of self," however. In the 1988 campaign, by comparison, he aired biographical ads that told the story of his upbringing in a public-spirited family that instilled in him a sense of public duty, his heroic record in the Second World War, his rich and rewarding family life, and his long service in public positions. In 1992, his campaign did not really present any coherent narrative of where he came from, what he stood for, and where he wanted to take the country. Indeed, a principal consultant on the Bush ad team complained after the fact that the candidate never provided any consistent direction on what he and his campaign were about (Castellanos 1993).

Thus, through the campaign, the three major candidates presented themselves to the public in different ways. Both Perot and Clinton pursued more direct and personal campaign communications than did Bush, possibly aggravating a sense of his being out of touch with the lives of the majority of Americans. Perot constructed an image of a nonpolitician and a simple citizen temporarily trying to straighten out things in Washington. His deliberately unconventional campaign with its plain-spoken style, apparent lack of big-time campaign smoothness, and common touch was both the means to communicate policy concerns and a message in and of itself. Clinton's constant enjoyment at being immersed in crowds, the apparent effectiveness of his "town hall" meetings and other direct interactions with voters, and his informal style all may have helped to forge a personal tie to the electorate. So while Clinton and Perot presented plenty of evidence of "what the candidate is like as a person," Bush conveyed far less of what he was about and made less of an effort to connect personally with the electorate.

Who Is Going Negative (and How)

In the aftermath of the 1988 presidential election, the press, the pundits, and many citizens strongly criticized negative candidate communications and ads in particular. Going into the 1992 election, the news media made conspicuous vows to hold candidates accountable for such attack campaigns. We have already noted that the citizens we interviewed also had a heightened awareness of such tactics and were ready to condemn them (see chap. 3). Did this climate constrain the candidates from making attacks? If they went on the attack, did they stick to criticisms of opponents' policies and leadership, which the public regards as more legitimate than personal attacks (Johnson-Carter and Copeland 1991)?

The most common nomination-phase ads were of the legitimate variety: those promoting the candidate's own character and issues at the same time and comparative ads that attacked the opponent on issues while promoting the sponsoring candidate's own issues. The general election produced a different pattern. Bush ran no biographical ads about his own character and experience. Clinton aired two ads touting his experience as a state chief executive and his remarkable up-from-humble-roots story. Ten Bush ads promoted both his own character and his issues, one was a comparative ad, and the other 11 of 23 were solely attacks on Clinton's character and/or issues. Clinton was equally on the attack in the general election period, with 10 of his 25 ads attacking Bush on both character and issues. Note, however, that only one Clinton ad attacked Bush solely on character, while Bush aired four character attacks on Clinton. Perot's ads did not directly and explicitly attack his opponents; in form, they spoke only of the candidate's own issues and character.[11] (See figs. 4.3 and 4.4.)

While Bush and Clinton attacked at similar rates, review of the emotional tones and themes used in the ads tells an important aspect of the story. The emotional tone of the ad was coded using the following categories, descriptions, and scale (see Kern 1989): 5 = very positive (hopeful, with children, lyrical music, etc.), 4 = positive (serenity, comfort, reassurance), 3 = neutral, 2 = negative (uncertainty, anxiety related), 1 = very negative (fear, repulsion, anger, sense of doom). Figure 4.5 displays the mean tone for each candidate's ads in the nomination phase. Buchanan's ads were by far the most negative of the primary, with a mean emotional tone of 2.0. There was a substantial difference between Bush ads and Clinton ads in the general election on this measure—as figure 4.5 shows. The mean emotional tone for Bush's general election ads was a negative 2.7; for Clinton's ads it was a more positive 3.2.

To better appreciate the proportion of each ad that was negative or positive the verbal tone of each message in the ad was also coded using the same scale (see fig. 4.6). In the general election ads when the candidates themselves were speaking, both Bush and Clinton were positive (mean

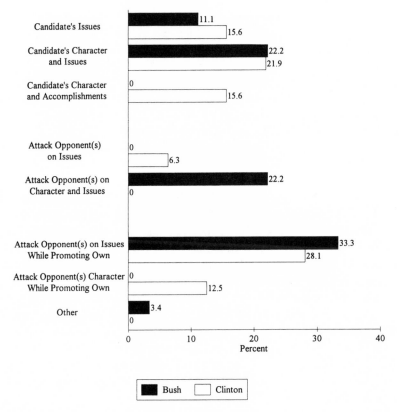

Figure 4.3   Percentage of nomination campaign ads promoting or attacking character or issues.

tone: 3.9 for Bush, 4.0 for Clinton). This is the classic pattern of not having the candidates themselves deliver the attack. However, when the *narrator* was the message source in the Bush ads, mean tone was a very negative 1.5. In the Clinton ads, narrator messages had a middling tone of 3.3. Another way to displace the source of negativity is to use average people to deliver the attack message, on the assumption that the attack appears more credible from nonpoliticians and does less damage to the sponsoring candidate's image as a decent campaigner. Several of the Bush ads used that technique for the entire ad, and two others used it for part of the ads. When average people delivered the message in Bush general election ads, the tone was a very negative 1.7 (in 78 message units). When Clinton ads used average folks to deliver the message, the tone was quite negative (1.8), but Clinton only used the device in 14 messages. Perot's personally delivered messages had a middling tone in his ads (mean: 3.4),

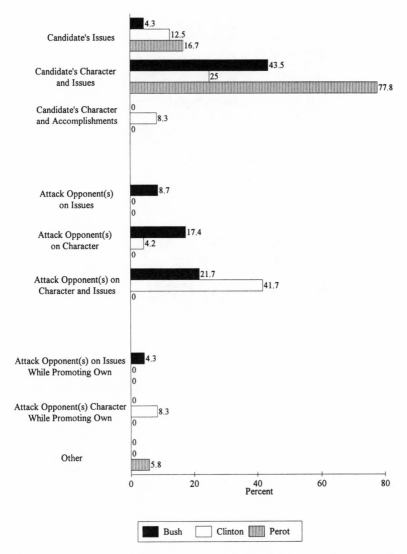

Figure 4.4 Percentage of general election campaign ads promoting or attacking character or issues.

and the narrator was similar (mean: 3.2). Clearly, if the public perceived Perot as a less negative campaigner, they had good reason to do so.

Analysis of the emotional content of the ads reinforced the negative valence of the Bush offerings. The candidate, however, tried to distance himself from negative emotional content. When Bush himself conveyed

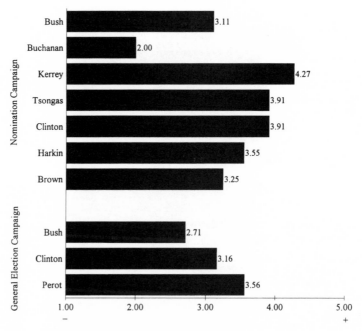

Figure 4.5   Average emotional tone of ads.

the message, the single most frequently employed emotion was categorized as "hope/optimism/enthusiasm" (in 23 percent of his messages) and the second most frequently used was "pride" (12 percent). The narrator and average people were the source of half of all messages in the Bush ads, and they delivered the bad news (aimed at Clinton): "distrust" was used in fully one-third of the emotional messages from average people, and "distress/anguish/worry" was used in another 15 percent. The messages delivered by the narrator used "threat" in 29 percent and "distrust" in 27 percent.

Most intriguing, the Bush ad buys reveal different patterns in placing national and local ads.[12] Perhaps because the national media were monitoring candidates' ads in 1992, Bush ran what might be called a stealth campaign in the general election. On the networks, the ads were balanced between positive and negative. The Bush campaign's most frequently aired ads were "Agenda" (on his domestic policy) and "What I Am Fighting For," which listed the basic areas of concern to him. The other half of the national ad campaign consisted of attacks on Clinton, primarily about trust. The stealth strategy came in the three local campaigns that we mon-

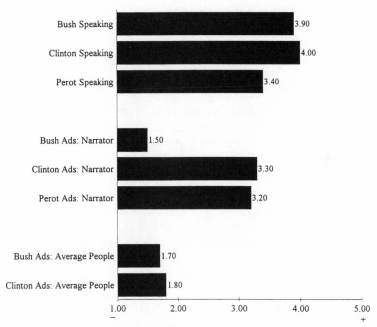

Figure 4.6 Average verbal tone of ads.

itored. The most frequently aired Bush ads on the local stations were all negative. Most of them attacked the personal character of Clinton, or used a thin veneer of issues to do so. The heaviest local ad buy (never aired nationally) was "Arkansas Record," which suggested not just that Clinton's policies were bad but also implied disaster if Clinton were elected to office.

Bush specifically reinforced the distrust theme in his convention speech and in the first debate, as well as coordinating the visual backdrops for campaign stops with ad messages. For example, right after the vice-presidential debate, the advance team at his events began displaying large banners reading, "Who do you trust?" directly behind Vice-President Quayle so that the cameras would include the words in the shot.

Clinton concentrated ad buys on the swing states and made only modest national buys. His campaign staff ignored states in which they either were far ahead or thought they had little chance. As Clinton media advisor Mandy Grunwald has pointed out, this enabled the Clinton campaign not only to make heavy ad buys in the 20 states they targeted but to "run two messages [ads] every week we were on the air. . . . That meant that from the day we went on we ran at least [one] positive ad every day—so that there was never a point when our advertising was solely negative" (Annenberg School of Communication 1993).

The Clinton campaign certainly did run negative ads. But they were not as negative, on the whole, as the Bush ads, and particularly in the targeted states, they were paired with positive ad messages. Further, the attack principally focused on policy issues and the performance of the incumbent on policy issues, rather than on the personal dimension, which people see as more objectionable (Johnson-Carter and Copeland 1991, 11–12). And the techniques used (principally the video of Bush himself) made the Clinton ads seem more credible. In addition, those ads also served a powerful "defusing" function. As West has pointed out: "Candidates often have problematic features. . . . It is obviously in their interest to defuse their shortcomings. They can do this either by lowering the overall salience of the topic to the public or by shortening the [perceived] distance between the candidates to the point where the subject no longer affects the vote" (West 1993, 125–26). Clinton had a major trust and character problem coming out of the nomination phase, which the Bush ads sought to exploit. But the Clinton ads fought back with video of Bush to raise questions about Bush's own trustworthiness and credibility on the matters that most affected people's lives: the economy, jobs, and taxes.

In the second debate, Clinton summed up and reinforced such advertising efforts aimed at countering and defusing the trust issue. When two successive citizen-questioners asked the candidates to stop "trashing the opponent's character," Clinton answered: "I'm not interested in [Bush's] character, I want to change the character of the presidency. And I'm interested in what we can *trust* him to do, and what you can trust *me* to do, and what you can trust Mr. *Perot* to do for the next four years" (emphasis in voice).

In his response to the questioner who asked the candidates to stop the mudslinging, Bush also attempted to reinforce his ad message: "I believe character *is* a part of being president; I think that has to be part of, uh, a candidate for president." His answer showed that he had missed the public disgust with attack politics and suggested that Bush would continue to engage in negative campaigning. Indeed, that night and for days immediately following the debate *every single ad* the Bush campaign aired on the networks included harsh personal attacks on Clinton.[13]

Clinton deflected these attacks on his character in two ways. During the early primaries Clinton countered the scandal stories by redirecting attention to the economy and blaming media scandalmongering.[14] In one of his ads Clinton himself, looking directly into the camera, addressed the public: "Look what's at stake in this election: your home, your job, your future. On Tuesday, you can send a message to Washington, to Wall Street—and to the *tabloids*. This is *your* election, *take it back!*" In the fall, Clinton countered Bush attacks with media reports that the Bush ads were inaccurate. For example, one Clinton ad featured visuals of newspaper articles in the *Washington Post* and the *Wall Street Journal* describing the Bush ads as "misleading."

Conclusion

E. E. Schattschneider (1960), in his classic *The Semi-Sovereign People,* warned that we should not expect candidates to behave as if they were members of a college debate team arguing the pros and cons of agreed-upon topics. Instead, he argued, most of politics consists of disputes over what the issues will be. Schattschneider's insight about politicians' attempts to displace conflict has been admirably upheld in many elections since. But the 1992 campaign provides an unusual variation.

We noted in chapter 3 a remarkable consensus among the public that the economy was at the top of the agenda. As a result, presumably, George Bush could not displace the conflict to matters that would be more beneficial to his candidacy. Our results suggest instead that a "tag team" of competitors—Buchanan in the primaries, Perot in the late spring and early summer, and then Clinton following the Democratic convention—forced Bush to discuss the economy even in his ads. There was, in short, evidence in 1992 of a convergence of all candidates on the issue that mattered most to the citizens.

Nevertheless, we also see that the three major candidates ran what we might call "crosstalk campaigns," carefully oriented toward distinct concerns and issues. In particular, all three cases are noteworthy for focusing on particular issues that dovetail smoothly with the candidate's story of his life and his presentation of self. Given that these linkages were made in a variety of campaign communications—Bush's and Clinton's convention speeches, the debates, the ads, and the biographical films—the three candidates sought to run highly integrated campaigns that centered on a single message that brought together issues with the candidate's character.

Thus Bush's ads sought to return to his forte, foreign policy, to which a whopping 77 percent of his primary ads and 70 percent of his general election ads made some reference; such an emphasis was geared to his presentation of himself as an experienced public servant who, unlike his opponents, could be trusted. Likewise, Clinton's communications stressed jobs and unemployment above all, along with a story of his tough past and his determination to succeed, all of which reinforced a message of empathy and compassion for those suffering hard times. Perot, for his part, spoke volumes simply through his unconventional campaign. His decidedly unslick ads and his self-portrait as the maverick reluctant hero trying to clean up Washington fit with his chosen issue, the budget deficit, which he blamed on politics-as-usual.

Citizens watching the campaign thus had three quite different candidates from which to choose, and importantly, these candidates diverged not only in their assessments of what the key issues were but also in what a president should *be*. Indeed, as the ads moved from the primaries to the general election, such interlinking of issues and character became more pronounced. The primary ads are more diverse in approach, with 23 percent focused on character and issues combined, and 10 percent attacking opponents on both dimensions combined. Compare this to the results for the general election, where 45 percent of the ads focused on character and issues combined, and another 22 percent attacked an opponent on both dimensions combined. These patterns within particular ads are reinforced by the candidates' efforts to remain "on message" across different forms of communications.

Political science has made much of the distinction between voters who decide on the basis of issues and those who opt for candidates on more personal grounds. From the evidence provided here, it seems that candidates do little to facilitate decisions exclusively on the basis of issues or exclusively on the basis of character. Instead, candidate messages are almost inextricably about both issues and character at the same time, as they gravitate toward issues that amplify their self-presentation, *and* as they stress aspects of their pasts and their personalities that reinforce their policy concerns. This raises two intriguing questions. First, is the divide between issues on one hand and personal qualities on the other far easier to talk about in theory than in practice? And if so, might that suggest both that issue discussion is not nearly as impersonal and that attention to candidates' personal qualities not nearly as apolitical as we have been led to believe?

FIVE

Media Coverage

Not so long ago, scholars felt no qualms about bypassing the role of the news media in the study of voting and elections. The failure of the first important voting study (Lazarsfeld et al. 1944) to find persuasive media effects led subsequent researchers to pay scant attention to news. For example, in *The American Voter*, Campbell et al. (1960) asked only a few questions about their respondents' news habits and then categorized the results as a measure of "vicarious participation" in the campaign.

Since the elections of the 1950s, of course, much has changed. Television has become virtually universal in American homes, displacing newspapers as the medium people claim to turn to first for news. Television spot advertising has given candidates a new way to channel persuasive messages to the electorate. Other political developments, notably the weakening of party ties in the population as a whole and the popularization of the nomination process, have made the role of the media more central (Bartels 1988).

Several researchers, using different methods and pursuing different concerns, have argued that "the political information environment" exerts great influence on public opinion (Sniderman et al. 1991; Page and Shapiro 1992; Lupia 1994). Zaller argues, for example, that "the impact of people's value predispositions always depends on whether citizens possess the contextual information needed to translate their values into support for particular policies or candidates" (1992, 25).

This study shares the concern for the political information environment, emphasizing that the media are a *resource* for citizens trying to make sense of the political world and reach electoral decisions. Our investigation of media coverage in the 1992 campaign is principally concerned with four issues—access, quality, candidate advantage, and news consensus. We ask, Is there a great deal of campaign information available? Is this information useful to voters? Is there a rough balance in the amount and favorability of the information? Last, do the media speak with one voice, or is there a variety of tones and interpretations available to the

89

public? In evaluating the campaign media along these dimensions, the study compares across media, including network news, local television news, and local newspapers in each of the four communities—Los Angeles, Boston, Winston-Salem, and Moorhead.

Access to information is the first step toward a healthy democratic debate. Given that politics must compete with other individual concerns, busy or not very interested citizens need a rich environment in which the costs of acquiring information are low or negligible. To be accessible to people with different styles, interests, and competencies, political information must be available in a variety of suitable formats. One measure of accessibility is the sheer amount of campaign coverage in different kinds of news media. How much is available in newspapers on the one hand, and on network and local television news on the other? Of course all communities cannot be expected to have the same information resources. Given the commercial basis of most American news media, one can assume that outlets in larger media markets have greater resources for covering the campaign than those in smaller markets. It would not be surprising if people in smaller communities, such as Winston-Salem or Moorhead, had less access to information and therefore higher information costs than people in large markets, such as Los Angeles or Boston.

Perhaps the important question is not so much where people live, but which media people actually use. Individuals who rely on newspapers, for example, may find more coverage of the campaign than those who rely on television (e.g., Patterson 1980). Even television watchers may find substantial differences in the offerings of local and network news programs.

Of course the amount of information does not tell the whole story. There is a long line of campaign studies that criticize the quality of news, especially the focus on the horse race instead of substantive concerns, such as candidates' policy positions (Patterson 1980; Robinson and Sheehan 1983). If citizens need a certain kind of information, do the media provide it? Are different kinds of campaign information available to people who rely on different media—network news, local television news, and newspapers?

Asking what kinds of news are carried in different media raises the question of media diversity. Do the news media speak with one voice, or is there instead a multiplicity of messages on which citizens can draw? After all, if the media present a consensual view of the campaign, then a greater burden is put on citizens to challenge the prevailing view (Noelle-Neumann 1993). If there is a variety of media views, then people have the opportunity to select, compare, and reinterpret the messages in making sense of the campaign. The news media fulfill an essential democratic function when they collectively provide a forum for lively political debate; but some observers complain that the very nature of the mass media homogenizes the content.

In general, scholars have viewed the news environment as largely homogeneous. The first systematic study of network news coverage of a campaign (Hofstetter 1976) found similar coverage across all three networks. Hofstetter observed little evidence of what he called "political bias"—namely, a more liberal or more conservative tilt—although he found substantial evidence of what he termed "structural bias," a preference for focusing on events and the horse race rather than on issues. Virtually every study of campaign coverage since then has reinforced Hofstetter's claims. More recent studies have also confirmed the essential similarity of the way in which events are covered across news media. Patterson, in his study of the 1976 election, concluded: "The public's acceptance of the press's version of the campaign is facilitated by the consistency of coverage by the various news outlets. . . . Although the press is not monolithic in how events are reported, it is in which events are covered" (1980, 100). Content analyses of the news were reinforced by sociological studies from the 1970s that found that different kinds of news organizations went about their jobs in similar ways.[1] Observational research concluded that news routines were the reason for similar products on television and in print, and in national and local television news, with variations accounted for by the outlets' different resources and news sources.

Of course, much has changed since the 1970s. Yet there have been few attempts to chart the impact of these new developments on election coverage. In particular, many recent investigations lump the three major networks together or treat one network as a typical example.[2] But the dominance of the three network news broadcasts in the 1970s has been succeeded by a more varied mix. Cable television now reaches about 60 percent of American households, providing increasing competition for the network share of the television audience. What is more, network news is being increasingly challenged by magazine-style news programming, beginning with CBS's long-running success, "60 Minutes." News programs are meeting the challenge by adopting some of the style and substance of magazine shows. Further, the network news programs are competing against their local affiliates, many of which have expanded their news programs from 30 minutes to one, two, or even more hours per night. Local news is increasingly characterized not only by its relentless focus on local news but also by its focus on crime, disasters, and feature stories rather than politics.[3] In the case of presidential campaigns, critics have expressed concern that new technologies allow ambitious politicians an uncritical celebrity spotlight.

We examine the news that is available to citizens in different places and through different news modalities and consider the richness of the coverage over the course of the campaign. Could people in different communities choose from a variety of interpretations of the candidates and the campaign, or was there a single media viewpoint? Do different news outlets concentrate on different issues? Or, in 1992, was it "the economy, stupid," no matter where you looked? Does the news coverage change during the campaign, becoming more complex as reporters dig deeper and analyze more complex issues, or does the range of discourse narrow as journalists develop a common vision of the campaign? Were the candidates covered the same from outlet to outlet, and similarly to each other? Or did some candidates have an advantage in one outlet or another, in one region or another, or in one kind of medium?

Implicit in that question is the issue of media bias. If there are differences in the way that the candidates are presented, where do they come from? Which topics or types of news stories lead to negative or positive coverage of the candidates? This question has important consequences not only for the way citizens evaluate the candidates but also for the way citizens evaluate the news media. The credibility of information is crucial to its use. The perception of bias, whatever its source, makes the job of the citizen more difficult. When people believe that there are reliable cue givers in the media environment, people can make effective decisions even with little information; however, when they are in doubt, citizens must take up the burden of interpretation themselves.

Access: Does It Matter Where You Live?
Does It Matter What You Use?

Our study provides an opportunity to see how much information is available to people in different regions of the country and different-sized media markets. Although few large American cities support more than one metropolitan newspaper the size of the advertising market can still affect the amount of news. Larger communities can be expected to have greater advertising demand, which in turn, provides the space for an expanded "news hole." Indeed, in the 1992 presidential campaign there was considerably more coverage of the election campaign in the three big-city newspapers—the *Los Angeles Times,* the *Boston Globe,* and the *Boston Her-*

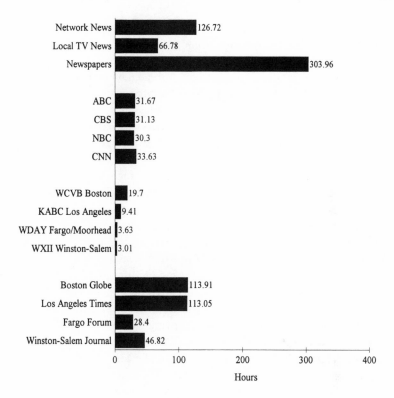

Figure 5.1   Total amount of campaign coverage. *Note:* For newspapers, 200 inches = 1 hour; every-third-day sample.

ald—than in the smaller-circulation *Winston-Salem Journal* and *Fargo Forum* (see fig. 5.1).

Similar dynamics might be expected to operate in local television coverage. And while the highest-ranked stations in Los Angeles and Boston did indeed provide more campaign coverage than their counterparts in Winston-Salem and Fargo/Moorhead, the difference was not linear. Boston, the sixth-largest media market, aired more stories about the campaign than Los Angeles, the second-largest market, and the relatively small market of Fargo (108th) had more coverage than middle-sized Winston-Salem (48th). During the primary season, the differences were even more marked: Boston had more than twice as many stories as Los Angeles, and Fargo had twice as many stories as Winston-Salem.

Factors in addition to market size appear to be at work in television news—in particular the local affiliate's ability to transform the national campaign into a locally relevant story. Much depends on the candidates' attention to the locale, the timing of the primary in that or a nearby state, and the extent of candidate advertising in the media market. In the search for a local angle, producers may go to great lengths to provide a local news hook for a national story. For example, the Fargo station, despite limited resources, sent a local reporter to cover the competitive early primary in South Dakota. Boston media were luckier. Not only is New Hampshire nearby, but the southern part of the state is in the Boston media market. As a result, all but one of the major candidates bought advertising time on the Boston stations. Another kind of local angle for Boston was Paul Tsongas, a former Massachusetts senator who was one of the leading early contenders for the Democratic nomination.[4]

Boston's lavish attention to the primary campaign was no doubt heightened by the fact that New Hampshire was the first major showdown of the 1992 campaign.[5] Given the greater attention to early contests compared to those later in the season (Patterson 1980; Adams 1987), the timing of the primaries resulted in more presidential campaign coverage in Boston and Fargo/Moorhead, whose primaries fell in March and April, than in the correspondingly larger media markets of Los Angeles and Winston-Salem, whose primaries came in the last weeks of the nominating season. Because local coverage depends on local events, however, media attention waned in locales with early primaries when the candidates stopped visiting sites within the media market. In fact, the most local event is not necessarily the most newsworthy: Boston media gave far more attention to the New Hampshire primary than to the Massachusetts primary, which all the other Democratic candidates conceded to Tsongas and for which only Buchanan bought any ad time. Conversely, visits by candidates or their surrogates produced a dramatic increase in local television coverage of the campaign wherever they occurred. During the primary season, for example, one-quarter of the February coverage in Fargo was taken up with a visit by Vice-President Quayle. During the late primary season coverage in Los Angeles jumped, as candidates visited the scene of the riot. In the fall, Winston-Salem coverage increased in part because it was in a competitive "battleground" state and barraged with candidate visits and advertising.

Notably, the amount of local television news of the campaign also reflects news production decisions. Even small local affiliates can cover the national campaign simply by using video generated by the networks. The network feed can be surrounded by local anchor "intros" and "outros," so that they become a seamless part of the local newscast. Among the stations we studied, the Fargo affiliate made extensive use of network video and network stories in its local coverage of the primary campaign. As a result, the Fargo station offered viewers considerably more campaign coverage than the Winston-Salem station, which preferred to air its own locally produced stories. An enterprising station such as Fargo's WDAY— which had the highest percentage of journalist-initiated stories of any of our four local affiliates[6]—can use its limited resources to provide a considerable amount of coverage. This is the counterpart of newspaper reliance on wire service stories, which was heaviest, once again, in the smallest of our four locales, where the *Fargo Forum* used the wires for 31 percent of its stories, compared to around 20 percent in the two Boston papers and the *Winston-Salem Journal,* and none in the *Los Angeles Times.*

Of course, people who live in very small communities, with limited print and local broadcasting resources, still have easy access to one national news source—network television. And indeed, throughout the campaign, network news carried more coverage of the campaign than did local affiliates. During the primary phase the network news programs carried four or five times as many stories as the local newscasts, and as figure 5.1 shows, the total airtime allotted to the campaign over the course of the year by the four networks was approximately double that of the four local broadcasts.

The difference between the amount of network and local coverage is not surprising. For many years, television's division of labor meant that the network broadcasts covered news of interest to national audiences— especially stories from Washington or New York—and only covered local stories when they represented national trends or possessed extraordinary news value. Local news programs were left to focus on close-to-home stories. This clear distinction between network broadcasts and local news shows has waned as local affiliates have begun to use satellite uplinks and video equivalents of wire service reporters, and as network news programs, in pursuit of audiences, increasingly focus on the bread and butter of local news—disasters, crime, health tips, and the like (Carroll 1992).

The increasingly common subject matter of network and local television news holds true for campaign coverage as well. While subject matter is becoming less distinctive, the quantitative difference is substantial. As the 1992 campaign wore on, both network and local news programs increased their coverage; nevertheless, the local stations aired far fewer stories than the networks. Consequently, a hypothetical viewer who watched only local television news was much less likely than a network viewer to run across a story about the presidential election at any point during the campaign.

Figure 5.2 shows that major newspapers remain a potential source of much greater access to the presidential campaign. Figure 5.2 contrasts our every-third-day sample of newspaper coverage with the total television coverage of the campaign. For the purposes of comparison, the newspaper sample has been placed on the same scale as television coverage, using a common rule-of-thumb conversion of inches to hours.[7] While the four-newspaper sample coincides with the peaks and valleys of campaign coverage on the four networks and the four local stations, the amount of coverage is twice as large for the print sample as for the total output of local or network news. It is important, however, to keep in mind in looking at the differences in the amount of print and broadcast news that the audience can be much more selective about the print news package than about the television package. While many people watch an entire news broadcast, very few read every article in the newspaper. Nevertheless, these quantitative differences mean that a citizen interested in following the campaign had much more news available in the newspaper than on television.

Quality: What Kind of News Is There?

It is clear that people have access to more or less news about the presidential campaign depending where they live and which media they use. But do people who live in different locales and/or use different news media get different *kinds* of information about the candidates and the issues? In the campaign, do some news media provide more useful information to citizens than others?

Our general approach to the content analysis of news was to code each story for any mention of dozens of aspects of the candidates or campaign. Most of our tables and figures combine these into broad, but distinct, categories. In addition, a subsample of all of the stories was analyzed at the message (sentence or clause) level, supporting and reinforcing the conclusions we reached on the basis of an analysis of whole stories (see Just, Crigler, and Buhr 1995).

One way to gauge the work of the media in providing an independent resource for voters is to see the extent to which journalists themselves initiated the stories, rather than simply following the actions of candidates and the events of the campaign. The distinction here is between

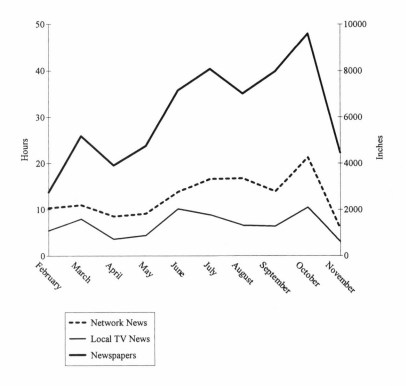

Figure 5.2   Amount of campaign coverage by month.

stories that mainly relate what a candidate said or did—including results of the candidate's own polls, news releases, press conferences, speeches, and ads—and journalist-initiated or "enterprise stories," which involve some investigation or analysis on the part of the reporter or news organization.[8] Media polls fall into the category of journalist-initiated stories.

One might expect that local news, with fewer resources for enterprise reporting, would be more inclined to rely on the candidates and their staffs to stage events and help make news for them, as compared with more proactive network news and newspapers. As figure 5.3 shows, this was indeed the case. In television, for instance, network broadcasts were almost evenly divided between journalist-initiated stories and candidate action stories, except at the end of the campaign, when the network journalists moved into high gear and the number of candidate action stories declined. By contrast, local news shows relied substantially more on the candidates to provide material for their campaign stories. Although resources may account for the difference in the preparation of enterprise

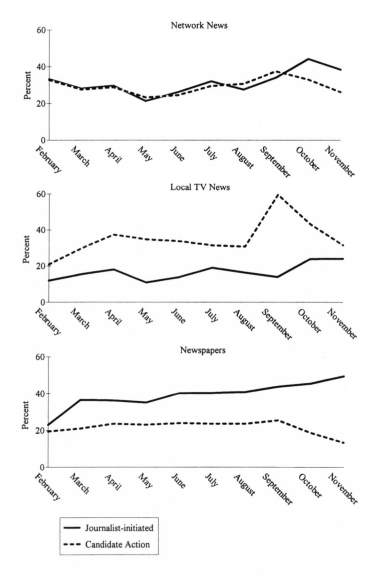

Figure 5.3 Percentage of journalist-initiated versus candidate action stories.

stories between local and network television news, the largest media market in our sample actually had the lowest percentage of journalist-
initiated stories, while the smallest market had the highest.

Newspapers differ from television news in giving far less room to stories about the campaign trail than to journalist-initiated stories, especially

news analysis. This too, represents a division of media labor. Because newspapers are less timely than television news, they have used their greater distance from the event to emphasize interpretation rather than description. The result is a somewhat different set of resources for voters. Television news provides a direct and immediate look at the campaign as it unfolds, while newspapers provide more analysis and interpretation of the events.

How the Media Construct the Candidates

Critics of campaign coverage have argued that horse-race/strategy stories tend to drown out the more democratically important coverage of policy questions (Patterson 1980; see also Brady and Johnston 1987; Sigelman and Bullock 1991). Figure 5.4 compares the percentage of stories that are mainly concerned with issues with the percentage that focus on the campaign process, over the course of the campaign. The results show the emphasis on the process rather than the issues, especially on local television news (Kaniss 1991). Issues came in behind the process/horse-race stories on local television news, except for the months of May and June, that is, at the end of the primaries and before the national party conventions. But there is considerably more coverage of issues on network news and in newspapers than on local television. On network news, issue stories predominate for most of the campaign, while in newspapers (which have more coverage overall), issue stories are especially prominent in the early fall. Issue stories get shorter shrift in all media when the horse race is most exciting (in the early primaries and in the last month of the campaign); but rather than completely upstaging issue coverage, campaign process stories appear to share the spotlight in all media.

When we looked at the "main focus" of campaign stories, we were not surprised to find that news was largely about the candidates, the individual protagonists at the center of the campaign narrative. To assess how the candidates were presented, we compared media coverage of the candidates along four dimensions: their personal qualities, chances of winning, organizations, and issue positions. (See chap. 2 for further description of methods.) The category "personal qualities" refers to the candidate's personality, personal background, or experience. Mentions of a candidate's expectations, chances, or strategies for winning were coded as "horse race/strategy." Yet another category deals with the candidate's campaign staff, finances, or organization. References to the candidate's positions on the issues was the last broad category. These four categories are distinct, but any mention of any one of these characteristics was coded for each story. Therefore, a given story may be counted in more than one

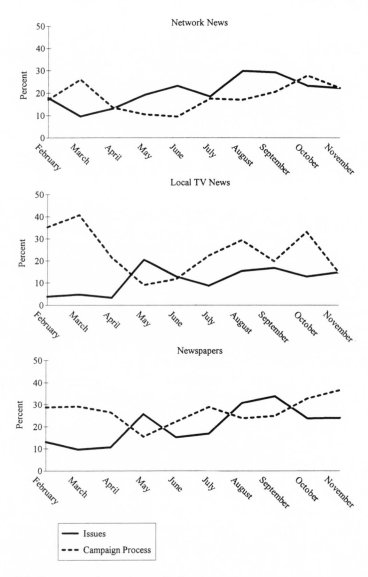

Figure 5.4 Percentage of campaign stories focusing on issues versus campaign process.

category. Our approach to the analysis emphasizes the potential information about candidates available to the news audience.

Was the way the news covered the candidates useful to voters? Were all candidates covered alike? As figure 5.5 shows, the overall pattern of candidate coverage is again very similar on network and local television

news and in newspapers. All three kinds of media put the greatest emphasis on candidates' personal qualities and their chances for election; issue
positions come in third, and the campaign factors (finance, staffing, etc.)
are last. This pattern confirms what other researchers (such as Patterson
1980) found in earlier studies of election news. Most dramatically, figure
5.5 shows that the particular candidates were covered the same way
across media. Bush was the candidate covered most on personal qualities
and issue positions. Perot was covered most in terms of his electoral
chances and his campaign organization. The emphases in Clinton's coverage fell between Bush's and Perot's on every dimension—personal qualities, horse race, campaign organization, and issue positions.

To be sure, these differences in the way the candidates were covered
was much less pronounced in newspapers than on television, which
tended to paint the three competitors in relatively broad strokes. Television, especially local television was more preoccupied with the candidates' strategies and chances. On local television news, stories about Clinton's and Perot's chances and strategies even outstripped stories about
their personal qualities.

The common pattern of candidate coverage demonstrates a substantial
news consensus. It is easy to explain why horse-race stories were especially newsworthy for Clinton and Perot, given the come-from-behind
drama of the Clinton nomination and the ins and outs and novel organization of the Perot campaign. But why was George Bush—surely a more
known quantity than his two competitors—covered so extensively on issues and personal qualities? One explanation for the emphasis on issues
in the Bush coverage is that all the stories that mentioned Bush during the
campaign year, whether the focus was on his activities as president or
as candidate, were included in the content analysis. Therefore, it is not
surprising that there were a large number of stories that mention policies
in which the president was involved. The explanation for the personal
focus of Bush stories is similar. Figure 5.6 breaks down the broad category of personal qualities into its components—stories about the candidate's ability as campaigner, personal background and character, and
leadership. In all three kinds of media, Bush, the incumbent president,
was covered predominantly as a leader, with Clinton and Perot discussed
more as personalities and as campaigners. Coverage of the president "act-
ing presidential" is, in fact, widely regarded as one of the great advantages
of office. The incumbent invariably receives the lion's share of media attention during the campaign and is necessarily cast in a prestigious and
respectable role. It is not so clear, however, that Bush received an incumbency advantage from the emphasis on leadership over personal back-

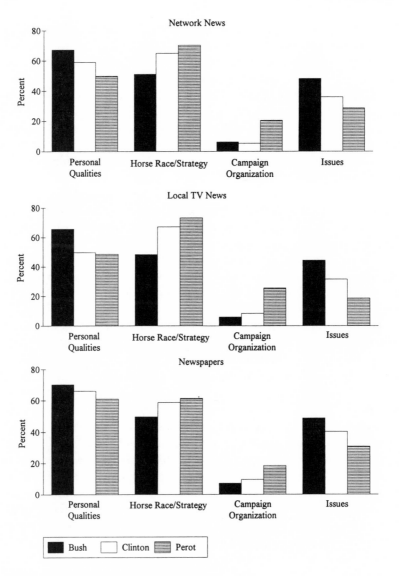

Figure 5.5   Candidate characteristics in campaign stories.

ground. In particular, the comparative lack of coverage of George Bush as a person may have undermined his ability to connect with the electorate.

The analysis of coverage thus far supports the view that local television news provides less coverage and is a less substantive source of citizen information in the election season than either newspapers or network news.

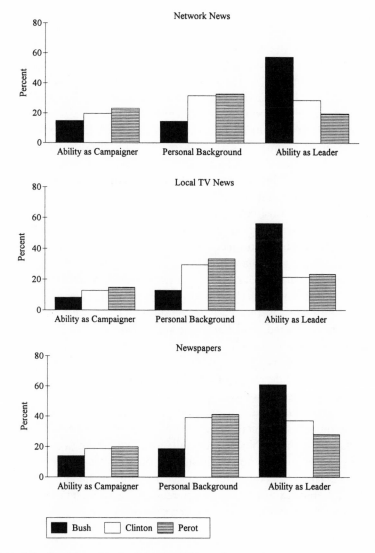

Figure 5.6   Candidate characteristics: breakdown of personal qualities.

Local television news spends less time on the presidential campaign; what attention it does give is likely to be instigated more by candidates' actions than by journalists' initiatives, and it is weighted more toward horse-race coverage, to the detriment of issues.

Yet there was a remarkably similar pattern of candidate coverage across media. Candidate coverage appears to be governed by shared understandings about what is a good focus for a story (candidates' activities or campaigning rather than issues), about what is newsworthy about candidates in general (namely, their personal qualities and strategies) and in particular (Bush's presidential decisions, Clinton's and Perot's chances for beating the incumbent, or Perot's unusual campaign organization).

Even during the primary stage of the campaign, there was an impressive news consensus about whom to cover. In particular, while the four networks diverged significantly in the extent to which they mentioned the various primary competitors, there were no significant differences among the networks in terms of which candidates were seen and which were quoted. In all of the broadcasts, Bush was mentioned in about two-thirds of the stories, Clinton in about half, and Tsongas, Buchanan, and Brown in about a quarter. Bush and Clinton were seen in about 40 percent of the stories, with Brown in about 20 percent and Tsongas and Buchanan in fewer. Likewise, candidates received differential visual exposure, with less credible candidates (Buchanan and Brown) given significantly shorter visuals on the networks. Coverage decisions, however, were not as straightforward as they might seem in hindsight. For example, Jerry Brown was not given as much coverage early in the campaign as his electoral success would have suggested, and Larry Agran, who did as well as Brown in early New Hampshire opinion polls, was virtually ignored.[9]

During the primary campaign, news organizations are forced to make choices about a wide range of candidates, and there may be no strong consensus about who should be covered. There are fewer choices once the nominees are established. During the general election campaign, the two major candidates were mentioned with equal frequency on all four of the networks, including CNN in the fall, although there was somewhat greater variation for the nontraditional candidate, Perot (see appendix C, table C.7). The news consensus on how to report each candidate means that the different candidates face different sets of strategic opportunities and obstacles in their attempts to reach the voters.

Candidate Advantage: It's Not What You Say, but How You Say It!

If there is a consensus concerning what is newsworthy about candidates, is there a consensus of interpretation? To paraphrase Schattschneider (1960), does the media chorus sing with the same accent? To see who benefited from the coverage, stories were coded for each candidate in terms of both verbal and visual tone, using a 5-point scale—negative,

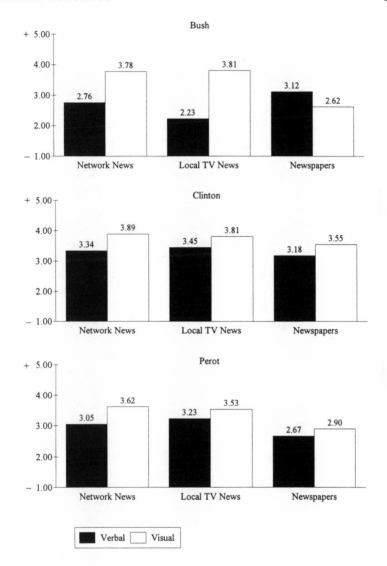

Figure 5.7 Average verbal and visual tone of campaign stories toward candidates.

somewhat negative, neutral, somewhat positive, and positive. The analysis shows variation between verbal and visual tone across candidates and media (see fig. 5.7).

Overall, the results provide vivid evidence of Graber's (1987) conclusion that television coverage of the candidates was made up of "kind pictures and harsh words." During the primary season, for example, virtually every candidate was presented on the networks significantly more favorably in the visuals than in the words of the stories.[10] If we compare Clinton, Bush, and Perot over the course of the entire year, their presentations are also significantly more favorable visually than verbally by the four networks, the local affiliates, and the newspapers. The only exception is newspaper coverage of Bush, whose verbal coverage was more favorable than his visuals in newspaper stories about him in his presidential role. It is intriguing that the text and visual tone were more likely to diverge in the audio-visual medium of television than in the word-driven medium of print. The difference between print and broadcast media is further evidence that news coverage is negotiated between candidates and journalists. Television's tremendous appetite for visuals may make television news more vulnerable to candidate control than newspapers. By carefully planning the locations of their speeches or engaging in well-chosen activities, candidates can help insure that the pictures shown on television will enhance their message, while newspapers can choose the single picture that reflects the text best. Clinton, for example, was especially successful in getting television to show him before crowds with his sleeves rolled up, reinforcing his message of "change" by projecting youth and vigor.

Taking the average over the whole campaign for the three leading candidates, the *relative* tone of the verbal messages toward the candidates shows a similar pattern across media (see figs. 5.8–5.10). The reporting about Bush tended to be the most negative, with Perot in the middle, and Clinton toward the positive end in all three kinds of media.[11] Only 2 of our 15 media outlets did not follow this ranking—WDAY in Fargo gave Perot slightly more positive coverage overall than Clinton, whereas WXII in Winston-Salem covered Bush generally more favorably than Perot. While, initially, one might guess that the tendency for Fargo and Winston-Salem television to wander from the media consensus might be based on local political conditions (the predilection for political independence in the upper Midwest or the greater Republicanism of North Carolina), the divergence was not found in the newspapers from those communities. Indeed—and most strikingly—while Winston-Salem's television station was the most favorable to Bush of any news outlet studied, the *Winston-Salem Journal* was the least favorable to him of all.

Yet, beyond the similar ranking of the candidates in terms of television audio and in newspapers, any hypothesis about a news consensus on tone of coverage is supported only in *relative* terms by our data. While the rank ordering of candidate tone was similar across media, whether and how much the tone was positive or negative varied greatly. The verbal

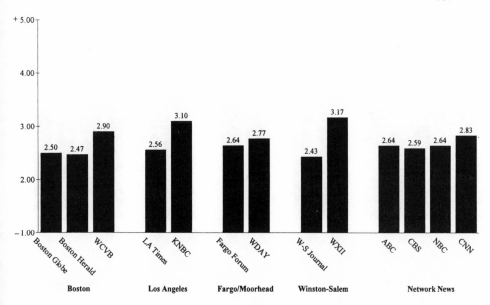

Figure 5.8   Average verbal tone of campaign stories toward George Bush.

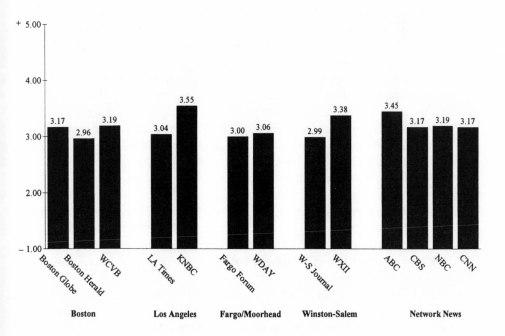

Figure 5.9   Average verbal tone of campaign stories toward Bill Clinton.

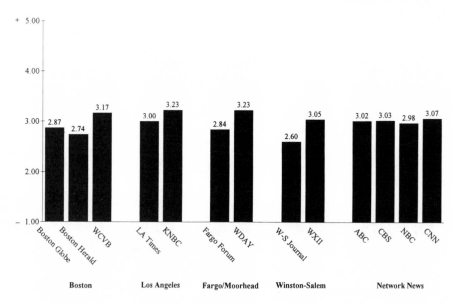

Figure 5.10   Average verbal tone of campaign stories toward Ross Perot.

tone of news about Bush and Clinton was significantly different on the four local television stations we monitored, as well as on the four networks. One network, ABC, was noticeably warmer to Clinton (mean verbal tone: 3.45) than any of the others, and CNN was somewhat kinder to Bush (mean verbal tone: 2.84) than the other networks, largely because its presentation of all of the candidates was more neutral.[12]

The data give little support to the notion that a community norm dominates the tone of coverage given to a candidate in a particular locale. There were significant differences in the tone of candidate coverage between different outlets in the same city. Note, for example, how much more harshly both Bush and Clinton were treated in the *Los Angeles Times* than on KNBC and how both Bush and Perot were treated far more negatively by the *Winston-Salem Journal* than by the local television station, WXII. In fact, all of the candidates tended to be treated better by local television news than by local newspapers. Network news coverage falls between the two—not quite so harsh as newspapers and not as favorable as local television.

These results raise an interesting question. If the news consensus extends from what to cover to how to cover it, there would be few significant differences among different kinds of media. Our results on verbal tone do not show that to be the case. If shared community values and pressures govern the tone of local coverage of candidates, then the evaluations of candidates by print and broadcast journalists in the same community should be more similar than evaluations by journalists in the same medium in different regions of the country. Clearly this is not the case either. Instead, the news consensus appears to be strongest *within* newspapers, *within* local television news, and *within* network news.

There are several ways to account for the discrepancy in tone toward the candidates between local newspaper and local television news in the same community. First, local newspapers are not so local. When they send their reporters to cover national events or use wire service accounts of the campaign, they take the local audience to the national story—while local television brings the national story to the local community. Local television news emphasizes the local angle of national stories far more than newspapers do. Sixty-two percent of the local television news stories about the campaign contained some sort of local angle, compared to only 37 percent of the local newspaper stories—a relationship replicated in each of our four media markets. But comparing the tone of local-angle stories to that of other stories about the campaign reveals an unexpected finding: while local-angle stories are indeed somewhat more favorable toward the candidates in newspapers, they are generally *less* favorable to the candidates on local television news.

A more satisfactory explanation for the less-critical view of the candidates on local television is that local television news is less journalist initiated than newspaper news. For example, 23 percent of local television news stories about Bush were journalist initiated, compared to 39 percent on the networks and 46 percent in the newspapers; 25 percent of local television news stories about Clinton were journalist initiated, compared to 41 percent on the networks and 46 percent in the newspapers; and 32 percent of local television news stories about Perot were journalist initiated, compared to 50 percent in the networks and 55 percent in the newspapers. And overall, journalist-initiated stories tend to be more negative toward the candidates than other kinds of stories.[13]

It is apparent, then, that the news consensus in individual markets breaks down when the focus turns from what is being covered to how the candidates are evaluated. In each of our four locales, people could find accounts that were good, bad, or neutral about the candidates, with local television news generally providing news favorable to the candidates and newspapers providing the least positive reporting.

Explaining Differences in Tone

In addition to these differences between types of media, we investigated the specific factors that led to positive or negative coverage of the candidates. Why was the incumbent president covered negatively throughout the campaign? Were there any factors that improved his coverage? Were these the same factors for all of the candidates? To answer these questions, regression equations were constructed to predict the tone of news stories separately for each candidate and each medium—verbal and visual tone for Bush, Clinton, and Perot in newspapers, on local television news, and on network news. The independent variables in all these equations included the following: the extent to which the candidate dominated the story (number of words quoted in print, number of seconds quoted or seen on television); whether the story was journalist initiated; whether the story referred to the economy as an issue; and whether the candidate was referred to by each of the following criteria: issue positions, campaign characteristics, the horse race, leadership, ability as a campaigner, or personal characteristics. Particular variables were included in the equations for each medium: for television, we included dummy variables for sources quoted in the story—persons in the street, journalists, or experts; for the two local forms of media, a variable was included that indicated whether the story had a local angle; and for newspapers, a variable showed whether the story originated with a wire service. The equations predicting news tone for Bush added an indicator about the content— was it about Bush as candidate or as president. Each of these equations was estimated with and without dummy variables for the research sites (for local television news and newspapers) and for each of the networks, to see whether particular news outlets accounted for the variation unexplained by other variables.

The point that stood out for the president was that the more he spoke in the story, the more positive the verbal tone in all three media. To the extent that Bush could persuade the media to focus on his own words, he was able to get more favorable coverage. Otherwise, there was no consistent pattern across media for verbal tone about the president. By comparison, the significant boosts to Clinton in all three media centered on the process of the campaign. The verbal tone was more positive for Clinton when the stories referred to the characteristics of his campaign or to the horse race or to his ability as campaigner.

The results for Perot varied even more from one medium to the next than did those for Bush or Clinton. For example, journalist-initiated stories about Perot were significantly more negative on local television news and in newspapers than on network news, person-in-street interviews made for more positive reports on television (both local and network), while mention of his personal characteristics was associated with more negative coverage in newspapers and on the networks. The differences suggest that the implicit threat that Perot posed to politics-as-usual was paralleled by a challenge to reporting-as-usual—and the different kinds of media responded in different ways.

Some patterns stood out for all three major candidates. On the networks and in newspapers, references to their personalities or background worked against all three candidates. When news focused on what the candidates were like as people, the stories tended to be unfavorable. On the positive side for the candidates, the number of seconds/words quoted significantly boosted the verbal tone (for Bush on all three media, for Clinton on the networks and in the newspapers, and for Perot in newspapers)—indicating that, in general, the more candidates were given a chance to speak, the better the story was for them. Horse-race coverage had more impact on tone toward candidates on the networks than in newspapers and on local television. In newspapers, the verbal tone was negatively affected by journalist-initiated stories and positively affected if the story contained a local angle.

What then makes reports more and less favorable to the candidates on the visual dimension? The differences in the equations for verbal tone and visual tone indicate that these operate on somewhat independent tracks. The variable with the most consistent effect across media is whether the story was initiated by journalists or by candidates. Journalist-initiated stories on local and network television news and in newspapers (with the lone exceptions of Clinton on the networks and in the newspapers) were significantly more likely to be visually negative than stories instigated by the candidates. It may be that when journalists originate the story, they can put together a consistent package with both critical words and critical pictures. On the other hand, when candidates stage the event they can at least insure positive visuals.

Intriguingly, visual tone was often positively associated with factors that made for more negative verbal coverage. For example, network and newspaper stories about Bush and the economy had the most positive pictures of the president, all other things being equal. It may mean that these stories are illustrated with footage of campaign hoopla or presidential activity that, in and of themselves, are more favorable to the candidate, regardless of the verbal spin. The tendency to illustrate journalist-initiated news with more positive footage may also be at play on the networks, which tended to pair soundbites by expert commentators with more favorable video of all three candidates. In any case, this visual-verbal mismatch meant that George Bush's overall image was unusually prone to "kind pictures and harsh words" when he was most under attack.

In general, our analysis of the verbal and visual tone of news reports about candidates demonstrates structural rather than ideological or partisan bias. The qualities that make candidates newsworthy can work for or against them, regardless of party affiliation. On the negative side, personal stories hurt all three candidates on network news and in newspapers, while on the positive side, campaign stories helped the front-runner, especially on the networks. For all three candidates, the more the candidate is able to instigate the story or control its elements, the more positive the story (both verbally and visually). Our analysis shows some support for the "bad news" thesis (most notably supported by Patterson 1993), in which journalists take a professionally critical posture toward candidates.

Although the favorability or unfavorability of tone toward candidates depends in part on the application of news values, there is still far more variation that is unexplained. Over and above the predictor variables, there were differences among the outlets in any particular medium.[14] The results show that news organizations had some leeway in adopting particular "lines" on all of the candidates, whether journalists or candidates initiated the story.

A News Consensus?

The evidence we have examined so far has largely been based on averages over the course of the campaign. We would like to understand, however, how the news consensus develops. Is news convergence another word for "pack journalism" or "beltway blindness," or does it grow over time as individual journalists, editors, and the public come to share a common understanding of the candidates and the issues of the campaign?

Candidate Coverage over Time

It may be helpful in thinking about the campaign to divide it into three seasons: the primary period (February to May), the summer season (June to August), and the fall campaign (September to November). The data show that variability in the verbal tone of candidate coverage was considerable in the nominating campaign, but notably diminished during the summer and fall periods of the general election. Apparently, as the campaign jelled in the late spring, reporters varied less in their assessments (explicit or implicit) of the candidates—with greater convergence of the tone of candidate stories over time.

The trends in candidate coverage over the course of the campaign are depicted in figure 5.11. The figure shows how much better both Bush and Perot did on the local television stations examined here than in the local newspapers or on network news. But the most striking pattern is the flat line for the tone of Bush coverage throughout the campaign year. It may be that because Bush was so well known to the press, his characterization in the media was made almost imperturbable by campaign events.

Analysis of the way candidates were covered reveals something about the tension between the shape of the campaign and the consistent demands of news. Figure 5.12 shows, for example, that on network news, mention of the candidates' issue positions in stories remained at fairly consistent levels throughout the campaign, rising to its height for all three candidates in August and then declining during the fall. The low points for issue coverage were unfortunately in March and October, when the nominations and election were most in doubt and many citizens were becoming attentive to the campaign. Issue coverage picked up in May and June, after the primaries, and again in August. Comparing issue coverage with horse-race stories, we see almost a mirror image. When horse race is up, issues are down, and vice versa. The evidence supports the contention that journalists spend more time on issues when the horse race is less exciting.

Network coverage of candidate personal qualities is, not surprisingly, most differentiated by candidate. For example, both Bush and Clinton received extra attention during their party convention months, while Perot peaked around the time of his abrupt withdrawal from the race in July. Figure 5.12 shows that Clinton's coverage focused on personal qualities and character early in the campaign, when he was facing charges about his draft history and use of marijuana. Coverage of Bush's personal qualities was also intense in the months of May and June when he went on the attack against Perot. Interestingly, the news media did not reopen the discussion of Perot's character in the fall, having done so in the early summer, and perhaps incorrectly believing that the electorate was already familiar with all three candidates by October.

Thus the news media converged in their candidate coverage over time. In the primary period, the news media winnowed the candidates by providing significantly less exposure to lower "tiers" of candidates based on judgments about their electability (Crigler, Just, and Cook 1992). The overall tone accorded to the candidates by different news outlets varied quite a bit, however. By the fall, with only two or three candidates to follow, the media shared a more consensual trend. Thus the paradox of campaign coverage was that as the coverage increased in amount, it de-

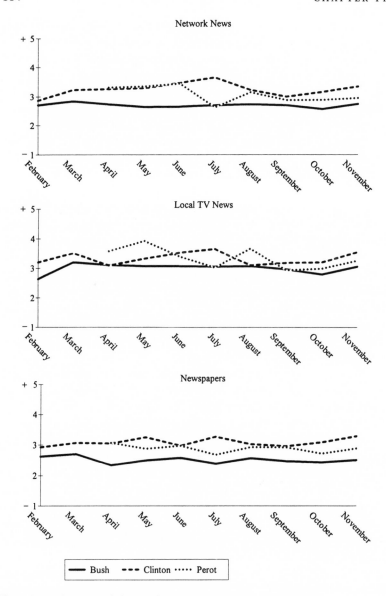

Figure 5.11 Average verbal tone of campaign stories toward candidates.

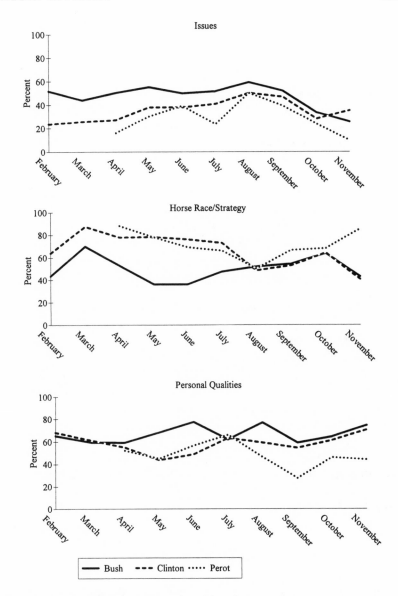

Figure 5.12   Network news coverage of candidate characteristics.

creased in variability. Not only did voters then potentially receive more news, but they apparently got more of the same.

The Issue Agenda over Time

It might be expected that inclinations and location would make the issue agenda less convergent than the description of candidates. Of course, 1992 is a somewhat atypical year, with polls showing a consistent focus of public opinion on the problem of the economy. Apparently, this concern was echoed and reinforced by the media coverage. Of topics mentioned the most in campaign news, the economy was clearly the leading issue throughout the campaign. This is not to say that other issues were ignored. Health care, the deficit, foreign policy, and a variety of social issues including abortion were also on the media agenda.

Figure 5.13 shows that the news concentration on economic issues became more important as the campaign unfolded. By comparison, coverage of other issues responded to particular flash points—for example, race (after the Los Angeles riots) and foreign policy (highlighted by international events during the summer months). There was no corresponding crisis, however, to produce the growing emphasis on the economy in the fall. The closer attention and focus of the news agenda on economic issues appear to have come from inside the campaign. One candidate, eventually two, increasingly made the economy the central issue of the campaign. It may also be that conviction was spreading among journalists that the campaign was about George Bush's management of the economy over the previous four years.

Conclusion: Judging the Richness of the News Environment

How then should the news environment be assessed? How much information was readily available to people living in each of these four media markets? What was the quality of that information? Was the news a resource for citizens in making informed judgments when they cast their ballots for the candidates?

The findings suggest that to some extent, access depends on where you live. Smaller media markets have less campaign news, but the association is not linear. A great deal depends on the editorial and marketing decisions in a particular place. Overall, market size is a more important factor for print than for broadcasting. Local newspapers vary far more, one from the next, than local television news programs. Although there is certainly variation, the news hole for campaign stories in local news broad-

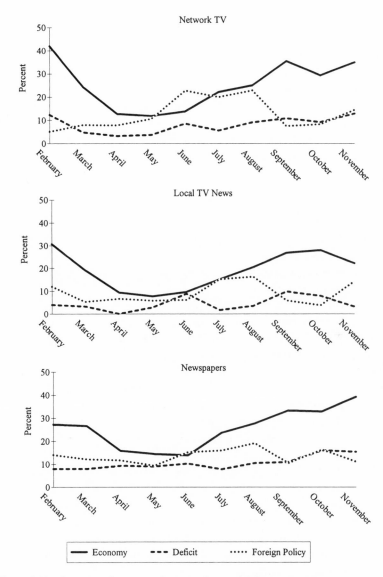

Figure 5.13 Coverage of economy, foreign policy, and deficit in campaign stories.

casts is simply restricted and the resources limited, whether in Boston or in Winston-Salem. But the stories that emerge in the larger markets are not necessarily more substantive than in the smaller markets—for example, there was a greater percentage of journalist-initiated stories on Fargo/Moorhead television than on local Los Angeles television. Nonetheless, it is clear that an average voter in Boston or Los Angeles will run across news about the campaign more readily than his or her counterpart in Moorhead or Winston-Salem.

Yet, while there is variation from one community to the next, there is substantial evidence that local television news and local newspapers handled the campaign in different ways according to format and medium. For example, in all markets local television journalists initiated proportionately fewer stories than their print counterparts. Local television was more inclined to focus on the horse race and consequently was easier on the candidates than were the networks. But there was no evidence of an intracommunity consensus on how to portray the candidates. Instead the results indicate more commonality within types of media than within communities.

During the campaign, candidates make special efforts to cultivate local news. The findings do not show that this pays off. The local angle may have won points for politicians in newspapers, a fairly negative medium, but it gained them nothing in local television news. When local television journalists initiated stories—although this was infrequent—they were significantly more negative toward the candidates than were local newspaper stories. Moreover, while small newspapers may have compensated for diminutive staff size by using wire services to cover national and international news, doing so both downplayed the local aspect of the news and imported the national press's viewpoint into local news coverage. In effect, the greater its reliance on the wire services, the closer a newspaper's tone was to the networks'. Our study shows that fewer resources need not mean "soft" media, but instead the penetration of national news sources and values into local news outlets, either print or broadcast.

While the quality of coverage may diverge between newspapers, local television news, and network news, the news agenda is fairly consistent. Many of these similarities in coverage presumably arise from standard routines, shared journalistic norms, and similar definitions of what is news and how it should be covered. During the campaign, there were similar amounts of attention to candidates across the news media, similar types of coverage for each candidate, and similar patterns in the tone of coverage. Moreover, in all three kinds of media, there was evidence of a struggle over news content; when candidates are allowed to speak longer or hold their image longer on television, they generally receive more positive coverage, but when journalists initiate stories, candidates tend to receive more negative coverage.

The diversity in presentation of candidates during the primary campaign and in coverage of Perot suggests that the guidance of "news val-

ues" is not so helpful to journalists in a fluid political situation. Furthermore, differences in the constraints on kinds of media—newspaper, local
television, and network—mean that the public has a spectrum of candidate presentations from which to choose. There is a range of assessments—albeit limited—about the candidates in the news media in a given
locale, and this range includes information about issues and the candidate's personal characteristics as well as about the horse race.

While the findings dispute the media monolith, they confirm the continuing unwillingness of journalists—in any medium—to spend much
time focusing on issues as the *main* topic of their reports. These data
show, however, that the horse race does not drive out all other kinds of
information. It may be that the preoccupation with who is ahead and
who is behind is the leading story, but in the process of reporting about
the campaign process, the news media do cover matters that are more
democratically relevant—the personal qualities of the candidates (which
voters can reasonably believe will help them predict performance in office) and their policy positions.

Returning to the question that began this discussion: what kinds of
resources do the media provide to citizens? The answer depends on the
candidates, the citizens, and the media themselves. Where candidates
choose to campaign makes a big impact on the total information environment available to the electorate—advertising as well as local coverage of
the campaign. Which medium citizens rely on also matters. Network
news is a rich and easily accessed source of campaign news—but more
and more Americans are neglecting it for the limited offerings on local
television. And, clearly, journalists matter. News producers determine, for
example, how much attention a local station will give to the presidential
campaign and whether it will attempt the coverage primarily using its
own resources (as in Winston-Salem) or through network feeds (as in
Fargo/Moorhead). Interestingly, the degree of market competition does
not necessarily improve news quality. For example, the *Los Angeles Times*
is the major paper in town and yet compares favorably with the *Boston
Globe*, which has a competitor in the *Herald*. There is fierce competition
among local affiliates in both Los Angeles and Boston for the television
news audience, but both Boston stations carry more campaign news than
either of the Los Angeles stations. The discrepancy between the amount
of issue coverage and news analysis between one local television news
program and another, or between one newspaper and another, suggests
that resources are not the only, or even the most important, constraint on
the quality of news coverage.

SIX

Shared Constructions: Ad Watches and Candidate Interviews

As was illustrated in the discussion of news coverage, the history of recent presidential elections has been a saga of ongoing negotiations between journalists and politicians. The most visible negotiations, of course, occur on the campaign trail itself, as candidates stage events that will present them in the most favorable light and journalists interpret them in ways that will fit their needs for interesting and important stories. But this negotiation is dynamic as well; at the end of each campaign, each side looks back on the previous year, determines not to be taken advantage of, and seeks new ways to increase their influence over the final product.

The 1988 election was not a happy occasion for either journalists or politicians. On one hand, journalists bemoaned the Bush campaign's predilection for stage-managed visual events, heavy on symbolism but light on substance, such as the candidate's visit to a flag factory in New Jersey. They were well aware, moreover, that by following the candidate and showing the pictures and accompanying sound bites, they were playing into a "photo opportunity" strategy perfected by the Reagan White House (Hertsgaard 1988). Various studies showed that television news coverage of advertising in the 1988 campaign provided free airtime to the candidates' messages and tended to amplify their content (Adatto 1990; Jamieson 1992a; Kaid et al. 1993; Kern 1993; Kern and Just 1994). Indeed, manipulative ads, such as Bush's "Revolving Door," which misled voters into incorrect assessments of Governor Dukakis's prison furlough program in Massachusetts, were amplified not only by having the ominous video repeated during the news program but also by the implicit praise heaped on the Bush campaign by reports of the ad's "effectiveness."

On the other hand, politicians claimed that their behavior was simply an adaptation to formats prescribed by journalists. In postmortems of the 1988 campaign,[1] campaign managers maintained that it was journalists' preference for vivid, terse, and colorful stories that forced candidates to stage events and to speak in soundbites. Journalists' preoccupation with the horse race rather than issues, the managers continued, also made it

120

necessary to turn to ads in order to talk about their candidates' policy concerns. Academic critics and the public objected to the condensation of political argumentation (Louden 1994) both in 30-second political ads and 9-second news soundbites.

In 1992, two new formats arose in reaction to these complaints. Journalists instigated a new approach to covering ads, termed "ad watches." In turn, candidates gravitated toward a burgeoning form of programming that we call "interview programs," which were more identified with entertainment than politics. Both ad watches and interview programs were formats that offered expanded analysis, exposure, and interaction. In the case of ad watches, the innovation was a conscious attempt by journalists to overcome criticism from scholars of the 1988 campaign as well as from within their own ranks (such as David Broder [1990]), to do a better job of covering campaign ads by checking for accuracy and analyzing messages. Candidate interviews represented an innovation that was negotiated early in the campaign between the candidates and media people outside the news, such as Larry King (with Ross Perot) and Phil Donahue (with both Jerry Brown and Bill Clinton). The public played an important role in bringing this innovation forward, by tuning in to these programs in sufficiently large numbers to encourage both candidates and media to expand these encounters into other media formats, including regular news broadcasts and MTV.

It is difficult to say whether these formats were dominated by those who initiated them. At first glance, ad watches would seem to be journalists' natural territory, inasmuch as they dissect ads on their own terms. But ad watches may amplify and reinforce the message of the ad. To the extent that they focus on the "effectiveness" of the ad rather than its accuracy, manipulative ads may be portrayed in a positive light. Likewise, control over candidate interviews was mixed. Journalists routinely criticized interview programs for supposedly "soft" questions from the audience or from interviewers more accustomed to entertainment celebrities, but at least candidates had to respond to the questions and had more than nine seconds to say their piece. As the campaign went on, journalists fought to find a place for themselves in the interview format. Sometimes they adopted the role of "follow-up enforcer," building on call-in and audience questions and seeking to pin down ambiguous answers.

This chapter looks at these two new forms of campaign communication noting the extent to which journalists or candidates dominate the discourse and examining how people responded. The discussion includes an assessment of ad watches and interview programs as a resource for citizens in their construction of candidates and the campaign.

Ad Watches

Keith Love, a reporter for the *Los Angeles Times,* developed the concept
of an "ad watch" long before Bush's "Revolving Door" ad was aired in
1988. He worried, as did others who followed him, that there was little
local television news coverage of political candidates. By default, therefore, political advertising was the voter's major televised information
source (Kurtz 1993). Although the news media increasingly covered ads,
the focus was on the role of advertising in campaign strategy (West 1993;
Kaid et al. 1993; Roberts and McCombs 1994). Portions of or even complete ads were included in televised news stories as "filler" (Rosenstiel
1994). Early in the 1990 midterm election cycle, *Washington Post* political columnist David Broder criticized ads for their "increasingly sophisticated insinuation" and issued a call to journalists to probe the accuracy
of advertising claims, as well as the use of sound and visual symbols in
ads (Broder 1990).

Ad watches suddenly blossomed in newspapers around the country,
and the week before the 1990 midterm election Broder suggested that ad
watches had affected the course of several electoral contests (Rothenberg
1990a). The consultants and spin doctors who created the political ads
swiftly joined the struggle for control over the format. Frank Greer, who
created 1990 ads for gubernatorial candidate Bill Clinton and went on to
work on his 1992 presidential campaign advertising retorted: "The press
[in critiquing political ads] gives us ammunition we can use on the air.
Most people won't read or see one article, but we can run it on the air [in
another ad] and run the hell out of it." Democratic pollster Paul Maslin
added, "A newspaper piece saying whether an ad is truthful or not that's
seen by 30 percent of the public isn't enough to reduce the actual impact
of a TV ad seen by 80 percent of the public" (Rothenberg 1990b).[2]

In the struggle for control of the ad watch format, a key question became whether local television news would develop ad watches as well,
and what type of ad watches would emerge. Beginning in 1989 and 1990,
a few local television stations worked with Kathleen Hall Jamieson, dean
of the Annenberg School of Communication, who argued that airing visuals in televised ad watches could enhance the ads' reach. The concern
was that rhetorically emotional visuals may enhance a message's memora-
bility and influence, despite a journalist's verbal critique (Pfau and
Louden 1994). Jamieson worked with the local stations to develop a format which would offer a critical evaluation of ads, as opposed to an assessment in terms of strategy. The local stations were "trying," as she ob-

served, "to do well what the networks weren't doing at all" (Jamieson 1992a).

Inaugurating critical ad watch formats became local television journalists' major planned innovation in news coverage in 1992, according to a national survey of news directors undertaken in the primary season (Wicks and Kern 1993). By wide margins, news directors believed that political advertising was "manipulative" and overused by voters who "rely too much on messages designed to persuade rather than inform." They planned ad watches that focused on accuracy and underlying symbolic meanings. Most local stations (57 percent) planned to critique advertising produced for state and local candidates, however, rather than for presidential candidates and on national issues (30 percent). Follow-up interviews with a randomly selected subsample of 48 local news directors indicated that indeed only one-third of them covered presidential-level ads. They argued that these were covered by newspapers and the national electronic media, including their parent networks, and that the need for ad watches was greater on the local and statewide level (Kern and Wicks 1994).

Entering the 1992 primary season, all of the national networks except ABC decided to increase their focus on political ads (Rosenstiel 1994). CNN inaugurated a half-hour afternoon program, "Inside Politics," which included a regular critique of political advertising under the direction of former *Wall Street Journal* reporter Brooks Jackson. Like NBC, CNN developed ad watch formats based on ideas by Jamieson.[3]

Ad Watch Formats
In their ad critiques, journalists believed that they must analyze not only the verbal claims made in political advertising but the visuals as well, and what Broder had called the "insinuations" of the underlying messages. While there was broad agreement to undertake ad criticism, there were differences in the focus of the critiques. The different styles of ad watches are illustrated in the critiques of one of the most controversial ads of the primary season. The ad, "Freedom Abused," aired by Patrick Buchanan in Georgia, criticized President Bush for supporting public subsidies of homoerotic art. The video in the ad was taken from a PBS documentary "Tongues Untied," partially financed by the National Endowment for the Arts. The voice-over blasted Bush for spending "tax dollars" on "pornographic art" that "glorified homosexuality."

On February 27, almost immediately after the commercial started running, the *Washington Post* printed a news article by E. J. Dionne, Jr., reporting the ad's airing and reactions from the Bush campaign calling the video a "blatant distortion of truth." Buchanan's response was that the ad "has nothing to do with anti-gay prejudice. It has to do with not spending people's tax dollars on values that insult them."

Analysis of the *Washington Post, Boston Globe,* and CBS critiques, all of which appeared February 28, clarifies the differences between "watchdog" and "campaign process" ad watches. Both styles of ad watch usually describe the ads and repeat, both visually and verbally, the ads' central claims. After that, they differ. Watchdog ad watches concentrate on the factual claims explicitly or implicitly made in the ad, while campaign process ad watches focus on the presumed effectiveness of the ad. The *Post's* watchdog ad watch, by Howard Kurtz, starts with a repetition of the entire audio of the ad, including Buchanan's charge that the Bush administration wasted "our tax dollars on pornographic art too shocking to show," together with a photograph from the ad, a close-up black and white "dead shot" (Kern 1989) of Bush's face partially covered with the text "This so-called art has glorified homosexuality: Bush used your tax $$$ for this." The rest of the ad critique is in two parts. In his first two sentences Kurtz analyzes the visuals used in the ad, as well as the underlying meaning: "By filling the screen with slow-motion images of dancing gay black men in leather harnesses, Buchanan tries to shock the viewer while linking the president to pornography, homosexuality, and disrespect for religion." He then evaluates the facts in the ad as well as the sponsoring candidate: "Buchanan unfairly suggests that Bush is personally responsible for each funding decision by the National Endowment of the Arts. The maker of the film shown in the ad, Marion Riggs, was given a $5,000 grant from the Rocky Mountain Film Institute, which received the money from the American Film Institute, which got it from the NEA." A comparable ad watch that appeared on the same day in the *Boston Globe,* by Renee Loth, was even more critical of the ad "for sheer appeal to intolerance and shock value" as well as its revelation of "an unattractive side of Buchanan." These examples show how watchdog ad watches critique ads and the candidates who air them for making a variety of claims based on factual, visual, and underlying implied meanings.

On the same day as the *Post* and the *Globe* published their ad watches, Eric Engberg of CBS aired an ad critique of two ads, including "Freedom Abused." Engberg's ad watch was in the campaign process style and focused on ad effectiveness. The Buchanan ad was placed in a comparative context, comparing it with other ads from the same contest and historical ads. The theme was negative advertising, and the Buchanan ad was compared with a Bush ad in which General Kelley questioned Buchanan's po-

sition on the Persian Gulf war. Its effectiveness was compared with that
of the 1988 "Willie Horton" ad campaign used on behalf of the Bush
candidacy. Engberg concluded,

> By staking a claim to the racially sensitive quotas issue and
> by coming on as a strong supporter of traditional values,
> Buchanan is cutting into Mr. Bush's base, something of a sur-
> prise for a president who was able to make effective use of "Wil-
> lie Horton" just four years ago.

As a result of the emphasis on strategy, the CBS ad watch ends on a positive note for Buchanan.

Our surveys indicate that a large number of viewers and readers were
exposed to ad watches. Beginning in March in Boston over 50 percent of
respondents reported having seen an ad watch in the previous week, and
the pattern continued through the primary season until June in Los
Angeles, where it declined to 41 percent. According to our pooled sample
in late September, reported ad watch exposure rose again to 48 percent.
By the end of October, with the increased airing of both ads and ad
watches, this figure rose to 61 percent.

If they were noticed, ad watches were viewed favorably by many of our
in-depth interview respondents—but they did not like campaign process
ad watches, which they often perceived to be "biased" media reporting.
They expressed concern about news reports of "effective" rather than
truthful ads. Participants were, however, positively impressed with watchdog ad watches, especially when they addressed factual claims and underlying implied meanings.

We used focus groups to gauge the reaction of people viewing segments
of news, ads, ad watches, debates, and candidate interviews. Analysis of
the subsequent discussion shows how voters used campaign information
in a conversational context. The discussion of campaign messages was
divided into units of conversational exchange around a specific topic. An
"exchange" is a dialogue between two or more people about a single
topic, involving either agreement of disagreement. These exchanges varied in length, but on the average there were six to eight exchanges per
media segment in our focus group discussions. (See appendix D.)

Boston focus group participants who saw campaign process ad
watches during the primary charged the media with sensationalism or
held the view that all candidates were being treated badly. As Jon pointed
out: "Well, they hit the negative ad thing. . . . They were focusing on 'let's
get the dirt going here.'" To which George responded, "When I see that
kind of a presentation, I would just turn to another channel."

They also worried about media bias. Viewing an ad watch on a local Boston station, participants argued that it favored Tsongas, "the hometown boy," as Bob called him. Earl concurred, disappointedly, "Of course, Harkin's out of it." Some people also expressed concern that the media were substituting their own views for those of the candidates and assuming unwarranted prominence in the political dialogue. As George noted, "It reminds me of years ago, the news anchorman after a presidential speech telling us what he said, even though we were watching him say it." With which Marty concurred sarcastically, "We weren't smart enough."

Focus group participants preferred watchdog ad watches. As Fred noted, "When they start making comments about it [a candidate's ad] pro or con, I would hope that the reporter would not do it from a personal or emotional [point of view] but do it from a scientific, factual—[Interviewer: Objective?] objective [perspective] and this is good or these facts are bad or these facts are not true." Benny summed up the positive sentiment for ad watches this way:

> When they [the media] know that an ad is misleading [they] come out and tell you. I have noticed that more during this campaign than I have previous ones. You know, they'll tell you why, you know, Bush did say this. But it is misleading. And they'll tell you what the source is, or where they got the information, or whatever.

Other participants suggested that ad watches had cut down on negative ads, which focus group and interview participants often said they disliked.

While the majority of comments favored watchdog ad critiques, campaign process ad critiques provoked talk about possible media bias. Still, the overall view of ad watches was less negative than of news generally. Figure 6.1 illustrates that in the focus groups, campaign process ad watches generated more comments about bias, but fewer remarks about manipulativeness or sensationalism than horse-race news, while watchdog ad watches were followed by more comments about how informative they were compared to news analysis pieces.

In evaluating the ad critiques, it is important to point out two problems that journalists faced in undertaking the watchdog effort. The first was dealing with what journalists saw as half-truths and misrepresentations. These included claims in ads that were accurate, but that were taken out of context. As Kurtz later pointed out, "subtle distortions," such as a claim made by Tsongas that Clinton was borrowing "from our children" to finance his proposed middle-class tax cut but that ignored Clinton's

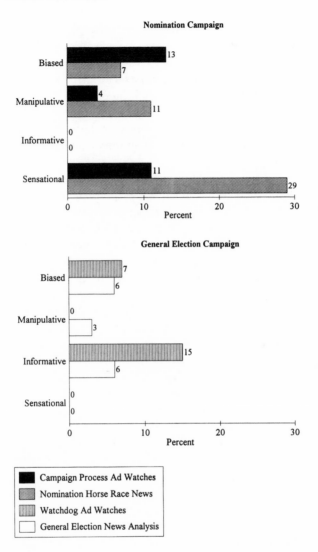

Figure 6.1 Focus group discussion of ad watches and news stories: percentage of conversational exchanges.

pledge to pay for his plan by raising taxes on the wealthy, "could slip through the [ad watch] net" because "it was hard to prove [it] literally false." The same was true of claims by other candidates, including Clinton. In the primary, for example, one of *his* ads quoted *Time* magazine as saying, "Much of what Tsongas proposes smacks of trickle-down economics." "True enough," Kurtz pointed out, "except that the same article said that on many economic issues, 'Tsongas is clearly the more courageous' of the two" (1993, 259).

The second problem stemmed from the fact that, as Kurtz noted, "calling a candidate a liar, in effect, required the press to break the shackles of objectivity that had long restricted campaign coverage" (Kurtz 1993, 259). This meant that news might be open to charges of "bias" against candidates, if the ads of one rather than another candidate were criticized more frequently.

Further, in a through-the-looking-glass fashion, the ad watches themselves played into the hands of the quick-response ad makers. As Clinton consultant Frank Greer forecast, newspaper ad critiques were shown in televised political ads to support candidate claims. Greer pointed out that in the 1992 general election he successfully prompted, through phone calls to journalists for major newspapers including the *Wall Street Journal*, ad watches that criticized the inaccuracy of George Bush's "Pipefitter" ad, which had charged Clinton with seeking to raise taxes on the middle class. Criticisms from the ad watches were then immediately aired by the Clinton campaign in counterattack ads (Greer 1993; Rosenstiel 1994), a situation which gives rise to some serious concerns.

The unrelieved negative tone of the ad watches implies that all candidates are deceptive, even when the criticisms are directed against things that are "mostly true" or "fair" but about which minor quibbles can be raised. Consequently, negative judgments, with the authority of presumably objective media sources, are readily available for candidates to use in subsequent attack ads. The result is to contribute to the overall negative tone of the campaign, which the people we spoke to during our in-depth interviews found so repellent.

The 1992 Ad Watches

Just how successful were journalists in creating ad watches that challenged candidates, rather than reinforced their efforts? Was it possible that, even in challenging candidate claims, journalists amplified their messages through the inclusion of ad visuals, even partial ones broken with all conceivable distancing and displacing devices? Was it possible that, as Jamieson pointed out at the height of the "Freedom Abused" controversy, "even if you do all of these [things to break the power of visuals] that might not be enough?" (Jamieson 1992a).

If ad watches were to serve as a counterbalancing resource for citizens, they had to be readily available in the information environment. Even if ad watches are defined broadly as "news stories about ads," there were

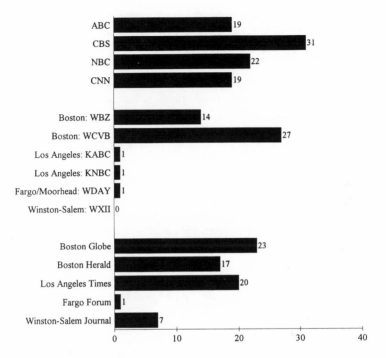

Figure 6.2 Number of ad watches.

still substantial differences in the number of ad watches aired by various media and locales. Figure 6.2 points to the fact that there were more ad watches in the newspapers than on either network or local television news, particularly in major-market newspapers such as the *Los Angeles Times* and the *Boston Globe*.[4] CBS aired more ad watches on the evening news than either of the other networks. It is important to note that CNN developed more ad watches than the other networks, but they aired them on the afternoon "Inside Politics" news program, and not so much, as these figures indicate, on their popular early evening news program.

While local television news directors from larger markets indicated greater overall interest in producing ad watch formats for the presidential campaign (Wicks and Kern 1993), comparisons of local stations in the four communities indicated that, although size of market was a factor, there were also major differences between news stations in the same market. The within-market discrepancy indicates that news judgment as well as resources played a role in the evolution of the format. One station, Boston's WCVB, clearly set out to make its mark in this area. Beginning with ads from the New Hampshire primary, it ultimately produced more ad watches than all of the other local stations we examined and all of the networks except CBS. Its Boston counterpart, WBZ, however, produced about half as many ad watches, while KABC and KNBC in Los Angeles, despite their greater resources operating within one of the nation's highest-ranking urban markets, aired one ad watch apiece.

Figure 6.2 also makes it clear, however, that ad watch "poverty" can exist in small and medium-sized market areas such as those in Fargo/Moorhead and Winston-Salem, where neither the local newspaper nor local television undertook presidential-level ad watches.

Control over the Format

Figure 6.3, based on multiple codings of ad watch attributes, points to significant variation in the development of different types of ad watches across media. It also indicates that candidate voices are still heard in ad watches. On the simplest, most basic level, two-thirds of ad watches describe the ads. Whatever else journalists may do, their descriptions facilitate the amplification and reinforcement of candidate messages. In Figure 6.3, ad description is categorized with other campaign process attributes because it clearly offers a platform for candidate voices to be heard inside the ad watch format.

Figure 6.3 also demonstrates that in other aspects of the ad watches there was a more equal struggle for control over the format. Newspaper ad watches made the most watchdog efforts, including evaluations of facts (40 percent) and visual symbols (35 percent), but they also evaluated ads for "effectiveness" in the campaign (35 percent). The picture is somewhat different on television news programs. Network ad critiques involved smaller proportions of evaluative messages, although they were also less likely than newspapers to judge ad effectiveness. Local television ad watches are similar to those of network news. Over all three media, most ad watches demonstrated shared control over the message, but the most substantive ad watch effort was in newspapers.

While all candidates were criticized in ad watches, our focus group evidence suggests that George Bush was hurt most. The damage to Bush did not arise because of the number of ad watches directed against his ads or the nature of the criticism. In our observation, journalists strove to be evenhanded to the two major party candidates (while mostly failing to critique Perot's ads along the watchdog dimension). The reason the ad watches hurt Bush was that people knew the most about him. They were able to relate new information in the ad watches to this prior knowledge, especially his broken promises and reputation for negative campaigning.

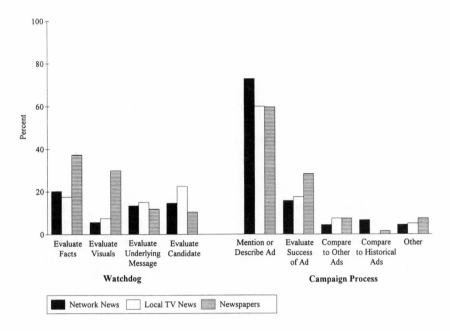

Figure 6.3   Watchdog and campaign process critiques in ad watches.

Clinton, although equally criticized in the fall ad watches, benefited from the public's hopeful attitude toward change. As one focus group participant pointed out in response to a fall ad watch: "I'm pretty sure the promises he [Clinton] spouts will—uh—come to life. Whatever he's said is going to happen." A second focus group participant disagreed: "Why are you so sure? Why should he be so different from anybody else [other candidates]?" Speaker 1: "Well, Bush is not going to do it [keep his promises]." Speaker 2: "We know that, but why is he [Clinton] going to do it?" Speaker 1: "That leaves him. . . . That leaves him. . . . I don't think anybody else's going to really [make promises which can be kept]. It's a process of elimination . . . whatever he says [he will do], I'm pretty sure it will be done."

By the end of the campaign, many participants in our focus groups chose to ignore the information in ad watches that criticized the distortions and exaggerations in Clinton's political advertising. They used arguments supported by the both-sides-are-doing-it assumptions that underlie the ad watch practice. But other participants rejected ad watch criticisms because they agreed with the underlying meaning of the accusations in Clinton's allegedly inaccurate ads about Bush.

For example, as participants viewed ad watches in the late October focus groups, there was wide agreement with the individual who concluded: "I think probably one reason [for thinking Bush's messages are more "hardball and negative"] is everybody's familiar with the 'read my lips' routine. So I suppose that gives a touch of truthfulness to Clinton's ads, but Bush's ads aren't anything like that." Overall, prior knowledge worked to Bush's disadvantage and contributed to participants discounting his messages in their interpretation of his ads. In the case of the less well known Clinton, however, when people found journalists criticizing a candidate with whom they agreed, they said, "all candidates do it [make inaccurate claims]."

But what about the visuals within the ad watches? Were the media able to regain control over the visual images that aired across the screen? One or more of Jamieson's three "Ds" were used in most of the watchdog ad watches that appeared on CNN and NBC, which attempted to follow her visual grammar. The two networks put ad visuals inside a box or used a big red "X" label for "falsehood" plastered on the screen. Some of the same devices were found on CBS as well. Other methods were developed by CBS reporter Eric Engberg. He often stopped a visual ad replay by calling "time-out" like a sports announcer, before evaluating the facts in an ad. Such practices were designed to contextualize the message.[5]

Analysis of our in-depth interviews and focus groups leads to the conclusion that ad watches tended to amplify candidate messages in spite of these efforts. During the Minnesota primary, Lisa remembers seeing an ad watch and complained, because the media were amplifying negative ads:

> They show a TV set on TV and say this is what Bill Clinton is saying about Brown and then they analyze it and they say, why would he do this? . . . I think that whole thing is inappropriate. . . . I don't think that needs to be done in that way, because in return they're slandering or showing something. I've never seen these commercials be on so I don't know why they're showing them.

The reason for the stubbornness of the amplification effect lies with the reproduction of salient verbal and visual information in the ad watches. Reinforcement could not be overcome by competing interpretations of candidates' messages by journalists or, in some cases, by their guests. Nor could the significance of the words and visuals be eliminated by displaying them partially, or by stamping the offending information with an "X." Indeed, the verbal and visual information from ads contained in ad

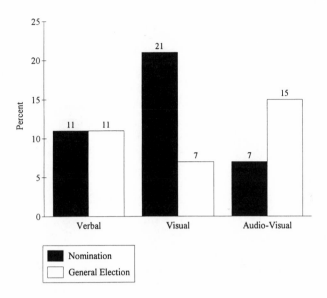

Figure 6.4 Focus group discussions of ad watches: percentage of conversational exchanges mentioning verbal, visual, and audio-visual messages.

watches offered strong cues for viewers, which they used in evaluating other information.

Conversational exchanges in focus groups were analyzed to determine whether they made reference to verbal, visual, or both verbal and visual stimuli (see fig. 6.4 and appendix D). In the nominating campaign ad watches, 20 percent of postviewing exchanges mentioned visuals. Participants talked about some audio-visual information (8 percent) but did not refer to the verbal alone. Although fall focus group participants cited fewer visual-only messages than the spring groups, their interpretations of the ad watches took account of more combined audio-visual messages. Altogether, twice as much visual and audio-visual information was picked up as verbal information.

The results suggest that journalists' verbal critiques in ad watches are much less salient to voters than the visuals that are included from the ads. For example, after seeing an ad watch about primary candidates' spots, including Tsongas's "Swim" ad, Jon remarked that Tsongas is "going to stay clean, because he's in the pool." Favorable ad visuals of Buchanan were also picked up and discussed after the ad watch. One participant noted, for example, Buchanan's "solid, low-key, look the camera square in the eye" appearance. The women focused on the fact that Bush looked, as Michelle says, "nervous," and "worried about being attacked."

Participants also commented on combinations of words and pictures in the ads being critiqued. One of the ads most likely to be seen through the ad watch was Buchanan's "Read My Lips" attack on President Bush. In the Boston focus group, George picked up on the ad's visual of an ordinary person in New Hampshire, "The man from New Hampshire said, 'You lied to me,' I mean, came out of the barn and said it." The women were equally attentive to the ad within the ad watch. Pam commented, "[Buchanan]'s got this little thing where he has the people saying 'read our lips.'"

Not only are people aware of the content of the ad within the ad watch, they responded to the ad watch as they did to direct ad messages. For example, four of the seven conversational exchanges after the showing of the Buchanan ad watch followed the Buchanan message and were negative to Bush. The president's integrity, leadership, and prior negative campaigning (the "Willie Horton" ad) were all censured. Susan observed, "Bush has finally become aware of what's been happening in the nation."

The same effect of ads coming through the ad watches occurred in the fall. Following a set of Bush and Clinton ad watches, the main topic was the failure of the Bush administration. The amplification that occurred was of Clinton's views about Bush. In contrast, Bush's views were discounted. As Jim in Moorhead noted, Bush was "hitting on some of Clinton's past things that really, if you think about it, don't have anything to do with whether he's going to be a good president." Bush's argument that Clinton would raise taxes and the journalist's criticisms of Clinton's advertising were ignored in the context of a general narrative about Bush. A different logic was applied to Clinton than to Bush. Rationalizations were used. As one participant in Boston noted, Clinton may raise taxes despite his promise, but taxes would "probably [not] get that high."

It is possible that watchdog ad watches aired early in the campaign, which criticize candidates on less universally salient issues about which voters have little knowledge, may have a different effect (Cappella and Jamieson 1994). In our series of focus groups, during both the primary and general election seasons, however, amplification of salient campaign messages often occurred despite the efforts of journalists to control them (see Pfau and Louden 1994).

Candidate Interviews

Whereas ad watches were instigated by journalists in an effort to counter candidate messages, interview program appearances resulted from candidate efforts to find a more congenial and open-ended venue for their messages. Whereas ad watches were planned by news media to provide better coverage of the 1992 campaign, candidate interviews surprised—not to say dismayed—journalists. As candidates sought out nonnews formats, journalists became concerned that candidates could gain access to large television audiences without the participation (called the "filter") of news specialists. Interview programs, like ad watches, however, represent a shared control—between candidates and media professionals—over the television content. During candidate interviews, media people and members of the audience ask questions, and candidates, more or less, answer.

There is nothing new about candidates seeking access to television. Since the early days of televised campaigning, candidates have sought television coverage of their campaigns. Free media time is a "best buy" for candidates. It is especially valuable for the candidate who does not have a big campaign budget to spend on television ads. Because free media usually involve news formats, coverage can lend even greater legitimacy to the candidacy than advertising. Historically, however, television news coverage has had its downside for candidates.

First, the traditional television news agenda, with its focus on conflict and horse-race issues, made it difficult for candidates to get airtime for the issues they thought were important (Patterson 1980). The journalists' control over how the candidates appeared on air could threaten a candidate's visual message as well. In the 1980s, however, the Reagan-Bush campaigns demonstrated how candidates could control the candidate's news appearance, by careful selection of background site, placement of candidate vis-à-vis news cameras, and preparation of irresistible photo opportunities (Deaver 1989).

The second problem of "free media" was the shorter and shorter time that was allotted for candidates to speak on television news. This limitation proved more intractable for candidates than control over the campaign agenda. As Adatto (1990) and Hallin (1992) have shown, the typical opportunity for candidates to be heard on network newscasts declined from about 40 seconds to less than 10 seconds between 1968 and 1988. The shrinking soundbite became a metaphor, not only for candidates but for critical observers of American campaigns, about the lack of substance on television news. Various studies confirmed that in spite of good intentions and a sensitivity to the issue, network soundbites did not get longer in 1992, averaging 9.8 second on the four networks.[6] The candidate interview represented an attractive alternative for candidates who wanted more than 10, or even 30, seconds on air (Kalb 1992).

Candidate interviews did not represent a dramatic new form either. Political interviews had been part of the television campaign since the 1950s.[7] Both Nixon and Ford paid for television question/answer programming during their campaigns in 1968 and 1976, and some candidates appeared on the "Tonight Show." By 1988, candidates frequently were interviewed on morning television news programs the day after significant primaries, during the party conventions, or following announcements of entry or withdrawal from the race. In the waning days of the 1988 campaign, Ted Koppel interviewed the Democratic candidate Michael Dukakis (with rather devastating results) on "Nightline."

What was new in 1992 was that candidate interviews were conducted with increasing frequency all around the dial and throughout the campaign. A conservative estimate is that there were more than twice as many candidate interviews in 1992 as in 1988. In 1988, the majority of the interviews were conducted on morning news programs and most were tied to breaking news events (Stevens 1993), but the dramatic increase in candidate appearances in the 1992 campaign was in entertainment programming. In 1992, 243 interviews were listed in the Legi-slate transcript service just for Bush, Clinton, and Perot and their vice-presidential candidates in the period January 26 (the date of the Clintons' appearance on "60 Minutes") to election day. An additional 11 interviews were listed in newspaper programming schedules and confirmed to have occurred. In total, these 254 listings involved 42 *different* programs.[8] The variety of programs involved in the candidate interview campaign meant that candidates appeared on programs with highly diverse audiences, including many viewers who do not normally follow the campaign.[9]

The expansion of candidate interviews in 1992 was in part a result of the rise in "hard" and "soft" television news programming in the years preceding the election. Newsmagazine shows, attempting to capitalize on the long-running success of CBS's "60 Minutes," blossomed on all three broadcast networks. In addition, popular interview programs thrived in virtually every time slot—early morning (e.g., "Today" and "Good Morning America"), afternoon ("Donahue"), prime time ("60 Minutes" and "Larry King Live"), and late night ("Nightline" and "Arsenio Hall"). The establishment of C-SPAN provided interested cableviewers with yet another alternative, offering plenty of live coverage of the campaign trail (see Mayer 1994).

As the campaign progressed, the barriers of prudence or conceit that kept candidates in the 1988 campaign from agreeing to appear on "Donahue" fell first for one candidate and then another. The frequency of candidate interviews even rose during the campaign, with increasing numbers of appearances on entertainment-oriented programs in the summer and fall. During the primary season, more than half of the presidential candidate appearances were on traditional newscasts or news interview programs. In the summer the magazine, weekday morning, and nighttime interview programs constituted half the appearances, and during the general election in the fall nearly three-quarters.

Candidate Strategies

Table 6.1 shows that candidates varied in their enthusiasm for the new venue. Of the three major candidates, President Bush, who by dint of office, had the greatest access to regular news channels, feared that participation in the candidate interview format would be demeaning. In May, he told a reporter: "I don't plan on spending lots of time on Phil Donahue shows. I'm president."[10] He did not surface on any of the interview programs during the primary season, but appeared 13 times in the three months between June and September, and twice as many times in the two months of the general election campaign—almost all on soft news and magazine shows (often called "infotainment"). The choice of programming reflected a conviction that the president should be made to appear more "in touch" with the people. Bush's vice-president, Dan Quayle, however, made a steady round of appearances on candidate interview shows from the beginning of the campaign, spending more of his time on straight news programs.

Probably the most important strategic use of the format was achieved by Ross Perot, who made his opening bid for the presidency on the cable program "Larry King Live." Perot was pressed by King to specify the circumstances under which he would run for president. After dancing around the point, Perot finally agreed that he would run if "the people" put his name on the ballot in all 50 states. When they left the studio, Perot asked King if he thought anything would come of the remark. King said he didn't know. The following day King's phones rang off the hook, and the Perot campaign was born.[11] As the campaign progressed, Perot appeared on a number of news interview programs such as "Meet the Press" but found the emphasis on policy so distasteful that he essentially withdrew from news programs to concentrate on the softer magazine, morning, and talk show formats. Perot sought out audience call-in shows, which he found particularly congenial to his populist style.[12]

While Perot's announcement was the most dramatic use of the candi-

Table 6.1 Televised Candidate Interviews, 1992

	Bush	Quayle	Clinton	Gore	Perot	Stockdale	Total
Primary (1/26–6/3)							
News[a]	0	8	27	N/A	13	N/A	48
Infotainment[b]	0	2	19	N/A	6	N/A	27
Entertainment[c]	0	0	2	N/A	1	N/A	3
Total	0	10	48	N/A	20	N/A	78
Summer (6/4–9/6)							
News	5	6	10	6	1	0	28
Infotainment	7	5	11	13	6	0	42
Entertainment	1	0	0	0	0	0	1
Total	13	11	21	19	7	0	71
Election (9/6–11/2)							
News	4	7	2	6	5	0	24
Infotainment	18	8	14	13	12	2	67
Entertainment	2	0	2	3	1	0	8
Total	24	15	18	22	18	2	99
Total	37	36	87	41	45	2	248

[a]News includes nightly news interview segments (on ABC, CBS, CNN, NBC, and PBS), news interview segments (on CNN daytime news and political shows, as well as primary and convention coverage), news talk shows (weekend morning shows and "Evans and Novak"), national town meetings, and late night news shows ("Nightline").
[b]Infotainment includes magazine shows ("60 Minutes," "20/20," "Primetime Live," and "Dateline NBC,"), weekday morning shows (on ABC, CBS, CNN, NBC, and Fox), and interview programs ("Larry King Live," "David Frost," and "Charlie Rose").
[c]Entertainment includes "Arsenio Hall," "Whoopi," "Donahue," MTV, and "Nashville Now."

date interview venue, credit for starting the trend actually goes to Bill Clinton. He and Mrs. Clinton appeared in late January on "60 Minutes" to respond to allegations of infidelity that threatened to derail his candidacy. Clearly this tactic posed a high risk, but so did the threat. The fact that the Clintons pulled it off demonstrated the power of a candidate interview to communicate the candidate's side of a story. Clinton followed up with an appearance on "Donahue" later in the primary season, reacting angrily to prying questions—and the audience took his side.[13] As Clinton's campaign picked up steam in July, he eschewed the entertainment shows and concentrated on the news-oriented programs, possibly to convey a more serious side to his candidacy.

The Public Tunes In

The public was attentive to the new format—as evidenced by program ratings that went up when candidates appeared (Stevens 1993). As the pace picked up in the general election campaign, 31 percent of the respon-

dents to our September survey reported seeing a "long candidate interview" in the previous five days, and by October, 58 percent said they had.
People were pleased with the extended access to the candidate that
the format provided. Our interviewees frequently complained that the
news gave them only little "snippets" of the candidates on television
and explained that they preferred the greater opportunity to see the
candidates.

Content analysis of the candidate interviews shows that there really
was a much greater opportunity for the audience to see and hear the candidates at length. Our analysis was made on a random sample of 35 candidate interview programs drawn from the Legi-slate archive (see appendix E). Our sample closely reflects the distribution of the major candidate
interviews by candidate, by season, by type of program, and by length.[14]
In our sample, the average length of a candidate's answer to a question
was 21 seconds, more than twice as long as the news soundbite (see table
6.2). There was some variation by candidate, which reflected their style
of presentation: Perot was the snappiest (averaging 16 seconds), Bush was
right on the average (21 seconds), and Clinton was by far the most long-
winded at 28 seconds. This variation suggests that control over the length
of the answer was far more in the hands of the candidate than on the
news, where the structural factors dictated the 9-second mean. More important than the longer soundbite, however, was the exposure that candidates received. Perot's exposure in our sampled interview programs virtually equaled his total exposure on the network news, and the major party
candidates spoke for an average of 8 to 12 minutes an interview. Exposure
was a direct function of the length of the program, which varied from less
than 10 minutes to an hour and a half. In some instances, the programs—
and the candidate's opportunity to speak—were actually extended when
viewer call-ins indicated high interest.

Citizens appreciated the "unfiltered" aspect of these formats as much
as the candidates did. Candidate interviews offered citizens a way to bypass "experts" and journalists and concentrate on the candidate's message. As Saul remarked:

> Here you have an opportunity to tune in "Donahue" or "Larry
> King Live" or whatever and see the candidates talking with real
> people, answering questions in a more casual format than a
> news conference, and people can better judge for themselves.
> It's one thing to read in the paper that X candidate was very
> slick in his performance. It's another thing to actually see the
> candidate and, despite the slickness of the performance, get

some nuggets about what the person intends to do, what he has taken responsibility for and what he hopes to accomplish.

Our interviewees generally liked the interview programs, because they allowed a longer and less artificial look at the candidates and often included questions from "real people." Frank had watched the "Today Show" interviews with the candidates. At the end of the campaign, he remarked:

> I thought they were really great. I like that. I was kind of disappointed that Bush, he didn't get involved in the "Today Show" until last week. . . . It's a little more relaxed atmosphere. They [the candidates] can't honker down to rhetoric.

Interestingly, citizens were also more likely to identify with the nonjournalist interviewer. They saw Larry King and Katie Couric as being more

Table 6.2 Candidate Exposure on Television

A. Interview Programs

Candidate	Number of Shows	Number of Answers	Total Seconds Heard[a]	Soundbite
Bush	5	172	3,688 (61.47)	21.44
Clinton	12	212	5,960 (99.33)	28.11
Perot	7	350	5,628 (93.8)	16.08
Total	35	734	15,276 (254.6)	20.81

B. Network News

Candidate	Number Stories Quoting Candidate	Number of Times Quoted	Total Seconds Heard[a]	Soundbite
Bush	947	1,807	18,579 (309.65)	10.28
Clinton	807	1,602	16,216 (270.27)	10.12
Perot	239	662	5,331 (88.85)	8.05
Total	1,993	4,071	40,126 (668.77)	9.86

[a]Numbers in parentheses are minutes.

like themselves. As Mike said in the fall: "It's funny, I trust more Larry King than I'd trust an anchorman, like an ABC, NBC or CBS. I trust more a person like Larry King. He's not even associated so much with that. He's like an average interviewer. He's just regular people."

Interviews provided candidates with opportunities to appear on programs that targeted diverse audiences. Audiences were segmented by time of day (afternoon shows get a mostly female audience, MTV attracts a teenage and young adult audience, while "Arsenio" drew a greater than average number of African Americans). The message conveyed by these appearances was that the candidate "cared" about the particular audience to which the show appealed. Young people felt acknowledged as political participants by Clinton's appearance on MTV's "Choose or Lose."[15] Similarly, blacks felt validated by Clinton's appearance on "Arsenio." As Luke, an African American, noted in the third wave:

> Clinton on race, when he showed up on "Arsenio," was probably one of his biggest statements to make. And they talked like they were buddies. They were talking like there was no color, O.K.? Clinton was portraying that I can talk to people and I don't recognize you as just being black and dumb but black and successful. Sure I want your vote but this is what I'll be able to do for your people.

During in-depth interviews, people noted that these interview programs provided access for people who might not normally watch the news. Maria said:

> I thought it [Clinton's appearance on "Arsenio"] was nice because that type of program appeals to a certain type of people. These people don't rush home and watch the evening news . . . [but] they were able to hear them talk about the election and hear the candidate.

While most of these programs had small audiences, the symbolic message of these television appearances was carried to the mass audience by regular news programs. For example, the actual ratings for Clinton's "Arsenio" appearance was in single digits, but audiences for all three network newscasts saw the clip of Clinton playing the saxophone and wearing "shades."

In addition to giving the audience a chance to see more of the candidates and specific audiences a chance to receive the candidates' attention, many of the candidate interview shows gave the public an opportunity to take part in the program. Many of the soft news programs featured audience participation, either by the studio audience or via telephone by the viewing audience. The interactive aspect made the genre new and exciting for the public. It was not necessary to participate oneself in order to appreciate the opportunity of citizens to interact with candidates in interview formats. People identified with the citizen-questioners, who asked questions in ways they could understand and about topics they were interested in. Linda noted about the second debate:

> I liked the fact that there were everyday people asking the questions. . . . It felt like they were talking to me, versus when there are reporters there. . . . Their way of phrasing, the reporter's way of asking a question may not be the way I would ask it, because I may not be that savvy. But the way the everyday people ask the question might be the way, if I had the opportunity, I would ask it. Not with a lot of jargon. Just something plain and simple, like if you were talking to a friend. You know, 'Listen, what do you think about his . . . or what is your opinion of this?' So that format allowed for it to be so that you could understand it and you could feel more comfortable that you knew what the questioner was even asking. Sometimes when the reporters are asking, we're like, well, what are they really trying to ask?

The popularity of this format was evidenced in the reception of the second general election debate. The "town meeting" structure, in which a studio audience questioned the candidates, had an even larger audience than the more traditional first debate, which featured journalists asking the questions (Buchanan 1993).

Questioning the Candidates

If the candidates were looking for a format that allowed them to state their views on policy, the interview programs provided that. In our sample, about half or more of the questions were about issues, even on the programs that were in the strictly entertainment category ("Donahue," MTV, etc.). The questions generally gave plenty of opportunity for candidates to talk about themselves, their personalities and backgrounds, which was the particular aim of the Clinton strategy. Questions about the candidate were the focus of 15 to 20 percent of the questions on the news and soft news shows and 25 percent of the questions on the entertainment shows. About one-third of the questions dealt with the campaign, except on the entertainment programs, where the figure was only 10 percent. The major difference between the exposure of the candidates on the news and the interview programs was primarily length and secondarily the emphasis on issues. The interview programs gave citizens the opportunity that democratic critics have been hoping for—a format that people enjoy and that gives candidates plenty of time to talk about their positions on the issues. In our focus groups, participants paid close attention to what candidates had to say in the interview segments they watched. In the case of Clinton, who focused on salient issues such as jobs and health care, many participants talked about their agreement with his challenge to the status quo and echoed the candidate's message.

The candidate interviews prompted conversation about candidate positions as well as the problems facing the country. After exposure to candidate interviews, focus group discussion reflected the language of the candidate more frequently than for any of the other media. Participants talked, not about the visual or audio-visual messages, but used the candidate's own language and focused on his ideas. People referred to the candidate's words and used them in constructing arguments (see chap. 7, especially fig. 7.2).

For example, Edna in Los Angeles suggested that Clinton was a "good speaker." Others not only agreed, but offered Clinton's words to support the evaluation. Bill added that Clinton is not only speaking, he's "thinking . . . consulting eight economists, Nobel Prize winners and so on." Bill believed that Clinton was considering issues carefully and respected him for this, even though he, like many others, did not always agree with the substance of Clinton's health care proposals. Bill in fact suggested that he did not "know what can be done about it [health care]." But it is clear that, like other participants in the focus groups, he was interested in hearing what the candidate had to say.

In another focus group discussion, Janine, in Moorhead, started off with this favorable reiteration of a Clinton comment: "Taxing the top 10 percent. God, I loved it!" Later on, Erik picked up on what Clinton had to say about insurance companies. Clinton, he concludes, "stresses insurance companies are getting away with murder. I guess that jumps out at me."

While the public was enthusiastic, many journalists looked down on the candidate interviews because they believed that the questions would be easy, "soft balls"; however, our analysis strikingly shows that the audience, not the journalists, asked the most issue-oriented questions. Fully three-quarters of the audience questions specifically addressed the candidates' positions on the issues, compared to half for the journalists and about 40 percent for the professional interviewers. Surprisingly, it appears that the journalists' reputation for concentrating on the horse race to the exclusion of everything else was not borne out on the interview programs. Our data show that journalist interviewers were less likely than the professional interviewers (morning show hosts, Larry King, Phil Donahue, etc.) to ask candidates about their campaigns. The result may reflect the fact that many of the "professional interviewer" questions were asked in a breaking news setting, for example, after a candidate won a primary election.

While the audience's questions were just as, or in fact more, issue oriented than the questions asked by journalists or professional interviewers, there were other ways in which the audience's questions could be considered "softer." First, the audience was less likely than the interview hosts or the reporters to ask "follow-up" questions. About half of interviewers or journalists' queries involved asking the candidates to explain or expand their original answers, while less than 10 percent of the audience questions did. Members of the audience may have been reluctant to press candidates further because they had a smaller information base from which to launch the follow-up questions. Another explanation is that the structure of the interview shows did not permit members of the audience to go further. On some occasions a host would ask members of the audience whether the candidate had answered the question to their satisfaction, but more typically the host was in a hurry to make room for other questions. Given the structure of the interview shows, it is not clear whether members of the audience were in as suitable a position to press candidates for specific answers as the professionals were.

Structural reasons, however, do not account for the differences in the way questions are asked by professionals and members of the viewing audience. A 5-point scale was developed to evaluate questions for level of confrontation or hostility in style and substance. The assessment of confrontation was made using a videotape of the encounter. The analysis shows that journalists employed the most confrontational tone in their questioning of the candidates—the average was 3.3 on a 5-point scale— compared to professional interviewers, who averaged 3 or exactly neutral on the scale, and the audience, which averaged a nonconfrontational 2.75 (see table 6.3).[16]

Journalists were most confrontational when they asked candidates questions about their issue positions (mean: 3.4). This suggests that they may have pressed the candidates hard to provide specific programmatic information, but it also may reflect the journalists' tendency to attack nuanced differences in the way candidates represented their positions. In contrast, audience questions were virtually neutral on issues (mean: 2.9) and not confrontational on candidates' background or experience. The

Table 6.3 Mean Confrontation and Mean Tone: Questions

Category	Mean Confrontation	Mean Tone
Program group		
Aggregate	3.03	3.22
News	3.10	3.23
Infotainment	3.03	3.22
Entertainment	2.97	3.28
F-statistic	2.9	1.7
Questioner group		
Aggregate	3.03	3.22
News reporter	3.27	3.26
Professional interviewer	2.96	3.20
Audience	2.75	3.26
F-statistic	50	2

Note: Confrontation and tone are scaled from 1 to 5: 1—very low confrontation/very positive tone; 2—mostly low confrontation/mostly positive tone; 3—neutral; 4—mostly high confrontation/mostly negative tone; 5—very high confrontation/very negative tone. F-crit = 3.00. See table 6.1 notes for composition of program groups.

audience was more confrontational, however, when discussing campaign matters with the candidates. Audience questions about campaigns were significantly more confrontational than any other questions the audience asked (mean: 3.3), at about the same level of confrontation as campaign questions coming from journalists or professional interviewers. In general, people were not playing campaign "gotcha" with the candidates, but rather were complaining bitterly about the way the campaign was being conducted and expressing their frustration with the political process. These remarks were typified by the questions in the second October debate, when two different members of the audience asked candidates to stick to the issues and stop "trashing" one another.[17]

Candidate Exposure

The evidence suggests that regardless of the type of question, candidates addressed slightly different topics in their answers. The analysis of our candidate interview sample of questions and answers confirms that these shows were no different from other campaign discourse in focusing on the economy. The most commonly asked questions were about the economy generally, taxes, the budget deficit, and health care, then morality and values, abortion, jobs and unemployment, and finally, tariffs and trade, the Persian Gulf war, and foreign policy generally. The answers also focused first on the economy, taxes, the budget deficit, and health care, but jobs and unemployment was second only to the economy generally as a category of answers. After economic issues, the candidates' answers focused on education, the environment, and foreign policy. Clearly, these differences reflect the emphases that the different candidates gave in their campaigns. Clinton pressed hard on unemployment as a symbol of the deteriorating economic situation, and Perot made the deficit his hallmark issue. Even though questions often addressed issues of morality and values, the answers turned back to more substantive issues. It is also apparent that foreign policy, which might have benefited President Bush, was the last of the big issues both in questions and answers.

The dialogue of the candidate interviews was analyzed using a sample of 10 question/answer segments in each show in our sample. This part of the analysis evaluated every sentence, or clause, separately as a "message." This deeper analysis permits an assessment of the extent to which the interview shows addressed different aspects of the candidates. The message-level data indicate that issues were mentioned in half of all of the messages (49 percent), while the horse race was mentioned in only 6 percent, compared with personal qualities of the candidates in 22 percent and the campaign in 37 percent. The message data also tell a tale about what the candidates emphasized. Here the results show that Clinton was most likely to talk about himself in relation to issues (72 percent of his messages), with Bush a close second (65 percent), while Perot was much less substantive (only 39 percent of his messages referred specifically to an issue), preferring to talk about themes (such as responsibility) more than the other candidates did (13 percent compared to 1 or 2 percent for Bush and Clinton). All of the candidates devoted about the same attention to messages about themselves as people (about 25 percent) but varied a good deal in their likelihood to address their opponents' personal qualities. President Bush fulfilled the stereotype of the attack candidate that was evident in his advertising messages. Bush focused two-thirds of his remarks about Clinton on the candidate's personal qualities; in contrast, only 40 percent of Clinton's remarks about Bush spoke to his personal qualities and leadership. In line with his avoidance of personal attack in his advertising, Perot's remarks about his opponents tended not to focus on personal qualities (only 20 percent of his remarks about Bush were personal). The results show that candidates followed similar strategies and tactics in their ads and interviews.

Overall, what candidate interviews had to offer the citizens was a much broader canvas on which to picture the candidates than would be permitted by network news coverage alone. The lengthy and intense exposure to the candidates on interview programs provided viewers with the "parasocial" experience of television—allowing the audience to develop a pseudoacquaintance with the people on the screen and making it possible for citizens to judge the candidates much as they judge the people they encounter in their daily lives. Even low-interest, low-knowledge voters could take away information from a candidate's appearance on a candidate interview program, as in this example from our September panel:

> Eddy: I just know Dan Quayle—the three times I've paid attention to what he said, he seemed like he's kind of out in left field and he dodges questions.
>
> Interviewer: Are there any images or pictures that you recall seeing when you think of Quayle?
>
> Eddy: I guess it was on TV and the only one I can think of was he was on a talk show and sitting in a chair. He wasn't real sure-footed the whole time.
>
> Interviewer: "Sure-footed" meaning . . .
>
> Eddy: He didn't seem to know exactly what he wanted to say or what he was talking about.

Impact on Other Media

The interview shows appeared to meet the needs of the candidates and the public. Candidates sought out the new venues as a means of reaching the public, and the public responded by giving the programs good ratings. Candidate interviews added to the sense of displacement that some network news people felt as they were forced to share campaign coverage with local television stations and cable competitors. The journalists' role of chief interpreters of the candidates now had to be shared with more entertainment-oriented media professionals, even on their own networks.

One news response to the challenge of candidate exposure on interview programs was to address the soundbite problem. In July, after the notable expansion of the interview appearances, "CBS Evening News" announced a policy of lengthening candidate news soundbites to 30 seconds. CBS indicated that the decision had been taken prior to the primary campaign, but that was hard to square with the timing of the announcement. Six weeks later CBS announced that it was forced to retract the policy as unwieldy. Some time later in the summer, ABC News announced that it would not use any soundbites and would rearrange its resources to provide the audience with more analysis of the campaign and less coverage of the campaign trail. The "American Agenda" segment was launched in September and did live up to its promotion to provide analysis of issues, but in the news, the soundbites did not disappear or lengthen.

On another level, several news programs tried to integrate more audi-

ence participation and citizen agendas into their format. Both ABC and
CNN conducted focus groups on air and used audience evaluations of
the debates. It appeared that the "public agenda," which the interview
programs partially addressed, has gained increasing credibility.[18]

Conclusion

Both interview programs and ad watches gave candidates and media professionals greater opportunities to communicate with voters. Ad watches
increased exposure to candidate messages because, despite journalists' efforts, the ad descriptions and visuals were available to the audience. The
result was to increase the reach of candidates' ads. There is no doubt that
the interview formats met the candidates' needs for additional ways to
reach voters outside the limitations of a 30-minute newscast. To the extent that candidates appeared on nonpolitical programs they were also
able to target a more diverse audience than was previously exposed to
campaign television news.

From the point of view of citizens, there is evidence that candidate
interviews and ad watches met some of their needs as well. Although the
participants in our focus groups did not like the campaign process ad
watches, they did appreciate the journalists' watchdog efforts. In the case
of interview programs, although most viewers did not see more than one
or two, the public shared a sense that the candidates were more available
to them than in the past. In the pooled network exit polls after the election, respondents rated candidate interviews as second only to debates in
informing their votes.

One important additional advantage of candidate interviews is that
they often have high entertainment values. In Downs's (1957) terms, they
cut the cost of becoming informed. The reciprocal effect of information
and interest (Patterson 1980) suggests that some people gained entry-level
information about the campaign through interview programs. By breaking into the interest-information cycle, candidate interview programming
could account for some of the increase in levels of interest, information,
and voting that the public demonstrated in the 1992 election.[19] There is
good reason to believe that these new formats, in which people have an
opportunity to address their concerns to the candidates and in which
people are treated as capable of understanding complex information, created a feeling of connection with the process, and increased political
involvement.

THREE

Interpreting Messages and Voting

SEVEN

How Citizens Interpret Campaign Communication

Previous research demonstrates that people's expectations about a source of information affect how they use it (Lane and Sears 1964, chap. 5; Kosicki and McLeod 1990; Fredin and Tabaczynski 1994). In the context of an election campaign, the credibility and bias of the source of information are especially crucial (Graber 1994). This chapter examines what people think about and how they respond to various kinds of campaign communications: local and national television news, interview programs, and candidate ads. It might be expected, for example, that people would be suspicious of candidate advertisements, given the obvious partisanship of the source. While there is ample evidence that people discount advertising messages, Americans are also wary of information in the news. The public greeted a new source of campaign communication—interview programs—enthusiastically, while ad watches, another media innovation, received mixed reviews.

Given their diverse evaluations of ads, news, ad watches, and candidate interviews, do people use information differently depending on the source? To answer this question this chapter relies on evidence from focus groups, in which people were presented with different kinds of communication and given an opportunity to discuss what they saw. Analysis of the focus groups' interactions with media confirms that people use different interpretive tools, pick up on different channels of information, and accept or reject information based both on the source and on what they have already learned during the course of the campaign.

The evidence shows that people interpret ads, news, and candidate interviews by relying to different degrees on their prior knowledge, personal experience, and other media information. They acquire both visual and verbal information, which they integrate into the images they construct of the candidates. There are some surprises in the results. For example, participants in focus groups picked up on what candidates *said* in television interviews not on what they looked like; in contrast, people commented predominantly on the pictures in ad watches. In-depth interviews provide further evidence that people can interpret the same visual or verbal cues differently and often argue against the messages they receive from the media. In general, exposure to the media most often resulted in the audience ignoring or reinterpreting the message, rather then following its point of view.

Overall, the evidence from the focus groups and in-depth interviews depicts an audience that tries to use its own knowledge and experience actively to interpret media messages and construct candidate images. Given the interpretive and integrative role of the audience, it is not surprising that polls show little difference in favorability toward candidates for people who are exposed to different media during the campaign.

Exposure and Evaluation

Evaluating the News

Observers of the 1992 presidential election were struck by the historically early and persistently high level of public interest in the campaign. Notably, the campaign was marked by a number of media innovations, such as ad watches and extended candidate interviews, along with greater availability of campaign coverage on cable stations. Although the expansion of numbers and types of campaign channels had little effect on the level of public involvement during the primary campaigns, in June interest rose substantially, and by the time of the general election, citizens were highly involved in the media campaign. People reported significant increases in exposure to the media even in the last month of the campaign. Three-quarters of survey respondents reported exposure to local television, network, and newspaper news in September, and that figure grew to over 80 percent in late October.

Of course, not everyone is interested in the campaign, at the beginning or even in its final stages. In January, when asked to describe the presidential campaign to someone who knew nothing about it, Sondra said:

> That's hard for me because I haven't been keeping up with it myself. It snuck up on me. I've been so involved with the kids. . . . I feel like a typical housewife. I don't know anything but the kids. Come to the President, it's like, who is he, what's his name? I don't know.

By early October, Sondra knew that Bush was president, but admitted that she knew nothing more about the campaign.

Of the four communities examined, Winston-Salem, the one with the least news coverage in the nominating phase of the campaign also had the lowest level of interest. There, as elsewhere, uninvolved citizens tended to squeeze politics in around more pressing concerns. For example, in May, Lillian noted how the longer days of spring and the upcoming gardening season restricted her attention to the campaign. By the time of the general election in September she was busy canning her tomato "chow chow":

> Lillian: I haven't watched much of that in the last week or ten days.
> Interviewer: You haven't watched a lot of that in the last week or ten days?
> Lillian: Well, because of my chow chow [*laughter*] . . .
> Interviewer: You can't make a good chow chow—
> Lillian: Right, and watch TV. At least *I* can't. I've got to watch for the bugs and of course your late peas have got worms in them. You've got to watch for the worm holes so you can't watch TV and prepare vegetables too.

Those who did pay attention to the campaign in 1992 rated the media positively. Polls showed that assessments of the campaign coverage improved over 1988 levels. In the *Times-Mirror* "Report Card," the public upped the media from a grade of "C" to "C+." The surveys we conducted showed that the public's lukewarm assessments of the media improved slightly as the campaign wore on. In our spring surveys, respondents split evenly on whether the media were doing a good-to-excellent or fair-to-poor job; but by September a majority rated the media as good or better, and that figure actually increased in the last weeks of the campaign. National polls reinforced our findings; an ABC News/*Washington Post* poll in September showed that 64 percent rated the news media's job covering the election "excellent" (9 percent) or "good" (55 percent), an 18 percent increase from a nearly identical CNN/*USA Today* poll in April. The perceived improvement did not depend on which media people said they used.

In addition to survey respondents, our interviewees and focus groups also evaluated the media. The interview panel was specifically asked to describe how the media were covering the campaign. In focus groups, participants volunteered comments about the media after viewing particular video clips, in answer to the nondirective question, "What's going on here for you?" Ten percent of the 392 conversational exchanges in our 16 primary and general election focus groups dealt with the news media (see appendix D). We found remarkable similarities between the way people evaluated different media after watching them in focus groups and the impressions that they recalled during in-depth interviews.

Generally, praise for the press is grounded in the perception that journalists are doing an honest job of covering the election. As Selma said in a March interview:

> I think there is—to be fair to the media—I think there's an attempt on their part to try to show us what the differences are between the candidates. Every time I read the newspaper there is an emphasis on how one candidate feels about each topic, each area. And then you get their opinion as to whether it's true or whether it'll work or what they suggested would work.

People with less interest in politics appreciated the media's effort to distill information. Lillian, for example, commented in a late September interview:

> I get more out of the commentators than I do the press and Bill Clinton, because they go into all of this stuff and the commentators they condense it so. He tells me the whole thing without me having to listen to a 30-minute spiel.

Also in the fall, Sandra, who had been critical of the news media in an earlier interview, reported that the coverage helped her gain a "perspective" on the campaign:

> I couldn't [go hear him]. When Gore came here—I believe it was last week? A lot of people couldn't or weren't able to go listen to what he had to say in person, therefore television coverage is our favorite avenue to see it.

Several in-depth interviewees commented that they thought the media were doing a better job than in the past. Some called attention to innovations in the media, such as candidate interviews and debates, that gave them a greater opportunity to hear and see more of the candidates than in previous campaigns. Mike registered some surprise about the coverage in the spring:

> I think I'm actually not as opposed to [the media] as I thought I would be. I thought they would be more almost controlling. Like I said it's not so much in the soundbites any more, you see more quality, which I like. It's not so much give us your whole plan in 30 seconds so we can get on to something else. It's more like there's a debate. I think maybe that's cable. Maybe that's

why. You know maybe there's a difference between this election or maybe I'm watching more cable, I don't know. You get to have a longer look at people instead of a quick look.

Caren gave the media a backhanded compliment while criticizing Vice-President Quayle: "How else would I know he's an idiot, unless I heard it and saw it on TV myself?"

While the improvement in public assessment of media may reassure journalists that they are doing some things right, the disaffection of almost half the citizenry is still troubling. For some time now, media researchers have been particularly critical of news coverage that focuses on the horse-race aspects of the campaign, candidate strategies, and stumping on the campaign trail. Our surveys show that respondents were aware and equally disapproving of these trends in coverage (see chap. 5). Overwhelmingly, the public identified the horse race as the dominant theme in news. Queried in our September and October surveys about whether the news media was covering the horse race or the issues, roughly two-thirds responded "horse race," compared to less than a quarter who thought the media focused on "issues."[1] The complaint that the news media trivialize the campaign and provide too little useful information was echoed in our in-depth interviews and focus groups. Shortly before the primary in May, Sara, a low-knowledge and low-interest interviewee, criticized television news. She said:

> They don't tell you a whole lot about where the candidates stand or what they're saying. They say how many votes they need or where they'll be or what the next primary will be. . . . It's not very informative really. I guess they let you see what they think will interest you.

This theme, that the news media pander to the audience, recurred in in-depth interviews and focus groups throughout the campaign. People linked the media's taste for scandal and sensationalism to commercial motives that got in the way of useful information. As Saul put it in a January interview:

> . . . what they're doing in their quest to be number one in the ratings, they're not doing a good job. And not doing a responsible job of reporting [about] the candidates.

In early October, Mark complained that television coverage glossed over issues and focused on "slams" because of its commercial interests:

And it seems like you know going right back to the TV commercial thing, that all the things that they really went into depth about are, you know, are all the slams and stuff. Going way back to the whole Clinton and his mistress thing, I mean that was just absurd. That went on for so long and so many people wrote so much about it, and it really didn't mean much. You know, they just went further and further away from the things that they should really start explaining about. Because, as far as I know, I mean I suppose I know, there is supposed to be platforms that these people, you know, write up about "this is what I am going to do," but I have never seen one.

In both the in-depth interviews and the focus groups, voters saw the media as distorting what candidates had to say in order to get a good story. They believed that journalists took lines out of context, focused on controversial or catchy soundbites, and ignored much of what candidates had to say. Luis noted that television coverage in general and particularly coverage of Perot was "boom, boom, boom. And, it's not really what he said or what he's trying to put across."

The media's preoccupation with scandal particularly troubled people in the primary period, when the Clinton campaign was buffeted by one set of allegations after another. As Rose remarked in our first interview, "I think they go for the sensationalism first other than anything else to sell newspapers." Similarly, Luke argued in January:

It's like we're in this business to get the news out to most of the people, sure, that's one thing, that's your job. I think they want to stay on top. Basically, no matter what bit of evidence comes in, it's like, stay on top. First question is, "Did this guy sleep with somebody else? Is this guy into bestiality? Is he a sadomasochist?" But I think those are the first questions, then the second questions are, "Can he accomplish what's he's saying." It seems like that's secondary. Let's get the mudslinging in the limelight first, then we'll see if he can accomplish what he's doing.

Some members of the public recognize their own role in the market for sensational news. After all the coverage of the Clinton allegations, Vince said:

People talk about the tabloids all the time. It's garbage, it's this, it's that. Hey they get paid to write that stuff. If you're going to buy it of course they're going to write something that's juicy.

> They're not going to write something boring that people are go-
> ing to say, "What the hell are you reading that for," you know?

But some people feel that the coverage of scandal is manipulative. Like Selma, they blame the press for making them pay attention to things they would rather not think about:

> I think that some things ought not to be—the press shouldn't
> play up certain kinds of things that they do. And they say they
> do it because people want it, but I think that they make people
> want it. I think that's how it works.

Further, some individuals acknowledged that they would be disturbed if the journalists explicitly censored themselves once they got hold of sensational or scandalous information. In January, Gloria had criticized the news media for their preoccupation with scandal but then added:

> I wouldn't want things hidden from me, either, you know. If
> things have to be said, they have to be said. . . . I wouldn't like it
> if they didn't print it and I don't like it when they do print it.

Some of our interviewees were willing to give the media the benefit of the doubt because they were aware that journalists had to work with what the candidates provided—and understood that candidates would try to influence the coverage. Comments generally shifted from concern in the primary season that journalists expressed their own opinions toward a perception at the end of the campaign that the news media reflected what the candidates were saying and doing.

The criticism of the news that probably concerns journalists most, however, is not the emphasis on the horse race, soundbites, or scandal, but the accusation of bias. The view that the media are biased is fairly common among politicians, but social scientists have generally found various kinds of "structural" bias (e.g., favorable treatment of the candidate who is ahead in the polls) rather than partisan bias. In our surveys, most respondents agreed that the media were *not* biased, but the number of voters who believed that there was "bias in the news" increased from late September to October, rising from 38 percent to 47 percent. Among those respondents who thought the news was biased there was considerable agreement (50 percent or more) that George Bush bore the brunt of it. A declining proportion—33 percent of the sample in September and 26 percent in October—said there was a bias against Clinton, and 20 percent of the sample in October said there was a bias against Perot. Given the negative tone of news toward George Bush (see chap. 5), it is not surprising that Republicans were most likely to see bias in the press (55 percent, compared to 43 percent of independents and 35 percent of Democrats). Sixty-four percent of Republicans thought the press was too critical of Bush, compared to 44 percent of Democrats who thought the media were too tough on Clinton.

It is remarkable that while focus group participants expressed concern about bias after watching news stories from the campaign trail during the primaries, they did not find bias in the analytical news pieces they viewed in the fall, despite the fact that these stories made explicit comparisons among candidates. These findings support the conclusion that stories that critically assess candidates' positions on the issues are no more likely to be seen as biased than the more factual, horse-race stories.

Although some people were not very disturbed about outright bias, more people were worried about the unequal attention the media gave to candidates. Many citizens thought the press manipulated coverage to favor some candidates over others. Rosalyn complained about the *Los Angeles Times* even though she read it every day:

> I think it is very biased towards the Democrats, very liberal. I think they hardly give Bush an even break—or any Republican. They only print the news that they want you to read.

Social scientists have also been concerned that the media are not well equipped (as compared with political parties) to evaluate potential candidates for office (Patterson 1980, 1993). Members of the public, however, are simply concerned that the press is getting between them and the candidates. A few interviewees appreciated the media's role in screening candidates. Lars thought the media coverage of the campaign was "good":

> I think that the more media coverage we've got the better off we are. These people [candidates] are certainly going through a screening test, much more now.

Most citizens, however, worried that the news media designated front-runners and winnowed out contenders. Mike fumed in a January interview:

> I don't see what made Clinton the front-runner other than his looks. I really don't see what did he do substantially . . . that made him the front-runner and now they're all calling him the front-runner. . . . [The news] media irritates me.

Selma expressed similar concern that the media selected front-runners before she had a chance to hear what they had to say:

> We've been told that [the losing candidates are] not going to even be there shortly and it usually happens, just what [the media] said would happen. But you don't know whether or not they helped to move this along in that direction.

This concern was redoubled by the presence of Ross Perot as a third-party candidate. Rose protested in October:

> Some [media] have Bush first. Some have Clinton first and they all have Ross in the hole. . . . I don't think they have the right to tell people that if you vote for this candidate you are throwing away your vote, no matter how they personally feel.

The concern about manipulation of the political process, "gotcha" journalism, and scandalmongering was widespread. Perhaps this is the reason that citizens find it easy to reject so much of what they hear and read in the press.

Evaluating Political Advertising

Although people on our in-depth interview panel were much more likely to talk about campaign news than about ads, our surveys showed that in the last weeks of the campaign, exposure to political spot ads reached the same level as television news. More than 80 percent saw Bush and Clinton ads, and 85 percent of the sample reported exposure to Perot ads, which began to air in early October. The high rate of ad exposure speaks both to how often ads are shown on the air as well as to the attention-grabbing qualities of ads. In an interview at the outset of the campaign, Linda explained:

> I tend more to pay attention to the television ads. I'm not apt to get up during the commercial. . . . I want to listen and hear what the person has to say. . . . I don't want to read this long article. I'm tired now, you know. Or I'll save it [the article] and try to read it at another time or something like that, so that [the ad] does capture me to kind of [ask] "What's Kerrey all about, what is he saying?"

Interviewees often placed political ads in the context of commercial advertising and suggested that candidates were allowed to present themselves as they wished because they had paid for the time. Consequently, they expected that ads would be one-sided claims on behalf of the candidate. Vince put it this way:

The whole advertisement situation is—you have to be open-minded when you watch them on TV or when you read one in the paper because whoever it's about, him or his group has paid to put it there, so I mean you know it's going to be a plus for him and it's not going to be something negative. So I mean to me you can only take those things with a grain of salt.

Some people may try to tune out the ads of candidates they oppose. As Selma said in the last month of the campaign:

I don't pay too much attention to the ads because I know if it's a Bush/Quayle ad what it's going to say. It's going to say a lot of stuff about Clinton that's very negative and vice versa—Clinton is going to say things about Bush's administration.

Such efforts to ignore these communications do not always work, however. Somewhat later in the same interview, despite her claim to have devoted little attention to the Bush ads, Selma was able to describe three negative ads in considerable detail.[2] And Vince admitted in the same interview—after saying that he watched CNN and read the newspaper—that he could not overlook the ads altogether:

I don't want to say your paid political announcements [are something that I watch] but you learn a little bit of dirt here, dirt there, with that. Like I say, it's hard to turn them off—they're like regular commercials for kids' toys.

Because the ads are aired so frequently, people find it difficult to ignore their central claims. By the end of the campaign, many interviewees were able to recall and describe both the visual and the verbal messages of ads by Bush, Clinton, and Perot. Lenny, for example, remembered one Bush attack against Clinton:

They [the Bush ad] show the two guys with two different ties and they're both Clinton. They have a little thing over his head and you can't see who it is and all. I thought that was good. The guy on the right says he was drafted and the guy on the left wasn't. . . . Unfortunately, they're both Bill Clinton.

Sara vividly recalled a Bush attack ad about Clinton's "Arkansas Record." The ad was aimed at making voters distrustful of Clinton's tax intentions. The ad shows a vulture dominating a desolate landscape, likened to the devastation caused by Clinton's "tax and spend" policies. Sara, who was generally inattentive to the campaign, remembered the actual language used at the end of (another) ad, "And guess where he's going to get the money [to pay for his national social policies]." She commented:

> That commercial just really frightens me. It may be that I've seen it so much, you know. At first it wasn't too bad, but after it's been run and run and run it's really awful. . . . I think it's disgusting because I've seen it so much. I'm really tired of it. But I really want to know if it's *true* or not.

Just as with news, however, attention to ads was coupled with criticism. Some comments about ads were simply along the lines of "theater criticism" common to the strategy stories in the news (Adatto 1990). In October Mike reported that he was "left cold" by a Perot ad and commented in a vein similar to that of political consultants or other spin doctors:

> Mike: I don't think they were so effective. They were there and you have to read it. It wasn't a typical kind of commercial. It didn't have vivid images. It had a picture of the dawn or raining and then his text running up and over your screen.
> Interviewer: How did you feel about that ad?
> Mike: I didn't have any feeling. So I'd say it wasn't really effective. It didn't move me one way or the other.

Some interviewees were able to assess ads in aesthetic terms, even when they did not support the ad's sponsor. Eddy, who ended up supporting Bush, recalled a Clinton ad in October:

> It was when they said, "It's been four years," and they go back to '88 campaign and Bush is saying, "I guarantee you"—I don't know if this is verbatim but—"that you'll be better off in four years." And then it's, "How are you doing now?" That was kind of a neat ad. It makes you think. It's kind of open-ended. I remember it.

The more serious criticisms of ads focused on two dimensions: concern about manipulation and objections to "negative advertising." Commenting about a negative Bush ad, Jorge angrily said:

> It's just a way to cut another person's throat. I don't like those kinds of ads. I guess they're trying to make people believe and sway their vote. I've already made up my mind.

Citizens recognize that ads are partisan and worry about their impact, especially on others. While they did not often admit to being influenced themselves by political advertising, people in focus groups and in-depth interviews expressed alarm that others, perhaps less interested or sophisticated people, would be manipulated by ads. Lenny, referring to a Bush ad that praised Bush's presidency, said:

> Since that commercial, like I said, I can see through it and I think it is an effective commercial. I can see where you would get a lot of people who go, "yeah, ya know, geez, I remember when we were in, ya know, Desert Storm, and he is the best, isn't he." And kind of forget about the other stuff that's going on.

In one of many comments on this "third person effect" (Perloff 1993) in a Winston-Salem focus group, Tony reminded the other participants that, like commercial advertisers, candidates "wouldn't keep doing it [advertising] if it weren't effective." He continued, "a lot of people, because they're not willing to take the time to investigate, tend to be programmed by commercials like this." Michelle recognized that the reason that ads are effective is that they get the public's attention—including her own:

> People watch commercials. I mean how many actually sit down and watch the whole debate. . . . I watched some of it, but *I* wasn't going to sit there and listen to them [the politicians].

After watching a Perot ad in a Boston focus group, Rick explained: "At the end of the day I think people vote . . . based on a feeling that they have. It's effective." Similarly, Jeanne in Moorhead added that her own husband might be influenced by ads: "For my husband—who's disinterested in politics—I think these little 30-second zaps [negative ads] are going to zap him."

While concern about manipulation was generalized, viewers tended to describe ads as "negative" either when they did not resonate with their concerns or when they saw them as personal attacks that did not address issues. But when individuals agreed with the candidate's message, even in an attack, the comments were generally approving. For instance, just before the primary Linda, a Democrat who spoke critically of Bush at the outset of the campaign, recalled Buchanan's ironic "Read Our Lips" ad with approval: "When I saw the Buchanan one, I thought, well, Bush, you'd better listen up. I thought it was good."

On the whole, the audience discriminated among different sources of information. They criticized the news for sensationalism (which they saw arising from the profit motive) and for manipulation of the candidate field. With ads, their concerns focused on deceptive information and negative attacks. People recognized different, although not necessarily more praiseworthy, motives in the production of news and ads.

Did People Interact Differently with News and Advertising?

In light of the varying motives that they attribute to media sources, are there discernible patterns in the way citizens connect with news stories and ads? Are people more likely to ignore, follow, or transform messages about candidates depending on the source of the information? And how much depends on whether the information is contained in visual or verbal messages?

Since people have less political knowledge at the beginning of the campaign, we can expect impressions from the media to be more influential during the primary than during the general election. New media information, however, will matter only to the extent that people notice it and find it relevant—and the way it matters will be based on political knowledge and experiences that they already have. Popkin (1991) observed that candidate messages are most powerful when they bring together the lived experiences of voters with the larger discourses of the campaign. The same might be said of all campaign information.

Our analysis focused on how people interpreted the information presented to them and the way they supported their arguments in focus groups. Do people base their assessment of the information on broad political understandings or knowledge about political processes and leaders, particularly past and present candidates and presidents? Do they use direct and indirect personal experiences to evaluate what they saw and heard? How do they use different media sources to interpret new information (Gamson 1992; Kern and Just 1995)?

Resources Used in the Interpretation of New Information

The topics of conversation in the focus group discussions involving an exchange between two or more people were coded for what citizens brought to the discourse, which fell into three categories: political knowledge, personal experience, and recalled media sources (see appendix D). Political knowledge is a central resource that people use in interpreting new information. Significantly, as figure 7.1 illustrates, the stock of political knowledge that focus group participants used to evaluate candidates increased in the general election.[3] As the campaign progressed, prior knowledge became a more important resource and was more frequently applied to the interpretation of new information than in the primary period. During the nominating phase of the campaign, participants in focus groups relied on their knowledge of previous presidents and, to a lesser extent, other candidates in the 1992 election to help them form judgments about the current crop of competitors. In the general election, however, citizens' knowledge about the candidates was much greater, and they used more information about the two major party candidates themselves in making their evaluations. They were also more inclined in the fall to use their general knowledge about politics to interpret new media messages.

As Popkin has argued, voters can do a lot with relatively limited information. For example, in the absence of much knowledge about candidates, the women's focus group in Winston-Salem evaluated Bill Clinton largely through negative knowledge of two presidents—the incumbent, George Bush, and a past president from Clinton's own party, John F. Kennedy. The link between the other presidents and Clinton was purely associative. In the case of Bush, his failure to keep his 1988 campaign promise not to raise taxes became the prism through which they judged Clinton's promise not to raise taxes on the middle classes. As Elizabeth observed during the primary, "We were thrilled with Bush . . . but the first thing he did was raise taxes." Kennedy frequently came to mind as participants viewed news stories relating to Clinton's morals and trustworthiness. Deborah raised the question of whether a person who is unfaithful to his wife is responsible enough to be president. Participants immediately brought information into the discussion about Kennedy's personal life, provoking Phillis to comment, "I never thought that much of the man."

During the primary season, Ross Perot's record was even less available to voters than Clinton's was. Nevertheless, the May and June focus group participants made broad judgments about Perot's character and what he might do about their concerns. Some participants in the focus groups used media information about his Iranian hostage operation as well as what Perot said in television interview programs, although they had limited political knowledge about Perot, beyond familiarity with the book or the movie about him, *On the Wings of Eagles*. Some said they had heard him announce his candidacy on "Larry King Live." While some individuals expressed reservations about him, others were quick to articulate the view that Perot was a man of action who not only could get things done but might be able to do something about the nation's economy, based, almost exclusively, as one participant noted, on "statements that he's made."

Not surprisingly, throughout the election cycle more knowledge was used to evaluate the incumbent president than any of the other candi-

HOW CITIZENS INTERPRET CAMPAIGN COMMUNICATION   165

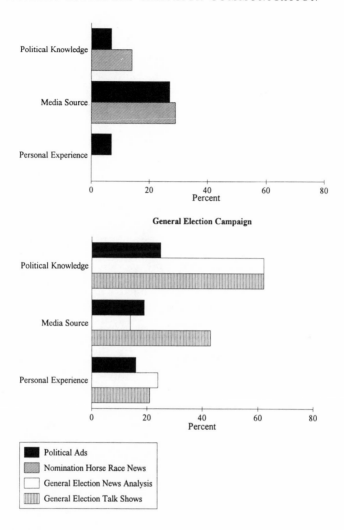

Figure 7.1 Support for arguments in focus group discussions: percentage of conversational exchanges.

dates. Participants remembered the Persian Gulf war, but it had lost its luster by the time the campaign was underway. They also noted that Bush had raised taxes. Such pieces of information gave people hooks into new information. Problematic information about Bush fell on fertile ground. For example, when Buchanan pointed out that although Bush declared in his January 1992 State of the Union message that he would lower taxes on families with children, he did not submit those changes to Congress as part of his next budget, participants who said they had not known this fact seized on it because it made sense to them in terms of what they already knew about Bush. The information about the budget was reinforced by a barrage of Buchanan ads and news soundbites (and ad watches that included clips of Buchanan's ads), making the point that Bush did not keep his political promises. In that way old knowledge was given new currency.

As the election approached, focus group participants drew more heavily on prior political knowledge and less on recalled media sources to interpret new information and to construct candidate images. Yet media sources remained important to them in building arguments. Public opinion surveys conducted at the same time as the focus groups showed greater reliance on television news than on any other medium. A Markle Foundation poll taken in the days preceding the election showed that more than twice as many people claimed to have relied on television rather than newspapers for most of their news and information about the campaign. In the focus groups, when participants named a particular source of information in constructing an argument, they most frequently cited televised news (though they did not usually distinguish between local or network news). Information from newspapers was mentioned about a third as often as televised news sources. Debates and radio lagged far behind, as did political advertising, although it may be noteworthy that political advertising was mentioned at all, since people believe it is a biased medium.

In the fall focus groups, personal experience also became more important. As people became more engaged with the election, they drew more on their own experiences—both direct and indirect—to evaluate campaign information. By drawing on a greater base of accumulated knowledge and relating their candidate assessments to their personal experiences, the participants' discourse became richer as the election neared.

Interpretation of Media Stimuli

Analysis of focus group discussions shows that as the campaign progressed, people brought more knowledge and experience to bear in interpreting electoral communications. By varying the stimulus, the focus groups were also designed to show how people used different formats of communication. Did topics in the news set the agenda for discussion—more or less than, say, advertising or candidate interviews? Did news framing of a topic carry over into the discussion, or did participants put a different spin on the material? Do some communications fail to stimulate discussion? Analysis of the focus group topics of conversation that followed exposure to different kinds of campaign media illustrates these various patterns.

Following, Transforming, and Ignoring Messages

We examined focus group exchanges for three patterns: following, transforming, and ignoring. A *following* pattern occurs when the group discussion is dominated not only by the topic but also by the kind of evaluation expressed in the media message. When such a pattern occurs, the exchange follows the evaluative frame of the media. A *transforming* pattern occurs when group discussion begins with a cue presented in the message but breaks through its evaluative dimensions. The topic of the stimulus sets the agenda for the exchange, but in the interpretation of information, participants frame the topic differently. Conversation after media exposure may also be completely unrelated to the message. An *ignoring* pattern occurs when focus group participants move away from media information to an entirely different topic.[4]

In focus groups, a moderator usually leads the discussion by using a set of loosely structured questions that follow presentation of a media message. Although open-ended, such questions directly or indirectly channel conversation toward the presentation. Nevertheless, the discussion often revolved around the participants' own concerns. Importantly, more topics of conversation, or conversational units, transformed or ignored media messages than followed them. The focus group results confirm the fact that media offer useful information that people use to build social discourse, but because the discussion so often moves away from the framing or evaluative position of the stimulus, the results lend little support to the idea that people are always "primed" to follow media interpretation of information. Participants tended to put their own spin on media cues, when they did not ignore the messages altogether.

Overall, as figure 7.2 indicates, there was a somewhat greater tendency to follow news and ad messages in the primary than in the general election (37 percent vs. 25 percent). Possibly because individuals know less in the spring, they were less likely to challenge information. Yet following is certainly not absent in the fall; the most dramatic instance of following the message resulted after viewing candidate interview segments.

In the preprimary focus groups, there were important differences in the discussions following the presentation of political ads and horse-race news. Figure 7.2 shows that participants frequently ignored messages in political ads but were more likely to stay on the topic, either following or transforming the evaluative frame. With horse-race news, participants

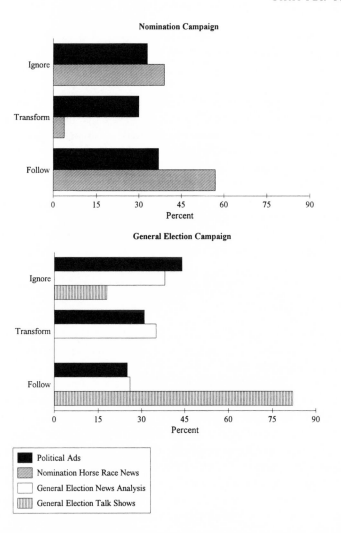

Figure 7.2 Focus group discussions that ignore, transform, or follow media messages: percentage of conversational exchanges.

either followed the story framework (57 percent of topics of conversation) or dropped the topic altogether and went on to discuss other things.

Interactions with Horse-Race News in the Nomination Phase. Horse-race stories are a typical form of news about candidates. Participants in focus groups seemed to think these stories had little to do with them, and they were unable to connect them with their personal experiences.

Most of the discussion of horse-race news concerned personal consider-ations of the candidate. (For an analysis of coding procedures and a sum-mary of results for the coding of all frames for topic of conversation, see appendix D.)

As an example of how people interpret horse-race news stories, note how focus group participants reacted to a news story about George Bush campaigning in the New Hampshire primary with Arnold Schwarzeneg-ger. After a Boston group watched the story, they talked about how Bush was performing as a candidate. According to Bob, "His campaign wasn't doing very well, and he needed the help of an actor." They also called on another media source to make sense of the news story. As Marty ex-pressed it:

> I mean, he had to bring in Schwarzenegger to help him out. I think I saw a *comment on TV* about that, his campaign was ba-sically lethargic at that point, they were bringing people out of the woodwork, and everybody likes Schwarzenegger, with his two Terminator movies. You know, he needs people like that to help him out. (Emphasis added)

Bob concurred, also referring to a "comment on TV" that indicated Bush's campaign was in trouble.

In this example, participants evaluated candidates according to the standards of horse-race news, either following it or ignoring it, but not transforming it. The example lends support to Patterson's contention that "voters behave much more like spectators than election participants when they encounter such information [horse-race news stories], usually re-sponding not to what the candidates represent, but to the status of the contest, if they respond at all" (Patterson 1980, 90). The focus group conversations often illustrated a process-oriented way of thinking about the election, which builds on the horse-race orientation of news stories. Patterson pointed out, and this study confirms, however, that people have the alternative of ignoring the news. As figure 7.2 indicates, after viewing horse-race news stories, discussion frequently abandoned the message al-together and turned to other concerns.

Interactions with News Analysis in the General Election. Partially in re-sponse to criticism that news focused too much on the horse race at the expense of issues, in the fall of 1992 "ABC Evening News" added a series of lengthy news stories, their "American Agenda" segment. These stories followed a problem-promise-performance format for discussing election issues (Jamieson 1992a). In one segment viewed by focus group participants in early October, the story focused on the question of jobs, one of the most salient issues on the public's agenda. First, the analysis assessed the seriousness of the issue, and then it turned to George Bush's and Bill Clinton's positions and what they had actually done about employment while in elective office. As focus group participants used this information, their conversation took in the personal qualities of the candidates, but discussion turned as well to the candidates' positions on the issues, and the broader economic issues facing the country. Participants frequently brought in their personal experiences with economic issues. For example, Jolene linked the issue of technological competitiveness with the American educational system:

> I have two children, still in grade school and junior high, and I've seen what they're learning. It's not enough to compete against the Japanese market; it's scary.

The "American Agenda" story addressed a salient issue from a variety of perspectives and stimulated a lively discussion. Everyone in the group had an opinion about the problems facing the country. While the news analysis piece was relevant to the discussion, it did not limit the participants, who often transformed and expanded the conversation. More topics were raised in the group interaction. As participants tried to make sense of the information in the news story, they contributed personal experiences and integrated experience with information from media sources to gain a more complete picture of the jobs issue and related problems. The discussion not only focused on the problems facing the country, but also questioned why the problems had come about, how to solve them, who should be held responsible, who would benefit, and who would be hurt.[5]

In one group, the discussion moved on to question the relationship between elections and the entire governing process. Kelly expressed the concern that "[they] are spending so much time building a soap box that they're not worrying about what they're saying once they get on top." In a pattern that completely reversed that of the horse-race news stories, there was no discussion of candidate strategy. Instead, the discussion offered an opportunity to assess not only candidates and their issues but the broader meaning of elections in relation to governance.

A number of studies of news have concluded that the way people interact with information depends on how much they know and care about the topic. The results of focus group analysis of campaign news confirms that people are capable of building on information that resonates with their concerns. News about candidate positions on high-priority issues is not cut and dried for the audience. In fact, it is the supposedly entertaining horse-race news that makes little connection with people. News analysis can stimulate people to connect the news to larger questions.

Interactions with Advertising. Just as the topics of news stories stimulated different levels of involvement, the same was true of ads. Participants in focus groups definitely followed the messages in some political ads more than others. For example, in the primary, Bush's ads provoked distinctly "ignoring" reactions—such as the North Carolina women who simply said, "I like Barbara better." Ads in the nominating stage for Paul Tsongas were also not followed in the focus group discussions. By contrast, Buchanan's and, to a lesser extent, Clinton's ads were followed most attentively, particularly in the early primaries. In both cases the ads addressed issues that were high on the voters' agenda—distrust of politicians and generating jobs.

In the general election, focus groups most frequently followed the messages in Perot's ads, which also focused on what was wrong with the country. But participants also followed the attacks by both major party candidates on each other. As Bush's campaign staff feared, Bush's attack advertising was heavily discounted in light of the perception that he was a dirty campaigner. In Boston in late October, the focus group debated the validity of a Bush ad attacking Clinton's integrity. Kitty offered the view that the ad "makes you think." Rick disagreed, referring to Bush's *1988* attack advertising, "Boston harbor, uh, it's still polluted." Christine, however, agreed with Kitty and supported her position with a more credible media source:

> There was an article in the *New York Times* a couple of weeks ago that was similar to that ad ["Two Faces"] and it pinpointed dates and promises he's made and groups that he talked to and then the dates that he did the opposite and I showed that to so many of my friends and people were just amazed and are not going to vote for him now, and that wasn't my goal. My goal was just to say "Hey, pay attention. You know, *read* these things."

The discussion suggests that the attack ads of the general election, which centered on questions of trust, engendered extensive discussion about the personal considerations of the candidates. The exchange also illustrates how ads can stimulate voters to question their beliefs, use prior knowledge to assess claims, and integrate different sources of information in the evaluation of candidates.

Ads played a greater role in stimulating conversation about issues in the primary than in the general election, perhaps in part because early in the campaign people had less knowledge of the candidates. Especially in many communities where voters have few alternative sources of information, primary ads constitute an important information resource.

In contrast to the primaries, where candidates from the same party compete against each other, in the general election, partisanship is an important filter for information. For example Tony, a Bush Republican from Los Angeles, developed a sophisticated counterargument to a Clinton ad:

> The one that gets me the most is this thing about "read my lips, no new taxes" and how they've [the Clinton ads] fixed on that thing. I wish that Bush would have come out and said, "The reason why that happened is because the Democrats proposed the budget, that was a compromise budget with the Republicans, and if [I] had not signed it, the same thing would've happened to the Fed that happened in California." [If the Fed] started putting out I.O.U.'s, if you don't think that'll start rioting in the streets, I don't know what will.

During the general election period, people in our focus groups used more political knowledge and a richer base of media sources to evaluate ads. The result was a more complex discourse in which some messages were followed and some were wiped out.

It must be concluded that, just as people evaluated ads as a unique information source, they also used ads in ways that were different from other sources of information. General election ads were rarely ignored; rather, ads stimulated argument and counterargument supported by a greater information base than in the primary period.

Visual, Audio-Visual, and Verbal Information

The analysis of focus group evidence shows that both news and ads generate discussion that follows or ignores the campaign message. But is the campaign a "war of words" or is a picture worth a thousand words (Crigler, Just, and Neuman 1994)? While most studies of campaign communication focus on texts (of speeches, ads, and news), research has demonstrated that visuals play a significant role in learning. Pictures enhance recall of information and help individuals assess people and events and clarify their judgments of situations (Graber 1990; Palvio 1991; Nisbett and Ross 1980). Visual information may also increase attentiveness to information (Neuman, Just, and Crigler 1992).

In politics, "most people have learned to draw inferences from physical appearance and movements," and visual information about candidates may be more accessible or useful to voters than verbal messages (Graber 1987, 167–68). Analysis of focus group topics of conversation (see appendix D), however, shows that people can be attentive to visual, verbal, and combined audio-visual cues, and that any channel, although rarely reinforcing channels, can provoke discourse that either ignores, transforms, or follows the message.

Some visual information may be heavily freighted with meaning and can be picked up independently of language. For example, focus group participants gathered from the Tsongas "swimming ads" that the candidate was "healthy"—a significant attribute given Boston voters' knowledge of his health problems. Visual cues may also be transformed in discussion. For example, in a Los Angeles focus group before the California primary, Colin wondered: "One thing that struck me was that we never *hear* Bill Clinton in these ads, we just *see* him. Who knows what he said?" While visuals alone can stimulate attention and inference, they may also raise questions that move the discussion away from the evaluative frame in the message.

Verbal cues alone also stimulate discussion. For example, the content of the voice-overs in ABC's "American Agenda" program on jobs and unemployment resulted in lengthy focus group conversation about the economy. Verbal messages were particularly important for extended candidate interviews. As figure 7.3 shows, fully 43 percent of all the topics of conversation after exposure to candidate interviews followed verbal messages.

Previous studies suggest that people are most likely to learn from television when the audio and visual channels convey the same message (Crigler et al. 1994) and resonate with voter concerns (Kern and Just 1995). Analysis of focus group discussions shows that even when audio-visual reinforcement does not occur, or the issue is not salient, either channel or both may be ignored, or the evaluative frame of the verbal or visual cue may be transformed.

Focus groups were presented with some reinforcing audio-visual messages in both news and advertising. For example, a Moorhead focus group was presented with a network news story during the primary. In the story, a journalist describes Jerry Brown's charge that Clinton golfed at an "all-white golf course" and was therefore a hypocrite on race issues. The journalist explains Brown's point of view in the voice-over accompanying a visual of Clinton riding in a golf cart with a white companion. The visual information reinforced Brown's message about Clinton's lack of commitment to racial equality. Focus group participants noticed and

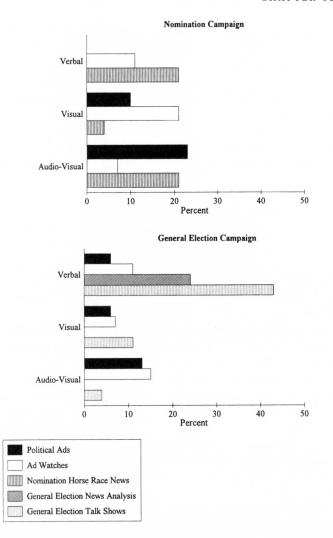

Figure 7.3   Focus group discussions of campaign media: percentage of conversational exchanges mentioning verbal, visual, and audio-visual messages.

talked about the issue, following Brown's frame, and repeatedly came back to the subject.

Another example of "following" a reinforced audio-visual message occurred in a local Winston-Salem news story about a new candidate—Ross Perot. The journalist's biography of the "son of a horsetrader" was set against the background of a log cabin. Local Perot activists were depicted on the screen engaging in political activities and talking enthusiastically about their grass-roots organizing effort. In part because of the local angle of the story, and in part because of the vivid visuals, participants in the focus group found the issue relevant and went on to express concern about the professionalization of electoral politics. The subsequent discussion followed the pro-Perot spin of the story.

While time and availability prevents many news stories from achieving a good match between audio and visual channels, ads are specifically designed to have reinforcing messages. For example, both Clinton and Buchanan used "read my lips, no new taxes" ads, which showed this mantra written out on screen, accompanied by audio-visual clips of Bush repeating the message. Not only did the "read my lips" ads represent reinforcing verbal and visual messages, but they also dovetailed the character theme with the salient issue of the economy. After watching Buchanan's Boston primary ads, Mark commented, "I think Buchanan again pointed out to everybody that when Bush said back in '88, 'read my lips, no new taxes' and then came up in '90, '91, with a tax increase, that was a total flip-flop."

Similarly, a Clinton advertisement emphasized verbally, in print emblazoned across the screen and in visual symbols of office, that the candidate had been returned to office by voters five times. Participants in the focus groups cited the audio-visual message that Clinton was "reelected five times" and used it as evidence of his credentials to govern. People also frequently picked up language from Clinton's ads relating to "caring" (about health care and jobs) with visuals of Clinton in a concerned or listening posture. Like the negative reinforced verbal and visual information about Bush, the information about Clinton was difficult to counteract in ad watches.

Not every instance of reinforcing channels, however, resulted in discourse that followed the message. Even in the case of a pointed advertisement about Bush's leadership in the Persian Gulf war, focus group participants were capable of rejecting the evaluative frame of the message. Tina inquired, "Wasn't there a line that said, 'George Bush changed the world?'" Others in the focus group confirmed that this was the case. Jolene ungraciously commented that George Bush may have brought about "changes," but they had taken the world further "back in the hole." Ginny concurred, "Sure. Iraq's moving weapons to the mountains of the Kurds—big deal." Focus group participants ignored the ad's visual symbols, focusing on the language but reversing the ad's message. While they heard the praise for Bush in the verbal message, they denied that the president had exercised good leadership.

Conclusion

The evidence from surveys, in-depth interviews, and focus groups is quite convincing that people have different expectations for news and ads. They want objective and substantive—"useful"—news. They are not convinced that the news is unbiased, they worry that the press intrudes on candidate selection, and they particularly object to sensationalism, which they attribute to the media's commercial motives. They perceive ads as inherently biased, but they expect them to be efficient and sometimes entertaining sources of information. Given the distaste for much of the subject matter of news and the discount on partisan advertising, it is not surprising that people do not follow many campaign messages but often reject the frame or ignore the topic. In focus group discussions, following, transforming, and ignoring messages occurred regardless of channel and, on at least one occasion, even in the face of reinforcing audio-visual cues. The only notable exceptions were candidate interviews, which generally stimulated discussion that built on what the candidates said, and news analysis, which resulted in lively and substantive discussions of the issues raised.

Analysis of 16 focus groups around the country in the spring and fall of the election cycle shows that counterarguing against media messages is particularly strong during the general election, when citizens draw on a richer knowledge base derived from mediated and personal experience and partisan interpretation. The campaign builds political knowledge that in turn affects how people interact with new messages—both stimulating the desire to make sense of new information and representing a filter through which new information is interpreted.

EIGHT

Media Use and Candidate Assessments

In contemporary campaigns, candidates devote considerable money and energy to constructing images of themselves in the media. Clearly, they expect that the way they present themselves in ads, debates, candidate interviews, and news coverage will pay off with voters. Likewise, the news coverage of the campaign aims to inform voters about the strengths and weaknesses of the candidates. But what do people make of the presentation of candidates in ads and news? This chapter examines how people use the media in weighing considerations and developing candidate constructs.

The findings are based on a range of data from in-depth interviews, focus groups, and public opinion surveys. The interviews help to explain the cycles of citizen attention and inattention over the course of the campaign and the difficulties people have in applying what they learn to the process of constructing candidate images. The focus group discussions show people talking about the impressions that particular ads and news segments made on their assessments of the candidates. Our public opinion surveys were conducted at the same time as the focus groups and extend the analysis of candidate perceptions and reception of ads and news among large random samples of citizens in the same media markets. The results show to what extent reported use of different media was associated with specific perceptions of the candidates. (The perspicacious reader will note that we do not talk here about media "effects" so much as we refer to information that may discourage or support particular conclusions.)

Voters and Information in the Nomination Phase

At the beginning of an election year, citizens often react to the campaign with confusion. At the baseline interview in January, almost all of our interviewees were able to name George Bush as one of the candidates for president (although one woman thought that Ronald Reagan was still in the White House), but few interviewees were able to name the Democratic challengers. For example, when asked to describe the candidates who were running, this Moorhead resident responded: "Well, Bush is the only one I know of running. I don't know of anyone else running. Who is? Do you know?" Our interviewees in four communities turned out to be typical of the public. A national CNN/*USA Today* poll taken in early January found the name recognition for all of the announced Democratic candidates was between 43 and 49 percent, except for Jerry Brown (72 percent).

The nominating field is a mystery in part because many citizens have not yet begun to pay attention to the campaign. A number of our interviewees said that they planned to attend to the campaign only later in the year, and several noted that by that time a number of candidates would be winnowed out. Strong partisans had the easiest time with the primary season, but their partisanship gave them reasons to delay any effort. For example, Cathryn remarked:

> I always vote when it's getting close to the time of the main election and stuff like that. But when I vote, like I vote just straight Democrat, so I really don't have too many opinions about it. We've got to have a president. I guess that's the way I feel.

Nonpartisans also reported that they delayed attention to the campaign. Eddy, a quintessential low-interest and low-knowledge voter, said in March:

> I don't pay attention to the election until it's kind of like three weeks before, or two weeks before. I've never been involved in politics. I don't like to watch a bunch of people tell me how they're going to change the country and stuff. I'm just kind of waiting for the politically active people. They're kind of going to like weed out the people. . . . I'll let them kind of make my decision for me as far as who the final two are.

Some citizens, like Madeline, used sports analogies to let themselves off the hook:

> What happens with me, it's like a lot of people and the Super Bowl—they don't pay attention to football until the Super Bowl is on. That's how I am with politics. When the big election comes, and it's getting closer, that's when I really get into it. But before that, I'm sort of out of it.

The willingness to postpone attention to the campaign was true even of interviewees who reported being very interested in politics. Herb initially claimed that he had "a lot" of political interest in January but did not pay attention to polls and horse-race stories:

> The charts and diagrams and percentages on the national campaign right now don't interest me because they're going to change weekly and change monthly. Wait until you get to August and they'll start becoming important. You got 30 percent now and you could have 50 percent in August or you could have 10 percent in August.

Herb claimed that he would begin to get interested once the Massachusetts primary was near. But when that time came, he decided to wait even longer before paying attention: "Right now, you know, I'm not as excited [as] if it was October 15th and the first of November. Nobody knows who the ball players are yet."

One of the reasons people tended to postpone attention during the nominating period was the sheer size of the candidate field. Vince was happy to have so much choice but noticed a trade-off: "I feel good for the simple fact that I see a lot of candidates that are running and I like that. The only thing—that makes it a little more confusing of who you want to listen to and who you want to believe." A couple even wondered why *six* candidates were allowed to run on the Democratic side versus only *two* Republicans.

In the face of a large number of contenders at the beginning of the campaign, people gather only discrete bits of information about the candidates. Take these examples from our Boston interviews in January: Linda could only say this about the candidates:

> I heard them talking about health care, I heard them talking about the recession. I heard them talk about tax cuts to, like, businesses or tax cuts for the middle class, or was that Bush? I guess it all goes together. But again it's about getting some relief to the middle class. Everybody's talking about that.

Gloria remarked:

> In the past couple of days it's become a circus because already one man's reputation is being attacked as being a womanizer. Another one wants to be the president who is going to rebuild the country, but no one knows how. Those are the two that are running that have made noise. The others I don't know. One of

them walks around a hockey rink. I have no idea what he's talking about and there's five or six more and I don't know anything
about them.

And Herb explained it this way:

> Interviewer: Where or how have you gotten your infor-
> mation?
> Herb: Mostly from I'd say newspaper. Not the article, just
> the bold type on the top of the article, and I don't know which
> statements go with which candidates yet, but one is going to be
> the health president, and another one is going to be the build-
> ing president. I can't even put the names with it yet.

According to our surveys in Boston, Bush was the best-recognized candidate at 90 percent, followed by Duke (87 percent), Tsongas (80 percent), Buchanan (77 percent), Clinton (70 percent), Kerrey (60 percent),
Brown (53 percent), and Harkin (52 percent). The people we interviewed
in Boston saw few distinctions among the Democratic candidates on the
issues. For example, Rose, who had moderate interest in politics, told us
just before the primary that she had paid close attention to a debate
among the Democratic candidates, but to little avail:

> I stayed through the whole thing and I found it so confusing be-
> cause as each man spoke he'd say "I agree with him and him
> and not with him." And the next one would talk about another
> subject, "And I agree with him, but not those two," and after a
> while each and every topic that they talked about, several of
> them did agree and several of them disagreed, but it wasn't the
> same people, and I found that after a while confusing. . . . The
> only one I found that sort of was all by himself on some sub-
> jects was Tsongas. I was beginning to think that he's slightly Re-
> publican in character because he didn't seem to fit the mold of
> the Democrats as much as the other three did.

And Gloria reported having seen a debate among the Democrats and being appalled at all the "foolish squabbling." The perception that the Democratic candidates held similar positions is evident in the answers to questions about the candidates in our Boston primary survey. We asked two
agree/disagree issue questions about all five active Democratic candidates
(Brown, Clinton, Harkin, Kerrey, and Tsongas). Even though Clinton ads
had emphasized his plan for a middle-class tax cut and Tsongas opposed
him, and Kerrey ads focused on fighting Japanese imports, the survey re-

spondents tended to think that all five candidates supported middle-class tax breaks and that all five would fight against imports from Japan. There was some variation from one candidate to the next, ranging from a high of 72 percent agreeing that Clinton favored middle-class tax breaks to a low of 59 percent saying the same for Tsongas, or from a high of 77 percent agreeing that Harkin would fight imports against Japan to a low of 66 percent saying the same for Brown. Yet the pattern of responses showed little distinction among the five Democratic contenders.[1]

Given the difficulty in making distinctions among the candidates, people coped in different ways. While some tuned out, others tried to clarify their understanding by honing in on a particular topic. The problem is that even if voters have a particular issue in mind, if the candidates all agree, the voter cannot distinguish them on the basis of issues alone. Take the case of Selma, who indicated her concern over abortion at her January baseline interview and commented:

> It's very early. I'm watching New Hampshire, I am watching, as to what's going on and the rumors that have surfaced recently. I'm aware of all that. I'm aware that they're all prochoice. Although, like I hear, I guess there's been some conversion along the way.

In the nomination phase, where all of the candidates have a common partisan outlook, it takes a canny voter to make distinctions. Saul noted that he was convinced that four of the Democrats—Kerrey, Harkin, Tsongas, and Clinton—shared his views and could make good presidents. But only Tsongas emphasized "conservation and renewables and solar energy," and he took that as an indication that Tsongas would take a long-term view of things. In an interview right before the primary election, Saul characterized his decision-making process this way:

> So given that all candidates are equally competent, equally appealing in general terms, I have to look to the more specific details and what will draw me to one candidate over another is something that really rings bells—as far as saying, yes, I like that. And then it's a matter of adding up the bells that have rung with this candidate versus that candidate.

Our primary surveys showed that public confusion about the large field of Democratic nominees helped the most familiar candidate, who, in the Boston survey, was the former senator from the state, Paul Tsongas. In a survey prior to the Massachusetts primary, the Boston respondents praised Tsongas, the hometown favorite, on every dimension we asked about, and a number of people in our in-depth interviews recalled seeing the ads showing him swimming. But Tsongas was not without problems.[2] After viewing local news in our Boston focus groups, several participants castigated his low-key personality and unkempt appearance. For example, Susan described Tsongas as having "the charisma of a bull dog." Pam said: "He looks like an unmade bed. He looks like he got out of bed in the morning, threw on the first thing that he picked up off the floor, like my son does sometimes, and combed his hair with a piece of toast."[3]

Our surveys showed that, although Tsongas was the local favorite, Clinton had already become a candidate to be reckoned with. Most survey respondents thought Clinton had strong leadership qualities. But questions about Clinton's honesty showed his Achilles' heel. Only 27 percent of the Massachusetts primary respondents thought Clinton was honest, while 48 percent did not.

In our Boston focus groups, news stories also reminded people about Clinton's integrity problems. Participants in the focus groups worried that Clinton was "in the middle of two or three different scandals" and that he was a "chameleon." Clinton's ads, however, provoked positive comments about his leadership abilities ("his stands on the issues are clear"), his credibility ("he seems believable"), and his overall appeal ("reminds me a lot of Kennedy").[4]

On the Republican side, the Boston survey results showed how much trouble the Buchanan challenge was causing the incumbent president, even among Republicans. Although Bush was seen by a wide margin as better able to handle the economy than Buchanan, the two were more evenly matched on honesty (36 percent for Bush vs. 31 percent for Buchanan) and caring (31 percent for Bush vs. 24 percent for Buchanan). What is more, the Boston Republicans were inclined to think that Buchanan, rather than Bush, would fight higher taxes and strongly believed that Buchanan would put domestic needs first (by a margin of 66 to 19 percent over Bush). Notably, these perceptions of the Republican candidates reflected the themes of the Buchanan ad campaign.

Our surveys aimed at identifying the resources people relied on for their opinions of the candidates. A series of regression analyses presented in table 8.1 show the association between evaluations of the candidates and exposure to television advertising, local television news, network news, and newspapers (see West, Kern, and Alger 1992 for additional details).[5] Regressions on the Boston survey data show that respondents' negative impressions about Bush were linked to their recollection of Buchanan ads and attention to news, but recalling Bush ads did not improve their rating of the president. Significantly, respondents who remembered seeing Buchanan ads were notably more likely to rate him highly on handling the economy and to express concern about Bush on that same dimension. In an interesting twist, respondents who reported heavy viewing of local television news tended to upgrade Buchanan's electability while downgrading Bush—exactly the opposite pattern of heavy viewers of network news, who saw Bush as the most electable candidate. The electability component may reflect Boston television's greater attention to the Buchanan candidacy in the preprimary period (Crigler et al. 1992). The Boston focus groups provided confirmation that candidate ads and campaign news stimulated negative views of Bush. After seeing a Buchanan ad, Roberta said, "I just think that Bush is out of touch with what is happening with the reality of this country and you know, that thing when he went and bought socks, the people in this country are in trouble." After seeing a news clip about a typical story from the campaign trail in New Hampshire, participants described Bush's efforts as "lethargic . . . he needs people like [Schwarzenegger] . . . to help him out." In the Boston focus groups even Bush's own ads elicited negative comments about Bush's leadership ("not presidential" and "sitting back"), his integrity ("how often does he talk to real people like that?"), and charisma ("looks like a geezer to me").

During the primary period, assessments of the candidates responded to alterations in their chances for nomination. By the time of our Winston-Salem survey in early May, Tsongas, Kerrey, and Harkin had dropped out of the race and Brown was the only remaining alternative to Clinton on the Democratic side. Assessments of Clinton improved markedly over the Boston results, especially in comparison to his remaining opponent. Survey respondents saw Clinton as more caring than Brown, as better able to handle the economy, and as a strong leader. But on the crucial dimension of honesty, Clinton and Brown were tied (Clinton was rated honest by 42 and Brown by 41 percent of respondents). Still, this figure represented a big improvement for Clinton over the 27 percent of Boston respondents who thought he was honest in early March.

In Winston-Salem, where news coverage of the nominating campaign was much sparser than in Boston or Los Angeles, people tended to use ads as a resource to identify Clinton's stands on the issues. Recall of Clinton's ads was associated with recognizing him as supporting health care and as being caring and best able to handle the economy. The Winston-Salem focus groups confirmed that Clinton's ads stimulated people to speak positively about the candidate—about his command of the issues, his professional experience, and his conduct of the campaign. The women's group was especially persistent in admiring his charisma. But even

Table 8.1 Ads, Local Television News, Network News, and Newspapers and Citizen Perceptions of Candidates, Spring 1992

Variable	Own Ads	Opponent Ads	Local TV News	Network News	Newspapers	N	R^2 or Correctly Predicted
Boston							
Buchanan electability	.27 (.24)	.27 (.24)	.48 (.29)	−.59 (.28)	−.23 (.19)	395	.91
Buchanan best handle economy	.26 (.15)	−.07 (.16)	.09 (.19)	.16 (.19)	−.20 (.13)	300	.73
Bush best handle economy	.03 (.16)	−.27 (.15)	−.08 (.19)	−.12 (.19)	.27 (.13)	300	.75
Bush electability	−.24 (.24)	−.37 (.23)	−.45 (.28)	.62 (.28)	.26 (.18)	395	.91
Tsongas supports middle-class tax cut	.11 (.05)	−.01 (.05)	.01 (.05)	−.09 (.05)	−.02 (.04)	319	.10
Tsongas best handle economy	.01 (.18)	−.39 (.17)	.23 (.15)	.07 (.15)	.19 (.11)	349	.72
Clinton best handle economy	.12 (.20)	.16 (.24)	.03 (.18)	−.11 (.18)	−.13 (.13)	349	.81
Kerrey supports affordable health care	−.41 (.18)	.08 (.24)	−.20 (.16)	−.03 (.16)	−.27 (.12)	298	.65
Winston-Salem							
Bush electability	−.58 (.21)	−.09 (.21)	−.12 (.24)	.40 (.23)	.14 (.18)	479	.92
Buchanan best handle economy	.25 (.14)	.10 (.14)	.36 (.16)	−.30 (.15)	−.01 (.11)	401	.75
Bush best handle economy	−.10 (.14)	−.25 (.14)	−.36 (.16)	.32 (.15)	.01 (.11)	401	.75
Clinton best handle economy	.40 (.16)	−.40 (.18)	.08 (.17)	−.02 (.26)	−.12 (.12)	345	.76
Clinton caring	.37 (.14)	−.31 (.15)	.19 (.15)	−.18 (.03)	−.10 (.10)	371	.62
Clinton supports affordable health care	.30 (.14)	−.11 (.16)	.18 (.15)	−.32 (.14)	−.07 (.11)	325	.64
Clinton honesty (b)	−.01 (.04)	.06 (.05)	.01 (.04)	.02 (.14)	−.07 (.03)	397	.13
Los Angeles							
Bush electability	−.26 (.18)	−.58 (.29)	−.24 (.16)	.15 (.17)	−.07 (.15)	213	.71
Bush best handle economy	.17 (.28)	.26 (.35)	−.04 (.25)	−.14 (.29)	−.30 (.22)	196	.90
Clinton electability	.50 (.22)	−.15 (.23)	−.18 (.20)	−.01 (.21)	−.22 (.18)	211	.78
Clinton best handle economy	.31 (.21)	−.47 (.27)	−.17 (.20)	−.16 (.21)	−.06 (.17)	195	.81
Clinton caring	.31 (.19)	−.58 (.25)	−.11 (.19)	.02 (.19)	.29 (.16)	201	.77
Clinton honesty (b)	.05 (.06)	−.06 (.07)	.18 (.05)	−.16 (.05)	−.07 (.05)	170	.19

Sources: Public opinion survey in Boston, March 2–9, 1992. Public opinion survey in Winston-Salem, April 30–May 3, 1992. Public opinion survey in Los Angeles, May 18–31, 1992

Notes: Entries represent regression coefficients with standard errors in parentheses. All models are logistic regression, unless denoted by (b); (b) indicates ordinary least squares regression.

after watching Clinton's ads, focus group participants continued to argue about Clinton's personal integrity and the possibility that he had engaged in scandalous behavior.

In our Winston-Salem survey, among Republicans, Bush was seen as better able to handle the economy than Buchanan, and Bush was also closing the gap with Buchanan as a tax fighter (45 percent for Buchanan vs. 40 percent for Bush). As in Massachusetts, however, the North Carolina respondents still thought Buchanan was more likely than Bush to put domestic needs first and to fight Japanese imports. Notably, putting America first was a prominent theme in Buchanan's ads. In our focus group in Winston-Salem, Elizabeth echoed this theme after seeing a Buchanan ad: "I think they should start focusing on the United States instead of sending money to foreign countries. We need to work on the people here in the United States first, 'cause there are a lot of people that don't have jobs and don't have homes and don't have food."

According to our Winston-Salem survey, people who were most likely to believe that Buchanan was better able to handle the economy than Bush were, as in Boston, those who watched local television news and those who remembered seeing Buchanan's ads. The power of the Buchanan message was illustrated in our focus groups. A Winston-Salem participant, for example, used a Buchanan ad theme to criticize Bush: "You know, we were so thrilled with Bush, you know, no new taxes, read my lips, and then the first thing he did was raise taxes. So the only people who got a break were the big companies and the richer people. The middle class and poor people here, we're paying more now than ever." Suzanne made the point even more directly by saying: "I thought it was kind of effective the way [the ad] showed 'read my lips' and George Bush, . . . that's probably a pretty good campaign tactic. . . . [Bush] just hasn't proven that he is able to do things." While the Buchanan ads hit home, the Bush ads missed their target. Indeed, one indication of how poorly the Bush message was received is that in our Winston-Salem survey, people who recalled seeing Bush's ads were much *less* inclined to think he would get elected.

In June, our Los Angeles survey showed little change in perceptions of the candidates on the Democratic side. Clinton received a substantial boost in electability. Overall Clinton was seen as the Democratic candidate best able to handle the economy; but more survey respondents in Los Angeles thought Brown was honest than thought Clinton was—when asked if Clinton were honest, 35 percent believed he was and 34 percent did not. It is interesting, however, that our Los Angeles focus group participants also criticized the news media for their inordinate attention to personal scandals.

As the nomination battle was winding down in June, Republican survey respondents in Los Angeles saw Bush as a strong leader and better able to handle the U.S. world role than Buchanan, but Buchanan still scored higher than Bush on honesty. Startlingly, only 30 percent of the Los Angeles respondents described Bush as honest, while 56 percent thought he was not. Bush's figures had actually become worse than Clinton's on this crucial dimension.

The major new theme that emerged in May and June in our Winston-Salem and Los Angeles focus groups concerned the presidential candidacy of Ross Perot. News clips about Perot engendered positive discussion about his campaign and his leadership abilities. Some participants raised questions about Perot's lack of tolerance for the views of other people—an issue that was not mentioned in the clip we showed them but was a topic heavily covered in the news. In our Los Angeles focus groups, women were more divided than men in their impressions of Perot; but overall, people in our Los Angeles survey saw him as an honest, strong leader. When respondents were asked who could best handle the economy, 27 percent named Perot, 18 percent cited Clinton, and 12 percent believed it was Bush. However, Bush was still seen as better able to handle the U.S. world role (32 percent) than either Clinton (13 percent) or Perot (12 percent).

In the primary campaigns, the findings from the surveys converge with the results from the focus groups: candidates' ads often encouraged viewers to hold some views more than others. But importantly, ads do not always gain the response the candidates want. While Buchanan and Clinton's ads seemed to provoke agreement, Bush's ads were generally ineffective—even in the locale where he was most popular (Winston-Salem). With Bush and Kerrey, we even found boomerang effects, by which ads seemed to garner negative reactions to the candidates.

What accounts for these differences in reception of candidate ads? One factor is that both Clinton and Buchanan focused clearly on the topic of the economy and dovetailed their issue and character claims around that issue, in contrast to the mixed messages of Bush and Kerrey. Second, ads may become more influential when other information is scarce. Bush's ads were interpreted in the context of what people already knew about him as the incumbent president. As the campaign proceeded, people were able to interpret new information about the other candidates against previous knowledge of them as well. We also found that lack of news coverage can leave another kind of vacuum. In locales that are news-poor, such as

Winston-Salem, for example, citizens' assessments of the candidates may hinge on what they glean from the ads.

News and Ads in the General Election

In comparison to the primaries with its bewildering assortment of candidates, spotty information, and confusing process, people were deluged with information during the general election. In fact, the problem is not one of costly information but information overload. By the end of the campaign, our interviewees often complained that they had had enough of the campaign and had begun to practice information avoidance, by skipping campaign stories in the newspapers, flicking the channel when ads came on, and so forth. Several people we interviewed in Moorhead said they were not watching much news. Selma, an informed and interested voter, said in October: "I have to say I am at the moment kind of saturated and that's unusual for me. I don't want to hear any more. I want Tuesday to come." Carlton, the only interviewee in Winston-Salem who reported devoting a lot of attention to the campaign at its outset, agreed at the end:

> It gets to be frustrating when you see all of these different—it's like if you turn the TV set on today at 8:00 in the morning and you'll see Bush and he's talking, talking, talking. The next time you turn the TV set on you see Clinton and he's talking, talking. It's like when does it stop? I think the media has caused people to suffer from burnout.

Others reported that they were starting to hear the same thing over and over again in the fall; J. D. said he felt "nauseated" and Paul found the campaign "dull, boring, nothing new. It's the same old song. The Democrats I heard on a commercial coming down here—the Democrats will spend it away. Clinton wants to spend 200 million dollars; Bush wants to cut back. Same song you've been hearing for the last 17 years."

The effect of this barrage of information was to produce more knowledge about the campaign. Whereas voters in the spring were often unable to say who the candidates were and what they stood for, they had no such difficulties in the fall—even after the reentry of Perot into the race. The survey data from all four communities confirm that by the fall, respondents were better able to match the candidates with their issue positions than they had been in the spring. As tables 8.2 and 8.3 demonstrate, the correlation between correct issue matching and exposure to the media

Table 8.2 Ads, Local Television News, Network News, and Newspapers and Citizen Perceptions of Candidates, September 1992

Variable	Own Ads	Opponent Ads	Local TV News	Network News	Newspapers	N	R^2 or Correctly Predicted
Bush best handle economy (b)	.00 (.03)	−.03 (.03)	.04 (.02)	−.04 (.02)	−.02 (.02)	1,276	.10
Bush caring	−.02 (.11)	.01 (.11)	.01 (.09)	.01 (.09)	−.02 (.07)	1,166	.80
Bush makes me worried	.06 (.09)	.03 (.09)	.03 (.07)	−.06 (.07)	.10 (.05)	1,314	.68
Clinton best handle economy (b)	.02 (.03)	−.02 (.03)	.01 (.02)	.02 (.03)	−.01 (.02)	1,210	.16
Clinton makes me proud	.16 (.10)	−.20 (.10)	.06 (.08)	.06 (.08)	.02 (.06)	1,245	.74
Clinton caring	.06 (.11)	−.01 (.11)	.00 (.09)	−.04 (.09)	−.05 (.07)	1,166	.80
Clinton honesty	−.02 (.03)	−.03 (.03)	.04 (.03)	.01 (.03)	.02 (.02)	1,152	.22

Source: National pooled surveys, September 28–October 4, 1992

Notes: Entries represent regression coefficients with standard errors in parentheses. All models are logistic regression, unless denoted by (b); (b) indicates ordinary least squares regression.

was much weaker, however, suggesting that by the fall, people have information from so many different sources that they did not have to be especially attentive to receive information about the candidates.

In one of only a few significant associations between candidate evaluations and media attention, September survey respondents who relied heavily on local television news were likely to feel that Bush would improve the economy, while those relying on network news felt that Bush would only make the economy worse. Individuals who relied on newspapers in the September survey, and those who relied on network news in the October survey, were also likely to report that Bush made them worried. These findings accord closely with the more negative tone toward Bush in network news and newspapers, as compared to the more neutral treatment of the president on local television (see chap. 5).

While in the nomination phase our in-depth interviewees usually responded to the question "What are the candidates emphasizing?" with scattered bits and pieces of information or references to the candidates as a group, interviewees in the fall were more inclined to respond with information about specific candidates emphasizing particular stances and issues. Even the images that people had in the general election campaign were more vivid than during the primary season, and they often encapsulated assessments of the candidates. In answer to the question "When you think about the candidates, are there any images or pictures that you re-

Table 8.3 Ads, Local Television News, Network News, and Newspapers and Citizen Perceptions of Candidates, October 1992

Variable	Own Ads	Opponent Ads	Local TV News	Network News	Newspapers	N	R^2 or Correctly Predicted
Bush best handle economy (b)	−.02 (.03)	.04 (.03)	.02 (.02)	−.02 (.02)	.01 (.02)	1,785	.10
Bush caring	−.03 (.11)	.14 (.10)	.02 (.08)	−.09 (.08)	−.03 (.06)	1,689	.80
Bush makes me worried	−.07 (.08)	.17 (.08)	−.01 (.06)	.16 (.06)	.02 (.05)	1,822	.68
Clinton best handle economy (b)	−.02 (.03)	.07 (.03)	.02 (.02)	−.01 (.02)	.00 (.02)	1,711	.13
Clinton makes me proud	.08 (.09)	−.11 (.09)	.06 (.07)	.11 (.07)	.03 (.05)	1,764	.70
Clinton caring	.02 (.08)	−.04 (.09)	.02 (.07)	.14 (.07)	.06 (.05)	1,689	.68
Clinton honest	.01 (.03)	.01 (.03)	−.01 (.02)	.03 (.02)	.01 (.02)	1,662	.14
Perot best handle economy (b)	.09 (.02)	−.01 (.03)	−.01 (.02)	.01 (.02)	−.02 (.02)	1,608	.04
Perot caring	.32 (.07)	.09 (.09)	−.03 (.07)	−.08 (.07)	−.02 (.05)	1,689	.73
Perot makes me worried	−.18 (.06)	−.05 (.08)	−.05 (.06)	.19 (.06)	.09 (.05)	1,781	.61

Source: National pooled surveys, October 23–November 1, 1992

Notes: Entries represent regression coefficients with standard errors in parentheses. All models are logistic regression, unless denoted by (b); (b) indicates ordinary least squares regression.

call seeing?" Saul offered the following picture of Clinton: "sleeves rolled up, smile on his face, talking to a mixed group of people." But Saul's explanation of the image took on elaborate meaning:

> I mean at various times a mixed group may be male/female; various shades of pale or black and at other times when I say mixed I mean blue collar/white collar, young/old. In other words, I picture him among everyone, not just standing there— like the image of Bush standing there in a suit many times— sometimes short sleeves—but he's wailing against the Democrats, how they'll bring the whole country down. . . . Clinton wants to bring us together. Bush wants to keep certain people apart.

A question about "images and pictures" of the candidates, however, did not simply elicit visuals from television news or from ads. Many of our interviewees actually used the question to assemble an original mental cartoon of their own. Thus interviewees talked about images like "Abbott and Costello, Laurel and Hardy," "Perot with dollar signs," or "two people in a pigpen throwing muck." When asked about images of the presidential candidates in October, Lisa responded:

> Well, with Clinton I picture a snake. Bush, I think of like a father figure, more of a . . . not dominating . . . but more of an authoritative . . .

Even if the picture was clearly derived from television coverage, the meanings of long-standing visual images shifted as new considerations were added to the mix. In the January interview, for instance, Vince recalled Bush fishing off Kennebunkport, but the picture was fairly neutral. As he became more frustrated about the economy in the fall, the same image took on a more negative interpretation:

> The thing that stands out in my mind is Bush in Kennebunkport waving, fishing. That's not doing anything for me. That just makes me believe "What a life!" However I realize that anybody needs a couple of days away. But can the average person afford to do that? As far as I'm concerned that doesn't win my vote.

Indeed, while the visual imagery was often very similar from one interviewee to the next—Bush, behind a desk or in the Oval Office, looking serious and distinguished; Clinton smiling and plunging into a crowd to shake hands; Perot standing behind a podium or wielding charts—the meanings of these images differed depending on one's political predispositions, particularly at the end of the campaign. Democrats, who favored Clinton, tended to see Bush's demeanor as an indicator that he was worn out, aloof, old, dull, gray, and out-of-touch, whereas Clinton's style suggested to them confidence, energy, an ability to communicate with a wide range of people, and a readiness to get to work. Republicans and conservatives, who favored Clinton less, tended to see in these behaviors that Bush was serious, experienced, and dedicated, while Clinton either was seemingly unwilling to admit the gravity of the situations facing the country or was programmed and slick. For example, several interviewees noticed Clinton's changing hair color, but the alteration was interpreted differently by Clinton supporters than by people who favored Bush or Perot. Ingrid, in a July telephone interview, said: "I think his [Clinton's] hair is getting grayer. I think he's being taken more seriously." Rosa on the other hand said that she would vote for Bush and not for Clinton. At the end of the campaign she said:

> The reason I waited until the very last minute was I wanted to see what they had to say, what all of them had to say. Clinton has been more evasive. He keeps changing for each group. He not only changes what he says, but he even changes his hair color and his clothing. He's not the same person each time. Maybe he wants to blend in with the people he's talking to, but all it does is give me the impression that he's dishonest.

Facial expressions can also be important to people. For example, Luke who was leaning toward the Democrats in a September interview, said: "I just think when you hear the name the first thing you get is the face and expressions on their face. Bush always looks worried or like he's caught in a lie. Clinton looks very much confident and aggressive even if he is lying, but it doesn't show on his face to me." Compare this to Kelly, initially a Bush sympathizer, in September:

> Clinton just seems to be trying to keep a big smile on his face like nothing is wrong with his campaign and everything will be fine and he will win. It's a very positive attitude but also a very blind attitude. . . . If you don't pay attention to the problems they're not going to take care of themselves. If you ignore a problem it won't go away.

By the time that the fall campaign came along, then, voters often reinterpreted particular events in ways that were at variance with what journalists and other observers might have thought obvious. For example, the coverage of Clinton's alleged affair and pot smoking was seen as immoral by a few interviewees, but many, even in Moorhead, felt that these events were "not a big issue" (Lisa) and should "not be held against him" (Cora). Jim in fact saw Clinton's admission of pot smoking as an example of his honesty:

> Jim: Bill Clinton, he seems like he knows what he's talking about. He sounds like he comes out more outstanding.
> Interviewer: Outstanding? How do you mean that?
> Jim: Uh, oh, he had that deal when he was in college days, or London, that he had smoked marijuana, whatever. I was watchin' that part and he just told—came out and admitted it truthfully, like, no sweat.

Most of our voters criticized the candidates, especially Bush, for "mudslinging," but in September Clinton's reluctance to enter into the

fray was troubling to Vince, who was then undecided but ultimately supported Perot:

> You read the—I don't want to say propaganda—but you read
> that Bush said this about Perot. Clinton, like I say, he kind of
> like is staying to the side. I don't think he wants to throw any
> mud for some reason. That's another thing that scares me about
> him. A guy that doesn't want to throw any mud at all—if you
> live in a glass house don't throw stones. There must be some-
> thing there.

Similarly, Mike, a prolife conservative, was left cold by Clinton's performance in the town-meeting–style debate; where most observers saw Bush
as hopelessly out of touch, he saw Clinton as slick and calculated:

> Mike: The Clinton debate that I call it. The one where it
> was a forum and how Bush looked so uncomfortable. Clinton
> looked too comfortable.
> Interviewer: Is this the one where they—
> Mike: Where the three of them were sitting and they were
> taking questions from the audience. I thought Clinton was go-
> ing to walk through the television set and come into my living
> room. He was too polished if he can be.

In short, although people were all participating (vicariously or not) in
similar campaigns, what sense they made about the election from that
experience differed, sometimes dramatically, from one individual to the
next.

Our surveys also found little consistent response to Bush or Clinton
ads during the general election campaign. The mixed reaction to the candidates' ads in the fall focus groups helps to explain why the associations
are so low. By the time the general election rolled around, people accepted
or rejected advertising information based on their accumulated knowledge and impressions of the candidates. Supporters tended to see good
things in the ads, and opponents judged them negatively. For example,
after seeing the Democratic candidate's ads in the September focus group
in Boston, one participant said, "I like the way Bill had his sleeves rolled
up in the ads, it made him look like he was ready to get right in there,
and work with you." But after seeing the same ads, other participants
criticized Clinton's leadership ability as well as the manipulativeness of his
ads ("valueless data"). After seeing Republican spots, some participants
offered negative remarks about Clinton's integrity ("out for himself") and
professional experience ("lack of world experience") and praised Bush's

demeanor ("seems more firm and positive") and his leadership on international issues; but other participants disagreed and claimed Bush was resting on his laurels and America's former strength.

Ads elicited similarly mixed responses in our September Moorhead focus group. Some participants criticized Clinton ads for taking facts "out of context," while others praised him for articulating the need for change. One participant said the music in the ads "is beautiful, it shows Bill Clinton with the blacks and the whites"; but his tax plans got mixed reviews. Republican ads led to criticism of Clinton's integrity ("don't trust him," "scandals," and "taxes"), but both positive and negative comments about the way Clinton conducted his campaign. Surprisingly, right after viewers saw his commercials, they criticized Bush's campaign ("insulting to your intelligence"), his integrity ("slippery" and "every time I watch one of these ads, I think, well, you know, he said this a couple of years ago"), and his leadership (choice of Dan Quayle as vice-president). Even his strong suit, foreign policy, did not elicit unmitigated praise, as some participants criticized Bush for abruptly ending the Persian Gulf war.

Evaluating Information

How can the mixed reactions to candidate presentations be explained? The evidence from our in-depth interviews points to a process in which voters begin with allegations or hunches about the candidates and then see how well those premises hold up against the evidence that comes along during the campaign. Where do these premises come from? Early in the campaign, citizens referred to previous elections and past and present politicians against whom they compared the current crop of candidates. Even candidates who were familiar, such as Bush, were compared with previous presidents, most notably Reagan; J. D. said in a January interview: "It seemed like the Reagans, they were still playing Hollywood, and seems like the Bushes are just ordinary, everyday people. That's what comes across to me." A number of Boston Democrats worried about the capacity of the Democratic candidates to stand up to a campaign against Bush, given their recollection of the way Dukakis folded in 1988, or referred to an ad as a "Willie Horton ad" when they saw a below-the-belt hit. If the candidate was well known, individuals drew on their prior knowledge to make current evaluations of the candidate. For example, when Tom talked about Brown's presidential bid during the primaries, he recalled the candidate's poor performance as governor of California:

Well, Jerry Brown is a flake in my mind. He's from California, you know. I just remember him as the guy who really screwed up the med-fly situation.

Other interviewees drew analogies to local politicians or saw new faces as reincarnations of old menaces, as when Richard, a social liberal, said in May, "I think Buchanan is another Jesse Helms," or when Selma, an African American, fumed in January:

> I'm disturbed about Pat Buchanan. I have never liked him. I heard what he's had to say for a couple of years now on television, I've read what he's had to say when I've had the stomach for him. I think that he is no different than David Duke. He's a polished David Duke.

These initial stereotypes of little-known candidates were tested and sometimes tossed out later by exposure to candidates' ads or news. Mike pointed out one ad in January:

> The Harkin one I thought was, I was impressed with Harkin because there was no fluff. He was sitting in a chair and telling what he thought and he was down to earth. He didn't look like some wild-eyed farmer like I first thought he was.

Or as Sara said: "They all look like leaders except for Perot. He don't look like a leader to me, but he's rich, so he must lead something" (September).

New premises for consideration may come from what the candidates' say about themselves or their competitors. Voters can compare the rhetorical claims of familiar politicians—especially the incumbent president—to knowledge they have accumulated about them over the years. Such comparisons did not work to the advantage of George Bush. For instance, in Boston, when Bush's ads showed him engaged in face-to-face conversation with New Hampshire voters, some of our interviewees were incredulous, arguing that Bush had never talked to people until he was in electoral difficulty. Later on, Selma derided Bush's campaign against "Washington": "He's against big government but that's all he's ever worked for his whole life."

By the end of the campaign, people were better able to test a premise about one candidate derived from the news or from the candidate's competitors. For example, Diane said about an ad watch: "Clinton has one [ad] out there where some of the news media were saying it is negative. I didn't see it that way. I thought they pretty much kept the election clean with the exception of the draft issues." Linda, an African American Democrat who began the year staunchly opposed to Bush, was asked in October about the ads and remembered, quite clearly, one of Bush's spots seeking to undermine Clinton's trustworthiness. She went on:

> I guess a big thing back and forth is people changing their standing on issues. You know, that's what Bush is saying about Clinton—that he waffles and often changes his position. But, everything to date that I've seen he's said the same thing. So, I guess I'm starting to see him as consistent.

Our interviewees often acknowledged negative considerations about their preferred candidate—but if their choices were secure, those considerations were rebutted and neutralized by other evidence they drew. Cora's support for Perot, for example, overcame her distaste for his "cockiness":

> Perot, I always thought he was very cocky and I think in a way he still is, but not in a disrespectful way. When he talks I have confidence, which I don't have when the other two talk.

Rose announced her support for Perot just before the election but felt compelled to explain away the disastrous performance of Perot's running mate, James Stockdale, in the vice-presidential debate:

> I wasn't too thrilled with the way his vice-president spoke when he had to get up and do public speaking, but then is one of the qualifications of a vice-president to be able to be a marvelous public speaker? Is that important? Especially when he was acting like a doddering old idiot I thought, "Oh, my God." I think it was just nervousness. Also he wouldn't participate in beating down the other candidates. So therefore he passed on a lot of things just because they decided to sour their campaign. Their campaign was not going to be harping on people's shortcomings. So that's what I've decided to do.

Or take J. D., who by September was leaning toward Clinton:

> Well you know they talk about Clinton trying to escape the draft. Well, by the same token didn't Quayle try to escape the draft? . . . And didn't thousands of other people try to escape the draft and did escape the draft? They went to Canada by the hundreds I suppose.

Individuals also assessed considerations according to the credibility of the source. A good example of this is the suspicion Bush engendered about his own integrity when he criticized the trustworthiness of his opponents. As Diane put it in October:

> It appears to me that Bush is not able to talk about anything unless he's talking about someone's character or trust. When the American people trusted him for four years they got absolutely nothing. The trust issue doesn't wash with me.

Sometimes considerations about the candidates were reinforced by other, independent information. For example, George Bush was viewed as "out of touch" in the fall campaign not only because of performance in the second debate (in which he appeared bewildered by a question asking how the federal debt had affected him personally) but because of his well-known blue-blood background. Selma said of Bush:

> I think also, and maybe it's not based on anything real, it's just how you get a feeling about people, but I think it's more than that, I don't think he's someone at all that growing up has had to deal with any adversity or diversity. Therefore I just don't think he has any sympathy or empathy for people like me or one much worse off.

In other instances, people considered the allegations of candidates in the light of information they gathered in their immediate environments or from their personal experiences. Tom's preference for Bush was supported by his own philosophy about limited government and his personal experiences with government programs:

> Although I can sympathize and empathize with those who are less fortunate and don't have adequate health care and insurance, I guess I'm such a pessimist about government handling of these things in terms of how I've heard how Medicare works from my own mother and in-laws and the problems they have and the cost and the service level. I just don't have that much confidence in a government controlled program. . . . That's why I would vote for Bush. I feel that Bush represents more the philosophy of business and letting the free market work.

And finally, people used their accumulated knowledge of politics to assess the rhetoric of particular candidates and their platforms. Knowledge of politics in general worked to deflect the impact of ads and other candidate communications. In September, Lillian remembered a Clinton ad that accused Bush of broken promises but went on:

> I don't think in my life I have ever known a political campaign
> that didn't make promises that were not fulfilled. I think every
> one of them has promised things that were not humanly pos-
> sible for them to do or that they didn't have any intentions of
> doing to begin with and I wonder how you define between the
> two?

As the campaign wore on, citizen disgust with exaggerated political
claims blunted the impact even of dramatic ads. In October, Sara rejected
as incredible Bush's "Arkansas Record" ad, even though she was a Bush
supporter:

> It first starts out with different things that they say Clinton has
> done in Arkansas. The thing that sticks out in my mind is the
> bird sitting on the twig in the dark. I don't remember all that it
> did say but it was like he destroyed Arkansas. *I'm sure he
> hasn't*. (Emphasis added)

The "Trust Thing"

Our opinion surveys suggest that the Bush attack ads actually may have
had a boomerang effect. In our late October surveys, 61 percent of our
respondents said that "most of Bush's ads attacked his opponent,"
whereas only 13 percent thought his spots "explained his own views." In
contrast, 30 percent thought Clinton's ads "mostly attacked," and 40 percent responded that Clinton's ads explained his views. Opinion surveys
done for the Times Mirror Center for the People and the Press in early
October also "found that voters who had been exposed to the commercials were more likely to rate Clinton's ads as 'more truthful and convincing.'" Indeed, fully 51 percent thought Clinton's ads "were basically
truthful vs. 35 percent who said they were not." Fifty percent thought
Bush's ads "were not truthful," while only 38 percent thought they were
(Arterton 1993, 101). These contrasting views of the candidates' ads
clearly had an impact on a more general conclusion. Fifty-four percent of
the respondents blamed Bush for being "more responsible for negative
campaigning," while only 15 percent blamed Clinton.

It should be noted that in the early months of the nominating season,
when Bush was having problems with his economic leadership, he was
still perceived positively in terms of trust. *New York Times*/CBS polling
in March found 56 percent of voters saying Bush "had more honesty and
integrity than most people in public life," compared to only 26 percent
who felt that way about Clinton. But by fall, perceptions about Bush on
the trust dimension had changed for the worse. A fall poll by the *Times*

Mirror asked respondents to "grade each candidate's ads as to their effectiveness in giving people a reason to vote for the candidate." Forty-five
percent gave Bush ads an "F" for failure, and this conclusion "was
directly linked to the ads' assault on Governor Clinton's character"
(reported by Donald Kellerman on the "McNeil-Lehrer News Hour,"
October 28, 1992).

The Case of Perot

Ross Perot was the candidate most successful in escaping negative campaign rhetoric and establishing his credibility through advertising, on
which he spent millions of dollars in the fall. He repeatedly stated that
the country needed to get away from politics-as-usual. In our focus
groups, these ideas were repeatedly expressed as essential aspects of the
Perot image. For example, just after Perot rejoined the race and was lan-
guishing in the polls, one participant in a Los Angeles focus group expressed the consensus around the table, "Perot is not a politician; he
doesn't dance around his answers."

The public response to Perot's ads was very striking. The *New York
Times*/CBS polling found that "voters who saw television ads said they
paid the most attention to Perot's. They rated his ads as the most truthful
and said the ads made [them] most likely to vote for Perot" (Frankovic
1993, 127–28). In addition, the *Times Mirror* polling found Perot ads
rated "the most informative" by far: 55 percent for his ads, compared to
20 percent for Clinton and 8 percent for Bush (Schneider 1992, 2814).

Our pooled October survey also shows that people who recalled seeing
Perot ads were more likely to say that he did *not* make them worried and
that he "cares about problems and needs of people like yourself" (and
rated Bush and Clinton correspondingly lower).[6] In our focus groups
and in-depth interviews, we heard that the unique form and style of Perot's ads helped reflect the widespread public perception that Perot was
the candidate truly dealing with important issues and was doing so in a
straightforward, plain-talking fashion. Combined with the perception
that Perot was the antithesis of politics-as-usual, the ads carried a powerful message.[7]

Comments from the focus groups provide deeper insight into why the
Perot ads stimulated such a response. People believed that Perot's ads
were straightforward and honest, and that they spoke overwhelmingly to
the issues. This sense was shared by some participants who did not intend
to vote for him, and even by a few who simply did not like him, because,
as one participant said after viewing Perot's campaign spots: "His ads are
just so good. He gets right to the point. There's no bullshit about him."

After seeing two ads for each candidate in the October round of focus groups, Larry in Moorhead said: "I think if we want to take those ads as they were presented to us, and if we were to take a look and say, 'Yeah, we believe what you told us,' Perot comes right up to the top in my viewpoint. Very, very high." Brenda concurred, "the others come out mudslinging with no actual answers . . . , just a bunch of junk." Chuck, referring to Perot's "Purple Heart" ad, pointed out that "there was absolutely nothing political about it." Bonnie noted, "I think just about everything I've seen, I think he comes out with a lot of very good stuff and something for us to think about." Brenda chimed in: "Yeah, actually the only good one, I thought, [was] for Perot, was a 30-minute paid advertisement where he sat down with his—what do you call it?—cue card type things; he sat down with his charts and he gave us exact numbers. Exact numbers, right down the list." A majority in the final Winston-Salem focus group and a sizeable minority in Los Angles held similar opinions. The Boston focus group varied more, but even there the majority opinion was that Perot was bringing to the forefront issues that the other candidates were not dealing with. The comments of one person in Los Angeles strikingly illustrated the power of the image Perot achieved through his ads precisely, because she disliked him. Twice, Rosaline said, "I think he's a weasel; I really do." But after the second remark, she said: "I've seen his commercials on the TV; we all have. And one thing I can say about it is the honesty in every commercial he has." Another group member immediately chimed in: "That's right! . . . And no pictures of him, just the writing—the writing on the wall." As important as what Perot said was the *way* he said it, which reinforced his image as a plain-speaking outsider, not another politician. In short, Perot was perceived as credible and honest in part because viewers did not think he was posing for the cameras in some slick spot.

Views during the General Election and Link to the Vote
The three candidates began the general election with high recognition levels in our pooled, four-site survey in September, with 80 percent recognition for Bush, 75 percent for Clinton, and 68 percent for Perot. But whereas Clinton was viewed favorably by 48 percent of the population, Bush was seen favorably by only 26 percent, and Perot by just 10 percent. Seventy-one percent felt Clinton was the most electable candidate, followed by Bush at 27 percent and Perot at 2 percent.

A month later, just before election day, the pooled survey showed that Clinton's recognition level (83 percent) had risen to match Bush's (83 percent). Still only 68 percent indicated that they recognized Perot. Favorability toward the two major party candidates remained the same (49 percent for Clinton and 30 percent for Bush), but Perot's favorability increased to 26 percent. This represented a 16 percentage point gain in favorability for Perot, the largest improvement for any of the candidates during the general election. Clinton was still seen as the most electable candidate (by 74 percent), compared to Bush (by 24 percent) and Perot (by 2 percent).

Perceptions of the candidates' personal qualities and issue positions in the fall were significantly different from those in the nomination phase. We have seen that Clinton's central focus was the economy and Bush's lack of compassion for the public's economic problems. Clinton's messages were largely reflected by public perceptions in the fall. In both the late September and late October surveys, far higher percentages claimed Clinton would "make the economy get better" (43 percent in September and 45 percent in October) than said so of Bush (16 percent in September and 19 percent in October), while 47 percent in October said Perot would make the economy get better. Clinton also scored well on perceptions that he "cares about people like you."

By contrast, Bush's "trust" messages attacking Clinton did not stick. In both fall waves and in all four communities, when asked whether each candidate "makes you feel worried," the number was greatest for Bush. By the end of the campaign in October, for example, 65 percent of respondents were worried about Bush, while only 45 percent worried about Clinton, and 45 percent worried about Perot. Surprisingly, for all the discussion about Clinton's character flaws, people generally rated the two major candidates as about equal on the dimension of honesty. By the end of the campaign 48 percent believed Clinton was honest, compared to 47 percent for Bush.

How did these candidate considerations match the vote itself? Our fall surveys asked about candidate preferences using the item "If the election were being held today, would you vote for Republican George Bush, Democrat Bill Clinton, or Independent Ross Perot?" Clinton led Bush by 51 to 28 percent in September, with 8 percent supporting Perot, 1 percent naming others, and 12 percent undecided. In late October, our pooled local surveys indicated that 45 percent chose Clinton, 28 percent Bush, 15 percent Perot, 1 percent someone else, and 11 percent undecided. The final vote on election day was 43 percent for Clinton, 38 percent for Bush, and 19 percent for Perot. The results indicate that our surveys came close to the mark, with most of the undecided respondents going to Bush.

The survey data were examined to see whether people's vote choices were linked to reported heavy exposure to particular media. A logistic regression model was run for each of the three major candidates (see table 8.4).[8] Overall, the models correctly predicted anywhere from 71 to 82 percent of the vote, depending on the individual candidate. The results show, however, virtually no association between voting for Bush or Clinton and reported exposure to television advertising or particular sources of news, although people who recalled seeing Clinton ads were less likely to say they would vote for Bush. There was no association between viewing Bush ads and either supporting his candidacy or opposing others. The Clinton vote was predicted by political interest, race, party, gender, ideology, education, and past family finances. Bush's vote was predicted by age, party, ideology, political interest, race, and past family finances. Not surprisingly, given his independent candidacy, neither party nor ideology were important to the Perot vote, although race and education contributed positively to his support. While past family financial circumstances were crucial to the fortunes of the other candidates, in Perot's case, future, not past financial conditions was linked to the vote. Perot's emphasis on the government's budget deficit apparently shifted people's financial anxiety from the past to the future. But there was a crucial difference between predicting votes for Clinton and Bush on the one hand and Perot on the other. People who said they had seen Perot's ads were significantly more likely to say they would vote for him (for fuller results, see Alger, Kern, and West 1993). Apparently, the high credibility of Perot ads, which we documented in our in-depth interviews, focus groups, and surveys, paid off in votes.

Conclusion

This chapter shows that citizens are slow to attend to the nominating campaign when the size of the field is large and candidates have similar political orientations. But when the field is small, stable, and polarized—as it was in the case of Bush and Buchanan—people can clearly distinguish between candidates. In either case, people use both news and ads in forming impressions of the major party candidates. The surveys show that reliance on particular sources of information was more closely associated with considerations of the candidates in the nominating phase than during the fall campaign.

Our survey data show that where the information environment is poor, people's perceptions of the candidates can be better differentiated on the basis of their ad recall than their attention to particular sources of news. So, for example, the relationships are stronger between ad recall and par-

Table 8.4 Effects of Ads and News on Vote Preference, Fall 1992

Variable	September		October		
	Clinton	Bush	Clinton	Bush	Perot
Own ad	−.02 (.11)	−.05 (.12)	−.10 (.09)	.01 (.11)	.22 (.09)
First opponent's[a] ad	−.02 (.11)	.07 (.12)	.06 (.10)	−.21 (.10)	−.09 (.11)
Second opponent's ad	...	...	−.08 (.07)	−.11 (.08)	−.09 (.10)
Local TV news	.05 (.09)	.00 (.09)	.07 (.07)	−.08 (.08)	.01 (.09)
Network news	−.10 (.09)	.03 (.10)	.04 (.08)	−.03 (.08)	−.01 (.09)
Newspaper	.03 (.07)	−.01 (.07)	.10 (.06)	.00 (.06)	−.12 (.07)
Gender	.09 (.15)	.17 (.17)	.22 (.12)	.08 (.13)	.39 (.14)
Level of political interest	−.17 (.10)	.15 (.10)	.18 (.08)	.25 (.08)	−.01 (.09)
Age	−.05 (.05)	.20 (.06)	.07 (.04)	.16 (.04)	−.28 (.05)
Race	.46 (.20)	−.35 (.22)	.97 (.17)	−.76 (.20)	.60 (.20)
Party identification	1.39 (.11)	−1.32 (.11)	.60 (.08)	−.71 (.08)	.07 (.09)
Ideology	−.73 (.11)	.75 (.12)	−.83 (.09)	.97 (.10)	−.05 (.10)
Education level	.20 (.07)	−.07 (.08)	.11 (.05)	.05 (.06)	−.22 (.06)
Region	.20 (.19)	.02 (.19)	−.04 (.14)	.08 (.15)	.01 (.17)
Past finances worse	.75 (.12)	−.89 (.12)	.60 (.09)	−.78 (.10)	.08 (.10)
Future finances worse	−.09 (.13)	.05 (.13)	−.11 (.10)	−.17 (.11)	.36 (.11)
Constant	−3.84 (.77)	1.80 (.79)	−2.43 (.56)	.12 (.60)	.26 (.65)
N	1,086	1,086	1,485	1,485	1,485
Correctly predicted	.77	.80	.71	.78	.82

Source: National pooled surveys, October 23–November 1, 1992.

[a]For Bush, first opponent was Clinton; for Clinton, first opponent was Bush; for Perot, first opponent was Bush.

Note: Entries represent regression coefficients with standard errors in parentheses.

ticular perceptions of Bush, Buchanan, and Clinton in the Winston-Salem primary survey than in any of the other local surveys. By September, however, when the information environment was richer everywhere, ad recall was not a strong factor in candidate perceptions. The only exception was Perot. In his case, ad recall was highly associated with positive perceptions of the candidate.

The Perot results reinforce the view that the amount and balance of information available to citizens makes a difference in their perceptions of the candidates. By spending $50 million on ads, Perot was able to counteract the lower level of attention to his candidacy in the news media and to encourage people to think of him in positive terms.

We also have evidence that candidate constructs evolve not only in relation to new information about the candidates but also in terms of the strategic environment. For example, as Clinton persisted in winning primaries, perceptions about his leadership improved vis-à-vis his challengers. Nevertheless, for a winning candidate, there remained considerable doubt about Clinton's honesty even in the last round of surveys. What our series of surveys and focus groups showed, however, was that the campaign—including Bush's own ad campaign—tended to increase the public's doubts about the president's honesty as well. The results suggest that in assessing candidates the public often infers character from the candidate's performance, ads, and positions on the issues.

Differences between our spring and fall results show that when the general election rolls around, people have developed at least tentative understandings of candidates, which they use in dealing with the late surge of information coming from candidates and the media. Citizens continue to accumulate knowledge about the candidates over the course of the campaign, but because they have so many sources of information in the fall, reliance on ads and news tends to be less associated with candidate constructs or vote preferences. Perot was a special case. He received substantially less news attention than the other major candidates, and he aired more ads, with the result that his ads were a substantial resource for his supporters. The Perot example suggests that if the weight of candidate communication and the nature of the appeal have a clear advantage, they can have a significant influence on the vote.

NINE

The Logic of Considerations and the Vote

Although observers agree that candidate constructs are important to voters, the jury is still out on how citizens develop and use images of the candidates in deciding how to vote. Survey analyses have tended to show that citizens *elaborate* constructs, judging candidates according to a number of different criteria. As the campaign continues voters' pictures of the candidates become richer and more complex. But experimental studies suggest just the opposite—*simplification*, by which voters limit their constructs to a bottom-line account of the candidates, even forgetting the information that led them to those evaluations in the first place. Experimenters find that the reasons people subsequently give for their evaluations are "rationalizations" of choices arrived at by a different process.

Our method for understanding candidate constructs relies on in-depth interviews and, as a result, acknowledges the social aspect of candidate evaluations. As Zaller (1992) reminds us, what people tell researchers reflects what they are willing to say to a relative stranger. These opinions about candidates are in a sense *public* opinions rather than private ones. The reasons that people articulate for favoring a particular candidate should not be dismissed as mere "rationalizations." Citizens often need to justify electoral decisions to others in a way that they do not have to defend purely private choices (such as preferring strawberry ice cream to chocolate). Information can be important to people as a way to justify their feelings.

Methods

To address how people form considerations, political scientists have generally drawn on the "likes" and "dislikes" toward candidates elicited in the presidential election polls conducted by the NES.[1] The NES analyses of candidate constructs are based on the following questions: "Now I'd like to ask you about the good and bad points of the two major candidates for president. Is there anything in particular about [candidate's name] *that might make you want to vote for him?* [Probe:] What is that? Anything else?" and later, "Is there anything in particular about [candidate's name] *that might make you want to vote against him?* [Probe:] What is that? Anything else?" (emphasis added). As one can readily see, such questions invite rationalizations of the vote and may bias or limit the scope of considerations that people say they take into account. Individuals may actually report only those considerations that might be perceived to be appropriate in the context of the vote. A more complete portrait of considerations may emerge if people are asked about candidates pure and simple, rather than in terms of reasons to vote for or against. For one thing, people might be more willing to express ambiguity and ambivalence in a more open-ended context. In addition, a less-directed question may allow people to offer considerations that might be part of the overall construct but that might not be considered "good" reasons to vote for or against a candidate.

To get the full range of considerations that people bring to bear, we asked our interviewees, "How would you describe the candidates?" The open format of the question aims at getting all kinds of considerations, political and nonpolitical, that our interviewees would have about candidates, without introducing any pressure to rationalize the consideration as a "reason to vote." In our analysis of what people said about the candidates, we categorized any mention of the candidate as a consideration. The considerations were coded in terms of: the candidate referred to, the kind of consideration, the valence (negative, neutral, or positive), and the time referent (retrospective, prospective, or neither) (see appendix F).[2]

Considerations were broken down into separate components. For example, if an interviewee criticized Bush for what she called "making too much" of Clinton's dodging the draft, this was coded as two considerations: one about Bush's campaign tactics and one about Clinton's draft dodging. Each one is a reason that might "induce an individual to decide . . . one way or the other" (Zaller 1992, 40). In this case, when the individual rebuts Bush's negative assertion about Clinton, she is bringing to bear considerations about both the candidates. Similarly, when an interviewee said that he admired Tsongas for honestly talking about the need for more nuclear power plants, he brought two considerations to bear: his assessment of Tsongas's integrity and his knowledge of Tsongas's stand on the issue.

Considerations were categorized as simply mentioning the candidate or event without inference, or as referring to the candidate's party, ideology, group affiliation (e.g., labor, the rich, the Ku Klux Klan), or issue or policy position. Considerations that referred to the candidate as a person were adapted from the Miller, Wattenberg, and Malanchuk (1986) categories to match the coding of candidate references in news and ads: integrity, reliability, ability as campaigner, ability as leader and professional experience, personality traits, empathy, personal background, and visual appearance.[3]

Considerations over Time

One way to begin is to ask the question: how many considerations of the candidates do citizens talk about over time? Figure 9.1 shows a substantial increase between the first (baseline interview) and second (primary election) waves, a holding pattern between the second and third (September) waves, and another substantial increase between the third and fourth (late October) waves. The upswing in the number of considerations between September and October suggests that people continue to accumulate information throughout the fall campaign, though there is little net gain over the summer.[4]

The average number of considerations reported per interviewee varied substantially by locale: Boston interviewees consistently averaged more considerations than Los Angeles interviewees, with Winston-Salem or Moorhead reporting the lowest average. Overall, the more stimulating the political information environment, the more considerations interviewees presented. An impressive indication of this association is the trajectory of considerations in Winston-Salem, which was both ad- and news-poor in the spring, but which saw hotly contested ad campaigns in the fall. As a result of candidate activity in the state, the average number of considerations reported by our interviewees in Winston-Salem between the primary (in May) and October almost doubled, an increase that far outstrips that in any other place.

What caused our interviewees to offer more or fewer considerations? How much of the difference between locales is the result of the political information environment, and how much of it is attributable to the characteristics of these interviewees? To answer that question, we measured the correlation between the number of considerations (logarithmically transformed to minimize outliers) from one interview to the next for each individual. We found high individual correlations between adjacent waves, but lower ones between the first and last waves.[5] The findings suggest that a significant portion of the variation comes from characteristics

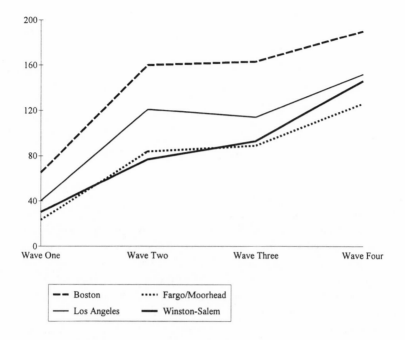

Figure 9.1   Average number of considerations of in-depth interviewees.

of the individuals. But the low correlation between the first and last waves indicates that other factors are also at work.

One explanation is that the campaign produces new information that enables people to talk more about the candidates, whatever their original level of information and engagement. To explore that possibility, we examined what characteristics predict the number of considerations an individual brings to bear (see table 9.1). Results for each point in the campaign show that the variation in number of considerations an individual uses is best explained by only three characteristics: the interviewee's self-reported political interest and the individual's attention to news, both measured at the baseline January interview, and whether the interviewee was a Bostonian.[6] This surprising importance of where people live, regardless of their individual characteristics, suggests that if a political information environment is very rich at the beginning of the campaign, it can provoke and sustain more discussion about candidates throughout the election campaign than environments that are initially sparse.

Intriguingly, the association between an individual's initial level of interest in politics and the number of considerations discussed declines in

Table 9.1 Characteristics That Predict Number of Considerations Used by In-Depth Interviewees

Characteristic	Wave One	Wave Two	Wave Three	Wave Four
Political interest	.40 (.16)	.22 (.10)	.10 (.10)	.08 (.09)
Attention to news	.40 (.15)	.30 (.09)	.22 (.09)	.16 (.08)
Boston (yes=1)	.61 (.30)	.36 (.17)	.35 (.18)	.25 (.17)
Constant	.79 (.52)	2.84 (.30)	3.50 (.31)	4.04 (.29)
Adjusted R^2	.37	.42	.24	.15

Note: Entries represent unstandardized regression coefficients with standard errors in parentheses.

the fall. This is not an artifact of using an old measure of political interest from the first wave. In the last wave, we again asked our interviewees to rate their political interest. We found that substituting the October self-report produced the same low correlation between interest and number of considerations as the January measure. These results, along with the gradual increase in the constant term in the equation, suggest that as political interest increases during the campaign, the rising tide raises all boats. The campaign enables most individuals to discuss candidates at some length, regardless of how interested they initially were in politics. The only individual characteristic that was associated with using a greater range of considerations throughout the campaign was an individual's initial attention to the news. The continuing significance of news habits underscores the relationship between the individual and the information environment. The more a person consciously paid attention to the media and the more campaign media there were, the more considerations the person brought to bear in discussing the candidates.

Which Considerations People Use

At first glance it is apparent that the nature of the discourse about candidates did not change dramatically over the course of the campaign. While there are some important shifts over time, these should be seen against a backdrop of stability. Table 9.2 shows the kinds of considerations people used at each wave of interviews. The first thing to note is that the vast majority of considerations that people used in each wave is connected to a substantive dimension. Only 8 percent of the considerations merely mention the candidates or refer to an event in which they participated, and just under 10 percent of the considerations refer to the candidate simply by a summary measure (either an explicitly emotional response or

Table 9.2 Average Percentage of Different Types of Considerations Used by In-Depth Interviewees

Consideration	Wave One	Wave Two	Wave Three	Wave Four
Nonevaluative	9.6	9.3	7.9	7.1
Event	2.7	2.4	3.6	3.6
Mention	4.4	4.1	3.6	2.6
Scandal	2.6	2.8	0.8	0.9
Policy/politics	15.7	13.8	13.8	10.6
Group/party/ideology	3.3	1.9	2.4	1.3
Policy	12.4	11.9	11.5	9.3
Competence	39.3	36.8	36.4	40.3
Ability as campaigner	19.2	26.3	23.9	27.3
Ability as leader	20.1	10.5	12.5	13.1
Character	14.7	17.8	21.6	23.8
Integrity	6.4	8.2	8.2	9.5
Empathy	4.2	4.7	7.1	8.3
Personality	3.1	3.1	3.2	3.4
Reliability	1.0	1.7	3.1	2.5
Personal qualities	10.0	9.9	10.1	9.1
Personal background	5.3	5.3	4.9	3.7
Visual appearance	4.7	4.6	5.3	5.4
Summary judgment	10.7	12.4	10.2	9.1
Emotional reaction	2.5	2.7	2.1	2.2
Evaluation	8.2	9.7	8.1	6.9

an evaluation). It is also clear, however, that very few considerations refer to party, ideology, or groups, suggesting that these have been overrated as considerations that people use in evaluating candidates. Instead, when people talk about candidates, they overwhelmingly talk about them as *people*.[7]

At every stage of the campaign, the most important dimension is the candidate's competence—either as a campaigner or as a leader. In the beginning of the campaign, people's considerations of competence are split about evenly between the candidates' abilities as campaigners and as leaders. Thereafter, as the campaign heats up, the candidates' abilities as leaders are mentioned less, and about one out of every four considerations refers to the campaign dimension. As Patterson (1980) found in the 1976 election, people tend to talk about the candidates as campaigners.

Beyond competence, a variety of considerations are discussed, mostly about character and policy. Apolitical references to the candidates as people—for example, to their personal backgrounds or their visual appearances—are much less frequent than references to personal considerations that are relevant in predicting the candidates' future behavior (just as previous studies would have predicted, e.g., Shabad and Andersen 1979; Miller et al. 1986).

Over the course of the campaign, considerations of the candidates' policies and political affiliations are cited less frequently (declining from 16 to 11 percent), while considerations of candidates' character becomes much more prominent (increasing from 15 to 24 percent). Moreover, the pattern holds for all four communities we studied. In short, there is a moderate but substantial shift in emphasis as the campaign advances: people talk less about policy and more about character.

This picture of aggregate stability may cover considerable individual variation, of course. How do particular individuals talk about candidates as the campaign proceeds? On one hand, one might expect that if the "rationalization" school is correct, people would not be consistent at all but would either invent random post hoc reasons or refer to whatever was the most prominent theme circulating in the media at that time. Alternatively, as Miller et al. (1986) and Lau (1989) claim, people could consistently apply particular considerations to candidates, whatever the stage of the campaign or whatever the current pattern of information. Following the constructionist model, however, we expect *both* effects— that citizens would be relatively consistent in bringing to bear particular considerations over time, but that they would not be immune to the discourses of the candidates and the media.

To investigate this possibility more closely, we concentrated on the three most frequently cited (and theoretically important) kinds of considerations: a candidate's policy positions, ability as a leader, and ability as a campaigner. In addition, we grouped integrity, reliability, personality traits, and empathy under one rubric entitled "character," given that these theoretically cohere and were mentioned too infrequently to examine separately. We did the same for personal background and visual appearance, combining them into Miller et al.'s (1986) category of "personal qualities." In order to control for loquacity (and remove the spurious association produced by the fact that some people talk more than others), the results are reported as percentages of the total number of considerations.

Table 9.3 indicates the correlations between the mention of a particular kind of consideration in one interview and in the next. As one can readily see, the panel was quite consistent in its use of particular considerations (with the one exception of "ability as leader," which showed no significant correlation from the first to the last interviews). In general, the results support the consistency hypothesis, that people who used one type

Table 9.3 Consistency in Using Considerations

Consideration	Wave 1–2	Wave 2–3	Wave 3–4	Wave 1–4
Policy	.49****	.31***	.54****	.21*
Character	.51****	.62****	.51****	.32**
Ability as leader	.50****	.43****	.39***	.18
Ability as campaigner	.53****	.34***	.39***	.26**
Personal qualities	.20	.45****	.33**	.23*

*$p < .10$ (all two-tailed).   **$p < .05$.   ***$p < .01$.   ****$p < .001$.

Note: Coefficients are Pearson's r between the percentages of considerations used in a given category from one wave to the next by each interviewee. $N = 48$.

of consideration about a candidate at the beginning of the campaign continue to use it at the end.

This consistent use of considerations does not arise simply because some sorts of people are more prone to use one kind of consideration than another. If it were the case, for example, that more-educated people used policy considerations more often than less-educated people, the results in table 9.3 could merely reflect a demographic difference rather than individual consistency. But, in fact, demographic and political characteristics of the interviewees generally fail to predict which considerations they emphasize from one wave to another.[8] Considerations are apparently available to and used by a wide range of people, who, having once found a way to gauge the political world, tend to rely consistently on the same set of considerations over time.

What about the valence and time frame of the considerations? We initially hypothesized that considerations would become more polarized over the course of the campaign (with increases in both negative and positive comments). Between the baseline and last interviews, people tended to speak about the candidates, on average, somewhat less neutrally and somewhat more negatively, but not more positively (see fig. 9.2). While the tone of considerations does suggest that modern presidential campaigns make citizens more negative about the candidates, the shift is not remarkable.

More surprising is how rarely people explicitly avail themselves of retrospective or prospective references. In every wave, over 80 percent of the considerations refer to the present or the very recent past of the campaign (see fig. 9.3). While it may be that present assessments are derived from unspoken information from the past (e.g., skepticism about Bush's honesty based on his breaking his "no new taxes" pledge the previous year),

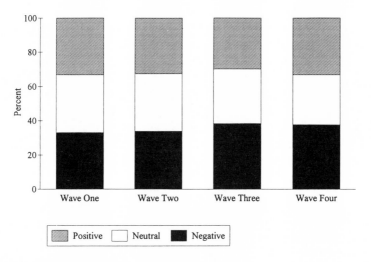

Figure 9.2   Tone of considerations of in-depth interviewees.

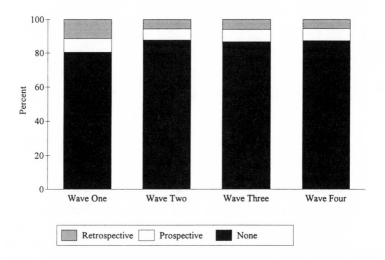

Figure 9.3   Time frame of considerations of in-depth interviewees.

it is still striking that individuals talk about the campaign so much in the present tense.

We had hypothesized that interviewees would begin by mentioning more retrospective considerations at the beginning of the campaign, when there would be little information available except the past, and would gravitate toward more prospective considerations of the candidates as the campaign advanced, but that expectation was only partially met. While the average percentages of retrospective considerations plummeted between the baseline and primary interviews, there was no counterbalancing rise in prospective considerations; instead, as time went on, the public's campaign discourse became more focused on the here and now rather than on the future.

This result is puzzling given the view that an election campaign involving an incumbent is often seen as a referendum on previous performance. Indeed, some interviewees did talk about the benefit of relying on the record, but many others expressed concern about extrapolating from the past. From these data, it appears that retrospective voting is not nearly as simple as some scholars believe. For one thing, people tend to be uncomfortable with an up-or-down vote on the incumbent. Instead, they must satisfy themselves that the other candidate is an acceptable alternative. The only exceptions to this among our interviewees were those who saw the situation as so dire that any option would be preferable; those individuals were generally strong, liberal Democrats (mostly African Americans), who took an early anybody-but-Bush approach. The only question for such voters at the primary is, who will be the strongest candidate? Carlton said before the North Carolina primary, "I think the last time we talked, we talked about what we could possibly do to get Bush out of office and right now it's Clinton." Likewise, at the primary interview, Diane viewed both Perot and Clinton as acceptable choices and concluded (in a sentiment she reechoed in October), "I'm just looking for changes, something different and anyone besides Bush is going to give me that."

But relying on retrospective judgments is problematic if there is no credible alternative to the disliked incumbent. Paul, in January, said: "None of the Democratic candidates have really impressed me that much. Right now, if I had to vote today, I would probably vote for George Bush. Because I really haven't seen anything that seemed better. But, like I said, I think he has a dismal record in domestic affairs." Vince was still torn in October because he could not come up with a credible alternative to Bush:

> I think that in all reality Bush should be there. However I feel that the four years tell me he shouldn't and my vote should go for Clinton. . . . I'm still confused because I know what I know. It isn't a whole bunch but I know that Clinton really hasn't got much of a positive record. He doesn't have a bad record but he hasn't done anything outstanding. But then again I look at Bush

who I say he looks like he should be president, but where have
we gone in the time that he's been here? If one of the questions
for you is "Where am I?" I'd have to tell you that I'm confused
and still waiting to see.

For our interview panel, retrospective assessments of the incumbent
were sometimes cushioned by a sense that some matters were beyond his
control. Sandra, in January, said she planned on being attentive to the
campaign:

> . . . cause right now, I don't feel like, I don't feel like it's all
> Bush's fault. And I just don't feel like another person can go in
> and move in the White House and take up where Bush left off
> and do any more better than he's done. Maybe they can, but I
> just can't foresee it.

The discounting of retrospective judgements occurred most frequently
among Bush supporters in January, who claimed that the poor economy
was not totally attributable to his actions. Eddy's assessment of Bush took
into account the problems he had to face:

> He seems to be on top of things. He hasn't done everything he
> said but he has done everything he can with his power I think.
> Of course this whole thing with Iran and Iraq and stuff is really
> probably going to make him look good. I think he's done a
> good job with what he's had to work with. . . . I mean he was
> given the country and there was a lot of people out of work, a
> lot of homelessness, and AIDS was happening, that still is, but
> he was given the country in somewhat of a bad time and it
> hasn't gotten any worse.

Some individuals accounted for faults in the president's performance by
acknowledging the competing demands of the office. Herb noted in a September interview:

> Well George can do a lot better. His foreign policy's all right.
> He probably should've taken a little more care with domestic
> policies and a lot of domestic issues in the last three and a half
> years. But he had a decision to make.

The link between retrospective and prospective assessments is also
troubling for a number of people. What a politician has done in the past
is deemed an imperfect gauge of what is going to happen in the future.
Luke put it this way:

It always seems like the person who has been in office has done a crappy job and the person coming up is always going to do a better job. Which one do you want to vote for? I know what he's done and I know what he's going to keep doing. I don't know what this guy's going to do. You know? It could be the type of thing like you don't know what you have until it's gone. He could've been doing a bad job but this new guy could do even worse.

The Logic of Personal Considerations

Previous studies have shown that voters' decision making is powerfully linked to their assessments of the candidates as persons, rather than to political considerations such as party, policy, or ideology. The same is true of our findings. Moreover, in their descriptions of the campaigns, our interviewees generally revealed an understanding of electoral choice that stresses a personal assessment as fundamental. As Eddy explained in January, "The people vote for the individual they feel most comfortable with and that's it."

Some of this emphasis on personal characteristics undoubtedly reflects people's ability to make an impressionistic "snap judgment" when seeing candidates in the news or in ads. Cathryn gave no reasons to back up her generalization in May: "I think that Clinton may make a good president. Certain other candidates that I see on TV, I will say I don't think they'll make a good president or they don't seem to be president material. But I can picture Clinton as being president." In January, Sandra, having said that all candidates engaged in mudslinging, concluded that all one can do is rely on impressions: "I was going by the tone of their voice. The look on their face when they are doing this mudslinging. Because you can look sometimes on somebody's face and tell whether they're telling the truth or not."

This snap judgment can, however, reflect political concern and choices in and of itself. Kelly, who generally had little knowledge and did not pay much attention to the campaign, provided an intriguing example of a "first impression" in her vague recollection of an early Kerrey ad ("somebody walking across what I think is a hockey rink"). Although she had no other memory of the ad—saying, "I don't even remember exactly what he was saying. I was helping my brother out at the time"—her political gut reaction tied in with her previous critique of negative campaigning: "All I know is I pick up feelings rather than the words and it was very— he seemed very negative and very angry about it. I don't think he was trying to push a positive 'what can we do to help it' but 'this is what has happened.' It didn't impress me at all so I didn't pay attention."

While conventional wisdom might suggest that the public's preference for personal assessments represents, at best, an unsophisticated shortcut to managing costly information and, at worst, a cop-out allowing a choice between candidates on the basis of irrelevant feelings about them as persons, it is by no means clear that personal considerations are so lazy, unsophisticated, and apolitical. Indeed, Campbell, Gurin, and Miller pointed out that people who relied more heavily on what they termed "candidate orientation"—"the structuring of political events in terms of a personal attraction to the major personalities involved" (1954, 136)— were actually *more* politically participatory, even after controlling for education. More recent work, such as Glass (1985) and Smith (1989), found that those who were more educated and/or more knowledgeable about politics were also likely to give more responses to the like/dislike questions in all categories and actually to have a higher percentage of responses that referred to candidates' personal qualities.[9]

Ample evidence reveals that, rather than using personal characteristics of candidates as cheap and easy information, our interviewees deemed personal considerations as good a predictor as one could find for what the candidate would do once elected. The trouble is that the campaign involves so much information about the candidates' personal qualities— for example, allegations of marital infidelity, actions in youth, moments of personal growth, health record—that it is difficult for people to know what is *not* relevant information, particularly when there is so much news about it. Far from mindlessly absorbing the latest gossip, interviewees indicated that they had to decide whether what they heard was or should be relevant to their political decision.

For example, Lars in an April interview, said he liked Tsongas but was concerned about news reports on his health: "The man sure has many, many good ideas and many things like that . . . his health could be another problem. I, I think someone I talked to was mentioning that he had cancer at one time, which should not disqualify him, but we're talking about four years here." In September Rose remarked on the ethical problems of some of Bush's children, and she wondered what that indicated about the candidate. She ultimately concluded that this news reflected on Bush's parenting ability and, by extension, his capacity as president:

> I know he's not responsible for his adult children but I wonder
> where he went wrong that he brought up adult children to do
> what they have done and they cost the government a lot of

money and they made big money at our expense. I think there's
something wrong when your kids want to do that. His character defects are coming out in the next generation even though I
do feel that as a parent you can't be totally responsible. But
since he's had more than one do it, it doesn't seem like a fluke
any more. Something's not kosher.

At other times, particular personal characteristics may be understood
as relevant to the circumstances that presidents may face. Sara, in January, noted:

I don't know this Bill Clinton guy. But, he seems like maybe a
good Democratic candidate. But, he acts like he's a little too
quick to respond, maybe. Kinda, half-cocked. . . . Like he
would easily rush off and not really take in all that was to be
considered. Like he would be kind of fast, you know. He looks
like—I don't know—he just ends up as an irritable picture to
me. I don't know maybe it's the way he moves his hands when
you watch him on TV or something. . . . He kinda moves, he
kinda moves fast. He kinda acts like he gets real mad easily.

Luke said, in March:

Their personalities are coming to light, like when you see Clinton can get upset. He's easily angered. I wouldn't want somebody who's holding their finger on a nuclear bomb to be able to
be that easily angered and then blow me to kingdom come by
pushing that button.

While the voters may then respond with "gut feelings" about the candidates, these rarely evoked the candidate as someone they would like to
have as a friend, so much as they referred to the candidate's professional
qualifications.

As Rahn et al. (1990) point out, individuals routinely assess people in
their professional capacities when they interact with physicians, lawyers,
professors, and the like. Although they may evaluate professionals as
people, the kinds of evidence they use may be quite different from the
kinds they use to choose a friend or a lover. Likewise, citizens distinguish
between the candidates as persons and as political actors. For example,
Herb rejected an interviewer's question about Clinton "How would you
describe him as a person?" He retorted: "I don't know him as a person.
But as a candidate I don't see him answering questions." Linda made a
similar distinction:

Character is important, but it doesn't hold a lot of weight. You know, what you did before, not character, meaning personal character, but professional character—I think that's very important. Personal character—if he and Hillary are having problems, well, it ain't different from anybody else.

Interconnecting Considerations, Or Using Issue Stances to Define Character (and Other Forms of Popular Inference)

One of the most striking conclusions that one takes away from the in-depth interviews is that it is impossible to categorize the individuals in our panel as party voters, issue voters, personal voters, and so forth. Instead, individuals have a wide range (if not always a large amount) of information about the candidates, which they try to integrate into a meaningful whole.

Considerations are interconnected in part because people would like to have a candidate that satisfies them on a number of different dimensions. In October, when Mike answered the interviewer's question "What's most important to you when you're making up your mind about for whom to vote as president?" a jumble of competing considerations emerged:

Lately I'd say character; character and do they agree with my ideals? Not that my ideas have to be the right way but it's my vote, do I feel comfortable in them? Do I feel they represent me? That's what it is. Do they represent my views?

Rather than choosing among competing considerations, people infer one aspect of a candidate from another. Issue stands and campaign events become opportunities to discern what the candidate is like as a person; in turn, information about personal background or candidate character may be used to deduce an issue position or an approach to the presidency.

Even when faced with news that focuses disproportionately on the campaign process, citizens may be able to use the day-to-day events as a way to make generalizations about the candidates' political capabilities and future performances. Many interviewees used a candidate's ability to run a campaign or his personal life as an analogy for his ability to be president. In January, Tom gave a very long explanation of what he looked for when deciding how to vote. Values similar to his own, willingness to compromise, ability to build a power base, and leadership qualities were key and could be seen in:

The way a person can organize a campaign makes a difference. I mean, that gives you an idea of what kind of person [he is].

> It's like waging a war of some sort. You've got to check out
> your competition, you've got to put together some kind of a
> plan as to how you're going to get known and make people
> think you're the best candidate. So, if you can wage a successful
> campaign when you run for election, I think that's a positive
> sign that you've got leadership capabilities.

Cora identified candidates' morality as important to her assessment of presidential potential:

> Well, I look for morals. I'm that age, you know. I think, if you
> can't, if a wife can't trust 'em, or, if we can't trust 'em person-
> ally, how can, ah, when he gets so big into the government and
> has a lot of power, how can you trust him then?

Cathryn, a strong Clinton supporter, used one incident to evoke Bush as being too high and mighty:

> Cathryn: President Bush was supposed to visit Greensboro
> [in September], but he didn't come because it was raining; so he
> didn't stop. So that should go over real big. . . . They're going to
> say, "Hm! He didn't even care enough to get off the plane in the
> rain to see us and make his visit after he done tell everyone he
> was coming."
> Interviewer: How do you feel about that?
> Cathryn: I feel about the same way. I mean he's too good to
> get off the plane in the rain to visit the people that helped, that
> encouraged their vote towards him. Hey, that's supposed to be
> the president of the United States.

And in May, Joseph viewed Clinton's fighting scandal news as a sign not only of effective campaigning but of seriousness of purpose:

> You can't hold that against a man the rest of his life. Everybody
> makes mistakes. They keep trying to dig up and throw some
> mud at him and he keeps on rolling. So you have to say he's got
> a lot of grit in his craw right there, you know.

In other words, campaign events are not understood exclusively in terms of what they say about the candidates' skills at campaigning, al-though that aspect is, as we have noted, the one most commonly dis-cussed. What a candidate does as a campaigner is also used to infer what the candidate is like as a person, and then as a potential president. Clin-ton's angry explosion on hearing the (false) news that Jesse Jackson had endorsed Jerry Brown thus can be transmuted into an indicator that he is trigger-happy; Buchanan's suggestion that Bush withdraw from the race is a sign of his being "very arrogant, very pompous and self-centered" (Kelly in March).

What is even more intriguing is how issue stances become opportunities to examine candidates' priorities and characters. The issue stand itself may be less important than what it says about the qualities of the candidate, which may, in turn, be a more proximate gauge to voting. Saul, who fell toward the high ends of interest, attention, and education, provided an example in a March interview of on-line processing. The candidate's position was less important to him than the fact that taking a stand demonstrated the candidate's willingness to grapple with the issues and provide specific remedies. Saul explained:

> I was happy to find in one article in the *Globe* that they said that Tsongas was clarifying two points of his economic policy. At the moment I can't remember exactly what they were but taking a look at it, it was like details coming out. I said, oh, yes, okay, I can accept that. That made me more supportive of Tsongas because it was not a generality, it was something more specific.

Similar to on-line judgment, when candidates discuss salient issues people get a simultaneous sense of the priority the candidate gives to that issue and what the candidate is like as a person.

Diane put it this way in an October interview in describing how she made up her mind to vote:

> What's most important to me is do they want to change or make a difference in the things that I think we need to change or make a difference in. Are they sincere in what they're saying? You can tell it by—I listen to what they're saying and the way they're saying it and the way they interact with people or tackle the question or issue head on. I just have to feel that you're sincere about what it is you're saying. I can feel something when you're talking and when you're talking about the issues that I think are important or that I would like to see improved on or changed.

What appears to be central to the evaluation of a candidate is the commitment made to a particular problem. The willingness to propose solutions to problems says something about a candidate's seriousness of purpose and ability as a leader.

Considering information, and finding a way to connect it with other information, is important for citizens not merely because it helps them in the individual task of deciding how to vote, but also because it enables them to participate as members of the public in the social construction of the campaign. How these predispositions match what the candidates and the news media say is our next subject.

From Considerations to Preferences to Choices

Constructing the Candidates: Case Studies

In order to better understand how people use considerations in reaching a voting decision, we examine how two individuals resolved conflicting assessments of the two major party candidates, Clinton and Bush. These examples illustrate the dynamic process of weighing and reweighing of considerations over the course of the campaign. In both cases two major considerations came into play, and the ultimate decision hinged on which was given priority. Both cases illustrate the importance of character in ascribing issue positions, and the importance of issues in inferring character.

In the case of John, an unemployed Vietnam veteran in Boston, the two criteria were Bush's past record on the economy and Clinton's draft record. John's initial fury at Bush for the state of the economy in the first wave, and his admiration for Clinton based on what he saw as a resemblance to President Kennedy, was thrown into confusion once he found out about Clinton's attempts to avoid the draft during the Vietnam war. His second interview, just prior to the Massachusetts primary, was filled with contradictory statements about Clinton and his chief rival at the time, Paul Tsongas. By the end of the interview he remarked that he felt betrayed by Clinton and was ready to sit out the fall election should Clinton be nominated. By the fall, however, John had returned to the Clinton camp. He reported that the state of the economy had convinced him that Bush had to be defeated, that he'd decided Perot was not a man of the people, and that he had talked to his fellow Vietnam veterans to establish that Clinton had made a principled choice in not participating in the war. Indeed, John's attempts to rethink the contest between Bush and Clinton even led him to question not only Dan Quayle's ambiguous history with the armed forces during the Vietnam war, but even Bush's record in the Second World War (Bush is a decorated veteran). In other words, the to-and-fro movement of John's voting preferences consisted of how much weight he was willing to put on Bush's management of the economy versus Clinton's evasion of the Vietnam draft. When he finally gave priority to the economy, he also reevaluated the character of the two candidates, casting aspersions on Bush's military record and reassessing Clinton's reasons for sitting out the war.

In the case of Lillian in Winston-Salem, the two criteria followed presidential prototypes: was the candidate moral, and was the candidate decisive? She began by noting during the January baseline interview that she had considerable ambivalence about Bush's past performance:

> I think that President Bush has done a real good job considering the drawbacks, and the things that he's had to, to work with. And there again, I can't elaborate, but sometimes I think that maybe things can be handled a little bit differently, on some of the issues that come up.

But this ambivalence was balanced by her strong Christian beliefs and her admiration for Bush as a "family man" and "one of the most moral presidents we've had."

Lillian reinforced this moral point of view in May. Although she then presumed that Clinton had committed the "hanky-panky" of which he had been accused, she downplayed it as a central criterion and noted that she was shifting her attention to another concern, that of active leadership, where she viewed Clinton more positively:

> As far as being honest I think he [Bush] is. I think he's a moral person and this means a lot to me. But there again, everybody can be forgiven and I'm becoming more impressed with aggressiveness and the determination to get a job done and not just saying I'm going to do this, but to follow up. I think Clinton has proved that he can do that during the years that he was governor.

By late September, the moral concern was still very important, with Lillian referring to Clinton as a "playboy type" and fretting over his draft record. But in addition to seeing Clinton more favorably when she viewed him through the prism of action, she now found Bush to be wanting on that dimension:

> I don't care for his attitude sometimes in that he'll veto things and sometimes I wonder if he does it out of spite because he can't think of anything else. Maybe he vetoes this one because they didn't pass that one. And I think that it's like the time he said, "No, no, no, read my lips," you know. And I still haven't

gotten over that. I think that's one of the most childish things I
have ever seen a grown man do. And I saw that stage and it just
turned me completely off.

Consequently, toward the end of the interview, she reported:

I'm getting concerned because I haven't made up my mind. I'm
hoping too to hear or see something that will tell me which way
I want to go. And so I've never been one to vote for the heck of
voting. I have to be convinced that—I mean I just won't vote if
I'm not convinced I'm doing the right thing.

Interviewer: So you're waiting for something that will help
you here?

Lillian: Something positive. At this point I haven't had anything to distinguish between the two that really sways me one
way or the other. They're running about neck and neck.

This balance between morality and action persisted in her late October
interview, just before the election:

Personally I'm about to decide to quit trying to rationalize on
what they're promising in my choice. I still think Bush is a good
man. He's a good family man and I think he's more moral than
Clinton. But I'm about to go past personal judgment and analyze the overall situation. I think too that Bush, bless his heart,
he hasn't done for us in the past four years and four more years
is all he can have to do anything. While I don't think he'll get in
there and sit down and do nothing I feel like he knows that if
he doesn't accomplish even what he's promised there's nothing
we can do about it. At the end of four years he's just out. If we
did give Clinton a chance to prove then he's at least going to get
in there and work hard for the four years hoping that he can
get in four more years. I'm leaning just a little bit more to forgetting the personal and realizing what's going to be best for
the country.

That last sentence proved to be crucial to her support of Clinton. In the
end, Lillian employed a standard of professional character in deciding
how to vote. Her decision process illustrated the logic of considerations
that citizens use to make voting decisions.

Weighing Considerations and the Vote

Looking across the panel of 48 interviewees, we explored how people
used considerations in making vote choices. We constructed favorability

scores for each candidate by subtracting the number of negative considerations an individual mentioned about a candidate from the number of
positive considerations. These scores were broken down by the kinds of
considerations people used. The candidate scores show, first, how consistently the panel applied considerations to candidates, second, how interconnected the considerations became over time, and last, how well the
consideration scores predicted the vote choice reported right before the
election.

Table 9.4 reports correlations of the candidate favorability scores on
different dimensions across the four waves of interviews. The table shows
how consistently people used particular kinds of considerations about a
candidate from one wave of interviews to the next. Beginning with Bush,
it is startling how little shift there was over time. In particular, the correlations between the first interview wave and last wave indicate that, by and
large, those people who viewed Bush favorably or unfavorably on the basis of character and leadership at the start of the campaign viewed him
the same way at the end. There was, however, less consistency in judgments about Bush in terms of policy, ability as a campaigner, or his personal qualities.

This contrasts sharply with Clinton, who was less well known at the
outset of the campaign. The panelists' vague assessments of Clinton at
the baseline interview in January did not hold over to the second interview, just before the primary. From the second interview through the fall,
however, assessments of Clinton on the basis of policy and character were
consistent, especially between our two fall interviews. By contrast, assessments of Clinton on the basis of his personal qualities and his abilities as
a campaigner were considerably less constant.

Finally, the ins and outs of the Perot campaign are reflected in the results, with no positive correlations on any consideration between waves
two and three (when the candidate dropped out and then into the campaign). In fact, the assessments of Perot's ability as a campaigner between
the primary and early fall waves, and between the two fall interviews,
were negatively correlated, which suggests just how topsy-turvy the assessments of Perot were. In spite of the volatility of assessments of Perot
over the summer, Perot's scores on policy and ability as leader are significantly correlated between the primary and last waves of interviews. The
results show that once Perot was definitively back in the race, people
tended to return to the assessments they had made in the spring rather
than start from scratch.

These various considerations of the candidates became more interconnected over the course of the campaign.[10] A factor analysis of the consid-

Table 9.4 Consistency in Valence of Considerations by Candidate

Candidate	Wave 1–2	Wave 2–3	Wave 3–4	Wave 1–4	Wave 2–4
Bush					
Policy	.15	.59****	.37***	.06	.36***
Character	.24*	.38***	.49****	.56****	.36***
Ability as leader	.65****	.40***	.69****	.50****	.48****
Ability as campaigner	.27**	.23*	.45****	−.06	.34***
Personal qualities	.39***	.37**	−.03	.15	.25
All considerations	.64****	.50****	.71****	.50****	.60****
Clinton					
Policy	.04	.27**	.49****	.08	.27**
Character	.01	.40***	.57****	−.02	.32**
Ability as leader	.01	.42***	.33**	.38***	.04
Ability as campaigner	.00	−.06	.09	−.05	.07
Personal qualities	−.23*	.09	.34**	−.01	.16
All considerations	−.00	.50****	.50****	.08	.47****
Perot					
Policy		.00	.07		.19*
Character		.04	.07		.16
Ability as leader		−.16	.28**		.44****
Ability as campaigner		−.25**	−.45****		.18
Personal qualities		−.10	.43****		−.00
All considerations		−.00	.28**		.23*

$*p < .10$ (all two-tailed). $**p < .05$. $***p < .01$. $****p < .001$.

Note: Coefficients are Pearson's r between each interviewee's favorability indices within a given category for each candidate from one wave to the next. Favorability indices were computed by subtracting the number of negative considerations in a particular category from the number of positive considerations in that same category and dividing by the total number of considerations in order to control for loquacity. $N = 48$.

erations used for each candidate at each stage of the campaign presents an intriguing pattern (see table 9.5). With Bush, one can see that these favorability indices are brought increasingly into line over the four waves. With Clinton and Perot, however, the pattern is curvilinear, beginning with a single factor at the initial interview (the first wave for Clinton and the second wave for Perot) but then diminishing at the next wave and only returning to that high level of interconnection late in the campaign. The analysis suggests that in the early stages of the campaign, assessments of new candidates may be consistent across a variety of considerations simply because people do not know very much. As the campaign proceeds, however, people accumulate more information, to the point that

Table 9.5 Convergence of Favorability Scores

Wave	Bush	Clinton	Perot
1	31.5	47.9	N/A
2	39.0	33.9	40.9
3	41.9	48.0	34.6
4	47.0	44.6	39.4

Note: This table reports the percentage of variance explained by the first factor in a vari-max rotated factor analysis performed on the favorability indices for each candidate on: policy, character, leadership, ability as campaigner, and personal qualities.

the assessments made by different considerations are less consonant and are only gradually reconciled as the citizens approach the voting decision in the fall.

Much of this move toward consistency is accomplished in the case of Bush and Clinton by bringing various considerations in line with party identification in the final wave. Party identification was significantly correlated with favorability toward Bush on character and policy only in the last two waves and with favorability toward Bush on personal qualities and with favorability toward Clinton on policy, leadership, and character only in the last wave ($p < .05$).[11] Prior to the fall, the only time that party identification correlated with favorability was for Bush's ability as a leader and his overall assessment. (None of the favorability indices in any wave for Perot were significantly associated with party identification.) Our analysis shows that party identification is important, not so much at the beginning as a guide to unknown territory, but at the end of the campaign when an individual is getting ready to vote.

Turning now to the vote, do these considerations predict electoral choice? The easy answer is yes. Interestingly, however, our panelists often mentioned considerations at variance with their candidate preferences. For example, 47 percent of our Bush voters expressed considerations favorable to Perot on leadership and campaigning, 40 percent of Bush voters talked favorably about Clinton as a campaigner, 36 percent of Clinton voters praised Perot on policy, and 33 percent of Bush voters made negative remarks about Bush's leadership.

These conclusions are reinforced by a series of logit equations reported in table 9.6.[12] Except for comments about Perot's and Clinton's personal qualities, knowing the number of positive and negative comments about each candidate along any single dimension predicts the panel's voting intentions significantly better than chance (as measured by the "model χ^2" statistics at $p < .05$). Not surprisingly, the best model for all three candi-

Table 9.6 Predicting the Candidate Vote from Consideration Difference Scores

Vote	Considerations					
	Character	Campaigner	Leader	Policy	Personal Qualities	All
Predicting vote for or against Bush						
Bush-Clinton	.18 (.08)	.10 (.07)	.20 (.12)	.53 (.22)	.20 (.19)	.07 (.03)
Bush-Perot	.20 (.08)	.10 (.08)	.14 (.10)	.02 (.14)	.29 (.19)	.07 (.04)
Model χ^2	24.74****	6.73**	14.07****	18.07****	7.72**	26.51****
Predicting vote for or against Clinton						
Clinton-Bush	.38 (.15)	.20 (.09)	.24 (.10)	.41 (.19)	.31 (.18)	.11 (.04)
Clinton-Perot	−.00 (.07)	.02 (.07)	.12 (.09)	.39 (.19)	−.19 (.17)	.03 (.03)
Model χ^2	31.46****	11.94***	13.73****	22.70****	3.99 (n.s.)	32.41****
Predicting vote for or against Perot						
Perot-Clinton	.23 (.08)	.22 (.11)	.31 (.14)	.22 (.15)	.00 (.22)	.14 (.06)
Perot-Bush	.08 (.07)	−.06 (.11)	.12 (.10)	.28 (.17)	.08 (.11)	.07 (.04)
Model χ^2	14.81****	7.16**	11.19***	8.06**	.77 (n.s.)	21.91****

$^*p < .10$ (all two-tailed). $^{**}p < .05$. $^{***}p < .01$. $^{****}p < .001$.

dates involves all of the considerations that our interviewees took into account. Yet it is striking to see how well a single dimension of considerations predicts the vote. Character alone predicted the votes for the two major party contenders, Bush and Clinton, as accurately as all of the other considerations combined. As table 9.6 indicates, some kinds of considerations, although frequently mentioned, are not so influential on the vote. The less-influential dimensions include the candidates' personal backgrounds and their abilities as campaigners. While citizens may pay a good deal of attention to these things, they apparently feel less discomfort at noticing discrepancies between their choice of candidate and their assessments of him as a campaigner or of his personal qualities. What seems to be most closely connected to the vote is candidates' character, policy positions, and leadership ability. In other words, citizens seem to pay attention to matters they consider to be politically relevant and work toward consistency between their assessments on those dimensions and their vote choice.

The importance of character is underscored by table 9.7, which shows the percentage of cases correctly predicted by each equation.[13] Decisions on Bush (pro and con) were best predicted by leadership, followed by policy and character; decisions on Clinton by character, followed by policy; and decisions on Perot by character more than anything else. In short, the most vital kind of consideration refers to the candidates' character—assessments of their integrity, reliability, personality traits, and/or empa-

Table 9.7 Percentage of Correctly Predicted Candidate Votes Based on Considerations

Consideration	For Bush	For Clinton	For Perot	Against Bush	Against Clinton	Against Perot
By chance alone	31	52	17	69	48	83
Ability as campaigner	33	68	25	91	83	98
Ability as leader	60	72	25	88	70	98
Policy	53	80	25	91	74	100
Personal qualities	33	80	0	91	43	100
Character	53	84	38	94	78	98
All considerations	67	88	50	91	87	100

thy. The most weighty consideration is character, but it is important to remember that character is connected to, and often inferred from, a candidate's policy positions and performance in office.

Conclusion

This chapter has explored the question "When people talk about the candidates, what do they say?" By examining a panel of 48 citizens across four waves of in-depth interviews, we have a clearer idea of how the discussion changes over the course of the election year and how the assessments that citizens made fit with their predispositions and their ultimate choices for president.

People did not have much difficulty—particularly once the campaign was at full tilt—in coming up with descriptions of the candidates. They approached their discussions of the candidates neither with cookie-cutter regularity nor with utter randomness. The results show that individuals have consistent ways of talking about candidates, but they vary their emphasis depending on the stage of the campaign.

What seems to shift most dramatically over the course of the campaign is simply how much people talk about the candidates, which increases during the nomination phase and again during the general election campaign. While those who start out talkative about the candidates tend to be among the more talkative later on as well, how much people have to say is not limited by initial interest. In fact, as political interest rises during the campaign, everyone has the resources to enter into the discourse. Likewise, the steep increase of considerations in Winston-Salem during the last month of the campaign suggests what can happen if an ad-poor, news-poor environment suddenly becomes inundated with political information.

The evidence does not support the view that candidate considerations become more polarized over the course of the campaign. Rather, when people talk about the candidates, both those they favor and those they oppose, they talk about them as persons with a mixture of positive and negative qualities, and they talk about the candidates in the here and now, not in terms of their past accomplishments or future possibilities.

What people talk about is, in part, remarkably stable at both aggregate and individual levels. At any of our four waves, for instance, the competence of the candidates was the modal consideration, although the touchstone of competence changed from their abilities as leaders prior to the campaign to their capacities as campaigners once the campaign was in high gear. Likewise, individuals tend to use similar types of considerations from one wave to the next, suggesting that these considerations are not merely post hoc rationalizations of the candidates based on whatever happens to be on the top of their heads, but are instead gauges that people return to time and again.

Within this overall portrait of stability, though, there are subtle shifts over the course of the campaign. Most notably, the talk about candidates shifts from a greater emphasis on policy at the beginning of the campaign to a greater stress on character by its end. Moreover, people's discussion of candidates' character tends to be more closely in line with their ultimate vote choice than their talk on other dimensions of considerations. Thus, assessments of character may be the bottom line for voters; they appear much more willing to voice dissonant points about their chosen candidate's ability as a campaigner or personal qualities than about that candidate's character. Finally, assessments are brought increasingly into line over time, with a boost from partisanship only by the last wave. Whether this emphasis on character reflects a response on the part of citizens to information across the campaign is difficult to say, given that, as we have noted in previous chapters, both the candidates' ads and the news meld policy concerns with messages about the candidates as persons. At the very least, candidates and the news media do little to discourage citizens from increasingly emphasizing character and may reinforce, if not instigate, that tendency.

These findings support our view of considerations as a process. Citizens during a campaign apparently feel comfortable considering new information about their candidates, including negative aspects of the candidate they prefer and positive news about the candidate they do not. Certainly, they do not approach the campaign with blank slates; yet it is impressive how willing people are to consider (if often only to rebut and reject) dissonant information, particularly at early stages of the campaign. Such considerations may be merely problematic at the beginning of the year but may later become transformed, through the constant reinforcement of the campaign, into facts that must be dealt with. A salient example from the in-depth interviews is the way early defenders of Bush, who made statements suggesting either that the economy was not so bad or that he was not responsible for the hard times, later in the campaign had to accept that Bush had not done a good job at managing the economy and had to find other reasons to support him.

This willingness to try various options and to bring them in line with previous predispositions such as partisanship late in the campaign is similar to the process sketched by Gelman and King (1993) in which voters only gradually reach what they call an "enlightened preference." But we would go further than King and Gelman in noting that if citizens run across new information that they cannot easily rebut, the new information may have a powerful impact on their assessments of and preferences for the candidates.

These results provide another piece of evidence that the capacity of the average citizen to enter into democratic deliberation has been underestimated by past research. It may well be that people rarely have an opportunity to regale a fellow citizen with a range of thoughts and observations about politics the way they held the attention of our interviewers. But that is a problem of political institutions and public space. Our findings show that ordinary citizens have the capacity to take in information, make inferences, and reach a comparative assessment of the candidates. Even if the institutions are lacking for people to deliberate collectively, individual citizens can and do deliberate over the evidence and its implications when it comes time to vote and select a president.

FOUR

A Constructionist Model of Voting

TEN

Discourse and Decision

Election research has seen cycles of optimism and pessimism, although the particular concerns have varied. Scholars have worried that election campaigns do not produce satisfying discourse because the people do not work hard enough at politics, the candidates mislead them, and the news media fail them. While this study does not contradict the weight of research about inattentive voters, strategizing politicians, or commercial media, by looking at all of the actors simultaneously it presents a different picture. We see the presidential campaign as a dynamic interaction in which each of the participants constrains and influences the others, leading to the election outcome. The interactions of the campaign, as well as who wins or loses, have important consequences for governance and for the robustness of the democratic process.

By examining the crosstalk of the campaign, this study has shown how powerfully the citizens' agenda can constrain candidate discourse, how news values constrain candidate coverage, and how candidates broke through the constraints of news to engage the citizens in new media formats. We have shown that for all of the participants in campaign discourse, the personal is political. And perhaps that is as it should be in a presidential campaign. Our study does not find the citizens to be captives of either the candidates or the journalists, nor even of their own political predispositions. They can reject or reinterpret media messages and consider alternative and even conflicting information. We found, of course, not only constraints but dependency. As citizens build constructs of the candidates, their information environment makes a difference in the range of considerations they bring to bear. The candidate attention to the locale, the resources and editorial choices of the local media outlets, the candidates' ad buys, and the citizens' news habits influence the richness of the process for better or worse. Below we detail our findings and discuss the implications for citizens, candidates, journalists, and democratic governance.

Campaigns and Citizens

Throughout this book we have seen how campaigns can provide people with an opportunity to see their own personal concerns in the context of the nation's problems. There is ample evidence that the presidential campaign informs people's vote choices and also provides occasions for participation beyond the simple act of voting. Citizens actively interpret communications, engage the attention of candidates and the media, and have opportunities to express their views in surveys, focus groups, town meetings, call-in talk shows, and even in candidate debates. To the extent that citizens believe that they can enter into the campaign discourse and that their concerns are being heard, the presidential election can be an empowering and democratic experience. But even if particular campaigns do not achieve that empowering and legitimizing effect, the campaign discourse sets priorities and expectations that have important consequences for governance.

Constructing the Candidates as Persons

Our findings triangulate evidence from surveys, focus groups, and in-depth interviews to show that voters select candidates as persons. The way voters decide substantially reflects the tendencies of all campaign communications—both news and ads—to focus attention on the personal qualities of the candidates. Our in-depth interviews and focus groups demonstrate, however, that citizens believe assessments of candidates as persons, especially their qualities of character, offer the most reliable indicators of how candidates will perform in office.

Our study of the 1992 presidential election provides persuasive evidence that assessments of candidate character were essentially political. In 1992, George Bush was deemed "out of touch," not merely because he had never seen a supermarket scanner, nor because he blithely boated off the shore at Kennebunkport, nor because he kept looking at his watch during the second debate, but because he would not admit the gravity of the recession and kept trying to steer the debate away from it. Bill Clinton, in turn, was judged caring and empathetic, not merely because he took a bus trip, nor because he hailed from "a place called Hope," but because he kept on addressing the problems that faced Americans in their everyday lives. And Ross Perot was deemed the most honest of the three, not because of his haircut, nor because he appeared on "Larry King Live," but because he talked directly to the public about a serious issue—the deficit—that the other candidates were perceived to be avoiding.

Interactions with the Political Information Environment

In our study we have been impressed by citizens' abilities to make the most of the information available to understand the political world. Our surveys, focus groups, and in-depth interviews all show that people gain information over the course of the campaign. Surveys showed that respondents were better able to identify the candidates' positions on the issues in the fall than in the spring. Focus group participants and in-depth interviewees increasingly used their own experiences and previous understandings to make sense of new information. And our interviewees in all four communities expressed more considerations about the candidates as the campaign went on.

Our evidence suggests that, at least in a presidential campaign, information is nearly omnipresent, so that people do not need to take information shortcuts. Instead, they can think about and extrapolate the implications of information readily available. As the campaign proceeds, people find new information all around them. Sometimes when they encounter new information, they note it and shrug it off. At other times, they may rebut it by referring to prior knowledge about politics or experiences from their everyday worlds. In dramatic instances, new information may require them to completely rethink the candidates and even to undertake new information searches. We saw this kind of reevaluation in the case of John, an unemployed Vietnam veteran, when he found out that his preferred candidate, Bill Clinton, had resisted the draft. Given the media environment, John did not have to look very far to find out more about Clinton and the draft.

Our examination of four very different information environments shows, however, that relative access to information is an important factor in candidate assessment. At every stage in the campaign, the interviewees with the widest range of considerations about the candidates tended to live in the area with the richest information (Boston), while interviewees who expressed fewer considerations tended to come from information-poor environments such as Winston-Salem. In a fascinating naturally occurring experiment, when Winston-Salem became a richer political information environment as a result of candidate ads and visits to North Carolina in the late fall, there was a corresponding increase in the number of considerations our interviewees brought to bear. As Huckfeldt and

Sprague (1988) would have predicted, political discussion is influenced not only by individuals' habits and preferences but also by the supply of political information. Our findings show that the ability and willingness of people to talk about the campaign and the candidates is closely linked to the richness of the political information environment, as measured simply by the amount of news and ads in the locale. Given citizens' haphazard and often inadvertent ways of encountering information, the more information available, the greater the chance it will get through.

Our investigation points out how valuable different kinds of information are to citizens. In focus groups, we compared the discussion that followed exposure to different "forms" of campaign communication. Notably, the standard format of horse-race coverage occasioned relatively lackluster discussion in our spring focus groups. By contrast, the discussion that followed a news analysis in the fall not only was more lively, but also allowed the participants to connect the larger political debate with their personal experiences. As far as ad watches were concerned, our focus group discussions made clear that people were suspicious of critiques that emphasized the candidate's strategy or the expected audience impact. But ad watches that focused on the verification of candidates' claims aroused attention and stimulated discussion of the issues. The ad watch format, however, did not completely deflect candidate messages. If the ad being critiqued contained information that resonated with their concerns, people talked about the candidates' messages just as they did after seeing an ad.

The focus group discussions also emphasize the power of the citizens' role in the interpretation of media messages. Focus groups commonly ignored or transformed rather than followed the meaning of messages to which they were exposed. By analyzing the groups' conversational exchanges, we found that discussion often moved away from the point of view of the message or moved on to other subjects. Interestingly, only the candidate interview programs (which, in reality and in our stimuli, tended to feature the challengers) generated discussion on the topic and echoed the point of view of the candidates being interviewed. Candidate interviews were also more effective in getting people to concentrate on actual words and ideas presented than either ads or news. Evidence from our in-depth interviews and surveys suggests that the Perot infomercials had a similar effect. In both cases the format's credibility seemed enhanced by an emphasis on issues that resonated with public concerns, presented with the fewest frills and least packaging.

While individuals in our focus groups and in-depth interviews actively

and variously interpreted campaign messages, the polysemy of the interpretation did not mean that there were no patterns of meaning. In fact,
our data show that the discourse of the election on the whole reflected
the relative frequency with which certain kinds of messages were accepted
or rejected. While individuals might have had idiosyncratic interpretations, people generally found some formats more credible than others (interviews, debates), some issues more resonant than others (the economy,
rather than peacetime foreign policy), and some candidates more credible
than others on certain issues (challengers can call for change more effectively than the incumbent). These overall patterns of interpretation and
dynamic interaction shaped the discourse and, ultimately, the outcome of
the election.

Lessons and Prospects

Anyone who expects performance to the standards of the *Federalist Papers* or the Lincoln-Douglas debates could not fail to be disappointed
with the discourse of recent presidential elections. The 1992 presidential
campaign was no exception. Key moments in the campaign included a
curious assortment—Clinton explaining that he did not inhale; a citizen
asking the president what the national debt meant to him personally;
Perot claiming Republican dirty tricksters were planning to sabotage his
daughter's wedding; Quayle misspelling "potato"; Stockdale wondering
in the middle of a nationally televised debate, "Who am I? What am I
doing here?"
    What made the campaign discourse more salutary than its recent pre-
decessors was *not* that it was somehow more edifying or well mannered,
but that this spectacle explicitly involved the American people as key participants.[1] During this campaign, the citizens received ample confirmation
of their potential importance and power, not only through the election
returns and the polls but also through their vividly displayed interactions
with candidates in interview programs and debates. Not surprisingly,
public opinion surveys showed that people felt themselves to be more politically effective than in previous elections—a rise that one team of scholars has suggested led directly to the increased turnout in 1992 (Rosenstone et al. 1993). What enabled 1992 to be different from its lamented
predecessor, the 1988 presidential election? We set forth our explanations
along with lessons that candidates, journalists, and the people might take
away from this campaign and this study.

Candidates

Candidates, of course, are preoccupied with one thing above all—winning the election. For them, the function of the campaign is to gain votes. Ads play an important role in getting the candidate's message across. The more resources a candidate can devote to ads, the more likely the message will be heard. Witness the surprisingly successful campaign by the wealthy independent candidate Ross Perot. Evidence in our interviews shows that the sheer repetition of ads can defeat a viewer's defenses and seep into his or her consciousness. For instance, Selma from Boston was a strong Democrat who claimed never to have listened to any Republican ads in the fall, but she was able to describe in detail three Bush ads; Sara from Winston-Salem noted that Bush's "Arkansas Record" ad had been run so many times that she was sick of it, but she also wanted to know whether it was "true."

Our findings suggest, however, that candidates do not have to be altruistic to want to mount substantive and responsive campaigns. Attention to the issues pays off. Evidence from our surveys, focus groups, and in-depth interviews confirms that successful ad campaigns integrate issue information. By "dovetailing" (Kern 1989) visual and verbal cues and integrated issue appeals with references to character, ads provoked focus group discussion that stayed on message. Less well crafted ads produced confusion and even derision. Bob Kerrey's "hockey rink" ad is a good example of a signal failure. The visuals of the candidate standing on an ice rink in front of a hockey net simply did not match his words about the balance of trade with Japan. Focus group participants and interviewees who remembered seeing the ad were generally puzzled by it. By comparison, it is surely no coincidence that the most successful ad campaigns during the primaries—Buchanan's and Clinton's, whether judged by our survey results, focus groups, or the recollections of interviewees—most effectively integrated sight and sound, issue and character. In fact, most general election ads referred to both issues and character. But ads that referred first and foremost to character were less effective simply because they seemed like mudslinging and politics-as-usual. Bush's attempts to push the message of "trust" in the fall may have increased Clinton's negatives; but the ads did not gain an advantage for Bush because they raised questions about his own integrity.

Our conclusion that effective candidate communications integrate issue and character reminds us of Richard Fenno's (1978) classic insights about how members of Congress communicate with their constituents. Fenno followed a number of legislators around their districts and concluded that their main goal was to establish and reinforce trust. But Fenno noted that in their interactions with constituents, members must talk about *something,* and they generally talk about the issues. Similarly, in an election campaign, even if candidates are fundamentally concerned with presenting themselves as persons, and even if citizens are most interested in making a personal assessment of them, candidates need to talk about the issues. Citizens then use what candidates say to infer not only what they stand for but who they are as persons.[2]

Of course, when candidates talk about issues they need not be specific. It is rational for politicians to be ambiguous, especially with heterogeneous electorates. Page's (1978) exhaustive examination of candidate communications notes how presidential candidates avoid detailed policy proposals and turn instead to broad policy areas, basic values, and consensual appeals. Although such communications may not allow anyone to predict just what a candidate will do if elected, they give people as good a sense as any of the *priorities* that a candidate may bring to the presidency.

Journalists

Journalists are in the information business. But given that the news is a business, journalists are under increasing pressure to make the product salable. In order to gain a large audience, journalists try to produce an impartial, if not objective, product. If they want audiences to watch the news every day, reporters must also find ways of presenting something timely, entertaining, or new. But the sheer necessity of cranking out a news product day in, day out leads journalists to "routinize the unexpected" (Tuchman 1973).

In the case of presidential elections, these news routines focus on the election as a game. By paying attention to who is ahead and who is behind, and what strategies each side is using to stay ahead or to catch up, journalists are assured new developments every day, something that might elude them if they reported for the umpteenth time that a candidate gave the same speech. This "game" mentality has been deplored in virtually every study of election coverage. Not surprisingly, we also find that the "horse race" is a key aspect of media coverage. In fact, the less news outlets cover the campaign, the more they emphasize the horse race; so we might even say that horse-race coverage is the sine qua non of election news. But our content analysis (which coded stories not by particular kind, but by whether they included particular content) shows that horse-race coverage does not push out issue coverage altogether. Just as candidates must talk about the issues in order to present themselves, so journalists must refer to issues when presenting news about candidates' strategies. Even when races are most seriously contested and horse-race news is at its height, there is plenty of information in the news about where the candidates stand.

But journalists might want to rethink the horse-race and strategy emphasis, not because of the scolding of some political scientists, or even because of public criticism of the media's preoccupation with scandal and trivia. Our focus groups reveal that horse-race news is neither useful nor interesting to the public. Judging from the results of our spring focus groups, horse-race news provoked little discussion, did not permit individuals to bring personal experience into their conversation, was difficult to build on as a topic for discussion, and was often perceived as biased. While horse-race news may well be helpful to citizens trying to identify the viable candidates, it is not good for much else. Our focus group participants responded quite differently to another form of news coverage: news analysis, a form represented in our study by the "American Agenda" segment on ABC News. Discussions of "American Agenda" were not only animated, but also enabled voters to bring their personal experiences into the political discussion. It is worth noting that producing such analytic stories may be cheaper for news organizations than sending reporters out on the campaign trail. By keeping reporters at home the news media could perform their tasks in ways that would save them money and produce the kind of journalism that is most desired and best used by the public.

We are somewhat cautious, however, in recommending more news analysis because our results show a significant and consistent tendency in all media for analytic, journalist-initiated stories to have a distinctly negative tone toward the candidates. It seems that journalists equate "enterprise" with "negativity." While we could easily imagine stories instigated by journalists that were positive toward candidates, this rarely occurs. We would argue that being "soft" on candidates across the board is not acceptable; neither is being invariably harsh. Evidence from our in-depth interviews and focus groups suggest that journalists' unrelieved "tough" posture diminishes their credibility and turns people off.

The negative tilt of journalist-initiated stories was one of many commonalities across the news. Our analysis amply confirmed that the coverage in 1992 was as homogeneous as Patterson's description from 1976. Candidates were covered the same way across media and modalities, although the tone across outlets in the same community often varied significantly. In particular, there was clear consensus during the primaries about who was worth covering and who was not, thereby winnowing the field. All news organizations also converged on similar narratives about the three major competitors in the fall. In the process, by sheer repetition for months at a time, the initial hunches people had about the candidates became indisputable facts. Notably, that the economy was in terrible shape and that George Bush was responsible for it might have been open to discussion, but by the end of the campaign in the face of the continuing barrage of news and candidate messages with that storyline, almost none of our interviewees, even those favorable to Bush, disputed it.

Our analysis of news indicates why candidates were stimulated to seek other venues in which to present themselves to the public. The success of the "talk show campaign" illustrates that journalists no longer have a monopoly on providing information to the American public. Some journalists quite reasonably felt threatened when politicians found a way to get around them—for example, shortly after Clinton's inauguration, UPI's Helen Thomas fumed on National Public Radio, "They feel we are expendable, and if they make an end run, they will get a better press, if you will, with the people. Eventually, they should realize the president has to be interrogated, and has to be accountable, and we're the ones to do it" ("Weekend Edition," NPR, January 24, 1993, as quoted in Cook and Ragsdale 1995).

But journalists do not have to be the *only* "ones to do it." While deceptive, ambiguous, or lightweight ads may require journalists to press candidates for more details and substance, interview programs were not deficient in that way. In fact, interviews focused on more substantive matters when ordinary people rather than journalists posed the questions, and provided longer opportunities for the candidates to explain their positions than the news. Our focus groups demonstrated that candidate interviews provoked citizens to grapple with ideas, rather than images, strategies, or personality.

As a result, the candidates' appearances on interview programs is perhaps the most salutary development of the 1992 campaign. By using an entertainment format, candidates found a way to communicate effectively to audiences they might otherwise miss and to present their views on the topics they wanted to emphasize.

Voters
The path-breaking campaign studies conducted at the University of Michigan and reported in *The American Voter* (Campbell et al. 1960) painted a bleak picture of elections as collective events, during which citizens discuss, debate, and deliberate about issues. Many scholars concluded that citizens were simply too inattentive to politics to participate much and could only make sense of the campaign through personal connection to candidates or party identification. Beyond partisanship, the possibility that people could project constrained or even consistent belief systems into the process seemed remote (Converse 1964, 1970).

There have been various attempts to revise *The American Voter*'s conclusions about the citizens' capacities to participate in democratic politics. Some scholars have raised serious questions about whether a person who has an ideologically constrained belief system is best equipped for democratic citizenship. Marcus for one, says no (1988; see also Krouse and Marcus 1984). Ideologues may not be able to enter into dialogue with anyone who does not agree with them; it is better, Marcus argues, to have a large stock of open-minded observers who will listen to debates among partisans, note the evidence, and make considered judgments. What might then strike Converse as an example of incoherence and inconsistency is instead an ability to consider more than one possibility and a willingness to listen and be persuaded. Others have found similar evidence of positive ambivalence among the American electorate.[3] Hochschild puts it this way:

> A democracy composed of consistent, tranquil, attitudinally constrained citizens is a democracy full of smug people with no incentive and perhaps no ability to think about their own circumstances. They know who they are, how things fit together—and woe betide anyone who questions or violates the standard pattern. Conversely, a democracy composed of citizens coping with disjunction and ambivalence is full of people who question their own rightness, who may entertain alternative viewpoints, and who, given the right questions, are more driven to resolve problems than ignore them. (1993, 206)

We are impressed with the range of considerations people bring to bear about candidates.[4] People seem to feel no discomfort about wandering and wondering. They wander through the information they run across, sometimes far from where they usually look, including the allegations and charges of opposing camps. And they wonder what its implications might be for their assessments of the candidates and the campaign. Only toward the end of the campaign do people use their initial predispositions—notably, partisanship—to help them craft their considerations into overall assessments of the candidates. The process of consideration that we observed speaks to the capacity of citizens to deliberate at least individually, if not collectively.

Governance
There are several indicators that tell us how well a campaign has succeeded as a democratic instrument: whether the candidates and the news media structured the debate so as to address the issues the people wanted

discussed; the amount of information and number of considerations the people take into account in their vote choices; and the degree of satisfaction that the people have with the campaign and the candidates. By those indicators, the 1992 campaign was something of a surprising success. But what did the campaign mean for governance? What mandate did the campaign convey to the new president?

On the surface, our findings seem to show that the campaign mandate is very personal. But our investigation demonstrates that personal assessments of a candidate's character invoke relevant political qualities. The public imputes good character in part to candidates who share their values, priorities, and concerns. Based on the campaign, it was reasonable for the public to expect in Bill Clinton a president who would focus on the economy, be accessible to the people, and empathize with their concerns. When Clinton began his presidency with attention to other issues, the public may have had good reason to register disappointment. As the new president's approval ratings fell, President Clinton learned what George Bush had before him, that campaigns matter. Candidates can be held accountable not only for the most publicized and generalized commitments—"read my lips"—but also for the implicit style of leadership that they conveyed during the campaign. The candidate's campaign construct itself, then, is part of the expectation of governance.

The subsequent trials and tribulations of the victorious candidate in 1992 (see Kumar 1995) should not discourage efforts to make future campaigns meet or exceed the standards of accessible information, high interest, and new popular involvement set in this election. Admittedly, that is no easy task. Election climates and candidates vary. The public will not always be galvanized by a single overriding issue that can set the boundaries of debate. Candidates may not want to expose themselves to the vagaries of television interviews or may face fewer liabilities in "going negative." In the future, journalists may not wish to yield pride of place to the public or less professional media personalities. But if elites trivialize the public's role, they do so at their peril. The downward slide of faith in government, political leadership, and journalism threatens the democratic process itself. The lesson of the 1992 campaign, and this study, is that together citizens, candidates, and the media have the capacity to engage in useful and substantive crosstalk and build mutual confidence in the democratic process.

Appendix A

Table A.1 Characteristics of In-Depth Interviews

Pseudonym	Locale[a]	Age	Race[b]	Education	Political Interest	PID[c]	Source	1988 Vote
Caren	LA	18–34	Wh	College	Some	R	Local TV	Bush
Carlton	W-S	35–54	A-A	College	A lot	D	Newspaper	Dukakis
Cathryn	W-S	35–54	A-A	HS	Some	D	Local TV	Dukakis
Cora	Moor	55+	Wh	Postgrad	Some	I	Newspaper	Bush
Diane	W-S	18–34	A-A	College	None	D	Local TV	Dukakis
Donald	Moor	55+	Wh	Some college	Not much	D	Local TV	Dukakis
Eddy	Bos	18–34	Wh	HS	Not much	D	Radio	Bush
Edith	Moor	55+	Wh	Some college	None	I	Newspaper	Bush
Frank	LA	35–54	Wh	Some college	Some	I	Local TV	Dukakis
Gary	LA	35–54	Wh	Some college	Some	R	Newspaper	Bush
Gloria	Bos	55+	Wh	Some college	Some	I	Newspaper	Bush
Grace	Moor	35–54	Wh	Some college	Not much	I	Local TV	Dukakis
Herb	Bos	55+	Wh	Postgrad	A lot	D	Newspaper	Bush
Ingrid	Moor	35–54	Wh	Postgrad	A lot	D	Networks	Dukakis
J.D.	W-S	55+	Wh	HS	Some	R	Newspaper	Bush
Jane	Moor	35–54	Wh	Postgrad	Some	R	Newspaper	Bush
Jim	Moor	35–54	Wh	Some college	Not much	R	Radio	Bush
John	Bos	35–54	Wh	HS	A lot	D	Networks	Neither
Jorge	LA	18–34	Lat	Some college	A lot	I	Local TV	Bush
Joseph	W-S	35–54	Wh	Some college	Not much	D	Radio	Bush
Kelly	Bos	18–34	Wh	Some college	Some	R	Other people	Bush
Lars	Moor	55+	Wh	Some HS	A lot	R	Local TV	Bush
Lenny	Moor	18–34	Wh	Postgrad	Not much	I	Networks	Bush
Lillian	W-S	55+	Wh	HS	Some	D	Newspaper	Bush
Linda	Bos	18–34	A-A	Postgrad	Some	D	Local TV	Dukakis
Lisa	Moor	18–34	Wh	Some college	Some	R	Local TV	Bush
Luis	LA	55+	Lat	Some HS	A lot	D	Newspaper	Dukakis
Luke	Bos	35–54	A-A	Some college	None	I	Newspaper	Neither
Madeline	LA	35–54	Wh	Some college	Not much	R	Radio	Bush
Maria	LA	18–34	Lat	HS	Some	D	Local TV	Bush
Mark	Moor	18–34	Wh	Some college	Some	I	Radio	Dukakis
Meg	Moor	18–34	Wh	Some college	Not much	D	Local TV	Dukakis
Mike	Bos	18–34	Wh	Some college	Some	I	Newspaper	Dukakis
Paul	W-S	35–54	Wh	Some college	Not much	R	Newspaper	Bush

Table A.1 *continued*

Pseudonym	Locale[a]	Age	Race[b]	Education	Political Interest	PID[c]	Source	1988 Vote
Pedro	LA	55+	Lat	Some HS	Some	D	Newspaper	Dukakis
Richard	W-S	18–34	Wh	HS	Some	I	Networks	Bush
Rosa	LA	55+	Lat	HS	Some	R	Newspaper	Bush
Rosalyn	LA	55+	Wh	Some college	A lot	R	Local TV	Bush
Rose	Bos	55+	Wh	HS	Some	I	Networks	Dukakis
Sandra	W-S	35–54	Wh	Some HS	Some	D	Local TV	Neither
Sara	W-S	35–54	Wh	Some college	Not much	D	Newspaper	Bush
Saul	Bos	35–54	Wh	College	A lot	I	Newspaper	Dukakis
Selma	Bos	35–54	A-A	Postgrad	A lot	D	Newspaper	Dukakis
Sondra	LA	35–54	A-A	HS	Not much	R	Radio	Bush
Tom	LA	35–54	Wh	College	Some	R	Newspaper	Bush
Tracey	LA	18–34	A-A	Some college	Some	D	Local TV	Dukakis
Vince	Bos	18–34	Wh	HS	Some	I	Newspaper	Neither
William	LA	55+	A-A	Some college	A lot	R	Several	Bush

[a]Locale: Bos = Boston, LA = Los Angeles, Moor = Moorhead, W-S = Winston-Salem.
[b]Race: A-A = African American, Lat = Latino, Wh = White.
[c]PID (party identification): R = Republican, D = Democrat, I = Independent.

Appendix B

Table B.1 National Ad Buys for July 1 to November 2, 1992: Most Frequently Aired Ad Spots

Title	Frequency
Bush	
Agenda	64
Gray Dot	40
Federal Taxes	25
What Am I Fighting For	25
Trust	19
Luke	10
Presidency	3
Guess	3
Total buys	189
Number of ads	9
Clinton	
Remember	41
Even	23
John	13
Senator Nunn	11
Billion	11
Gina	11
Change	9
Hit Parade Jobs	9
Industry	4
Total buys	143
Number of ads	17
Perot	
Storm	23
Purple Heart	16
We Can Win	14
How to Vote	14
Kids	12
Title Missing	11
Title Missing	11

(*continued*)

Table B.1 *continued*

Title	Frequency
Ticking Clock	10
Red Flag	10
Total buys	205
Number of ads	29

Sources: ABC, CBS, and NBC.

Table B.2 Local Ad Buys for July 1 to November 2, 1992: Most Frequently Aired Ad Spots

Title	Frequency	Cost ($)
Bush in Boston		
Arkansas Record	29	16,190
Trust	22	18,960
Federal Taxes	22	14,050
Crisis	19	8,480
Trust/CC	17	11,060
Total buys	173	111,390
Number of ads	12	
Bush in Winston-Salem		
Arkansas Record	40	12,870
Guess	34	6,315
Trust	28	7,520
Federal Taxes Ver. 2	23	5,200
Gray Dot	21	4,605
Total buys	294	79,935
Number of ads	20	
Clinton in Winston-Salem		
Billion	65	20,065
Curtains	60	18,210
Promise	51	15,075
Leader II	44	13,375
Morning	40	23,555
Total buys	499	175,080
Number of ads	22	
Perot in Los Angeles		
Storm	7	17,800
Kids	3	12,200
We Can Win	3	12,200
Unfinished Business	3	7,800
Clock	3	6,600
Best Person	3	6,400
Red Flag	3	5,600

Table B.2 *continued*

Title	Frequency	Cost ($)
Purple Heart	2	23,800
Total buys	39	146,200
Number of ads	16	
Bush in Fargo/Moorhead		
Trust	28	1,720
Luke	24	1,065
Peter	23	1,155
Arkansas Record B	13	1,325
Crisis	13	840
Total buys	134	8,205
Number of ads	9	
Perot in Fargo/Moorhead		
Trickle Down	5	600
How to Vote	4	650
Snap Shot	4	265
Graffiti Blue	3	1,170
We Can Win	3	620
Total buys	32	5,465
Number of ads	13	

Sources: WBZ in Boston, WXII in Winston-Salem, KNBC in Los Angeles, and WDAY in Fargo/Moorhead.

Appendix C

Table C.1 Regression Models of Verbal Tone toward Candidates on Network News

Explanatory Variable	Bush	Clinton	Perot
Number of seconds quoted	.007 (.002)	.007 (.002)	.003 (.003)
Expert soundbite	.04 (.060)	−.08 (.070)	.10 (.100)
Journalist soundbite	−.18 (.080)	.02 (.080)	.00 (.120)
Person-in-street soundbite	−.05 (.060)	−.09 (.060)	.34 (.090)
Journalist initiated	−.03 (.050)	.16 (.050)	−.11 (.070)
Economy as issue	−.11 (.050)	−.03 (.050)	.05 (.000)
Presidential action	.16 (.090)		
Candidate referred to by:			
Issues	.01 (.040)	−.01 (.060)	.18 (.090)
Campaign characteristics	.04 (.100)	.43 (.120)	−.09 (.100)
Horse race	−.11 (.050)	.23 (.050)	.14 (.080)
Leadership	−.11 (.050)	−.02 (.050)	−.00 (.100)
Candidate as campaigner	−.10 (.070)	.49 (.070)	−.38 (.090)
Personal characteristics	−.11 (.050)	−.24 (.050)	−.38 (.090)
Constant	2.81	2.98	2.82
Adjusted R^2	.04	.11	.07
Number of stories (N)	·1,195	1,109	581

Table C.2 Regression Models of Verbal Tone toward Candidates on Local Television News

Explanatory Variable	Bush	Clinton	Perot
Number of seconds quoted	.009 (.004)	.001 (.005)	.004 (.007)
Expert soundbite	−.04 (.150)	−.37 (.140)	−.01 (.220)
Journalist soundbite	−.11 (.230)	−.20 (.190)	−.18 (.270)
Person-in-street soundbite	−.08 (.130)	.12 (.130)	.51 (.160)
Journalist initiated	−.16 (.110)	−.09 (.110)	−.29 (.150)
Local angle	−.05 (.090)	−.07 (.100)	−.09 (.150)
Economy as issue	−.25 (.100)	−.09 (.100)	−.19 (.150)
Presidential action	.66 (.160)		
Candidate referred to by:			
Issues	−.14 (.110)	.20 (.110)	−.21 (.210)
Campaign characteristics	.11 (.190)	.39 (.170)	.19 (.120)
Horse race	−.07 (.100)	.45 (.100)	−.14 (.140)
Leadership	−.05 (.090)	−.05 (.110)	.44 (.180)
Ability as campaigner	−.07 (.170)	.26 (.140)	−.15 (.220)
Personal characteristics	−.13 (.100)	−.16 (.100)	−.25 (.160)
Constant	3.06	3.12	3.30
Adjusted R^2	.06	.09	.07
Number of stories (N)	409	418	199

Table C.3 Regression Models of Verbal Tone toward Candidates in Newspapers

Explanatory Variable	Bush	Clinton	Perot
Number of words quoted	.002 (.001)	.002 (.001)	.003 (.001)
Journalist initiated	−.36 (.050)	−.11 (.050)	−.35 (.070)
Economy as issue	−.02 (.050)	.08 (.050)	.10 (.080)
Presidential action	−.03 (.100)		
Local angle	.09 (.050)	.17 (.050)	.21 (.080)
Wire service	.14 (.060)	.14 (.070)	.00 (.100)
Candidate referred to by:			
Issues	−.01 (.050)	−.00 (.050)	.11 (.080)
Campaign characteristics	−.00 (.100)	.21 (.090)	.13 (.100)
Horse race	.05 (.050)	.24 (.050)	.06 (.080)
Leadership	−.18 (.050)	.02 (.050)	−.05 (.080)
Personal characteristics	−.18 (.050)	−.23 (.050)	−.31 (.080)
Constant	2.70	2.93	2.98
Adjusted R^2	.08	.08	.10
Number of stories (N)	1,456	1,440	619

Table C.4 Regression Models of Visual Tone toward Candidates on Network News

Explanatory Variable	Bush		Clinton		Perot	
Length of story	.01	(.020)	.03	(.020)	−.01	(.0400)
Number of seconds on screen	.004	(.001)	.001	(.001)	.002	(.0014)
Expert soundbite	.29	(.080)	.17	(.080)	.25	(.1000)
Journalist soundbite	.12	(.110)	.02	(.100)	−.21	(.1200)
Person-in-street soundbite	.02	(.090)	−.05	(.080)	.23	(.1000)
Journalist initiated	−.14	(.070)	.02	(.100)	−.15	(.0700)
Economy as issue	.19	(.070)	.23	(.060)	−.05	(.0900)
Presidential action	−.16	(.110)				
Candidate referred to by:						
Issues	−.01	(.070)	.11	(.070)	.18	(.0900)
Campaign characteristics	.22	(.130)	.16	(.140)	.08	(.1000)
Horse race	−.01	(.070)	.07	(.060)	−.07	(.0800)
Leadership	.15	(.060)	.14	(.070)	.17	(.1000)
Ability as campaigner	.16	(.090)	.47	(.080)	.24	(.1000)
Personal characteristics	.08	(.070)	.08	(.070)	.12	(.0900)
Constant	3.42		3.49		3.37	
Adjusted R^2	.10		.10		.13	
Number of stories (N)	686		726		380	

Table C.5 Regression Models of Visual Tone toward Candidates on Local Television News

Explanatory Variable	Bush		Clinton		Perot	
Length of story	−.02	(.030)	−.04	(.0500)	.04	(.050)
Number of seconds on screen	.004	(.002)	.004	(.0022)	.002	(.003)
Expert soundbite	−.11	(.170)	−.16	(.1500)	.32	(.180)
Journalist soundbite	.27	(.300)	−.44	(.2200)	.43	(.260)
Person-on-street soundbite	−.60	(.150)	−.15	(.1000)	−.12	(.140)
Journalist initiated	−.38	(.130)	.44	(.1300)	−.29	(.130)
Local angle	−.02	(.110)	−.04	(.1100)	−.00	(.130)
Economy as issue	.16	(.120)	.32	(.1200)	.00	(.130)
Presidential action	.24	(.170)				
Candidate referred to by:						
Issues	−.03	(.120)	.06	(.1200)	.13	(.180)
Campaign characteristics	.07	(.200)	−.06	(.1800)	.03	(.140)
Horse race	.32	(.110)	.33	(.1100)	.19	(.120)
Leadership	−.06	(.110)	−.11	(.1200)	.59	(.140)
Ability as campaigner	.04	(.180)	.06	(.1400)	−.37	(.170)
Personal characteristics	−.02	(.110)	−.15	(.1100)	.28	(.130)
Constant	3.76		3.69		3.15	
Adjusted R^2	.12		.13		.19	
Number of stories (N)	252		293		143	

Table C.6 Regression Models of Visual Tone toward Candidates in Newspapers

Explanatory Variable	Bush		Clinton		Perot	
Number of words quoted	.001	(.001)	−.000	(.002)	−.002	(.002)
Journalist initiated	−.81	(.180)	−.25	(.190)	1.04	(.240)
Economy as issue	.41	(.190)	.43	(.200)	.26	(.270)
Presidential action	.15	(.290)				
Local angle	.71	(.200)	.26	(.180)	.39	(.270)
Wire service	.52	(.320)	.25	(.390)	.73	(.330)
Candidate referred to by:						
Issues	−.14	(.180)	−.17	(.190)	.22	(.270)
Campaign characteristics	.66	(.300)	.43	(.260)	.05	(.290)
Horse race	.47	(.190)	.41	(.190)	.08	(.270)
Leadership	.18	(.190)	.19	(.180)	−.01	(.240)
Ability as campaigner	.12	(.200)	.08	(.210)	.01	(.330)
Personal characteristics	−.40	(.180)	−.02	(.200)	.13	(.250)
Constant	2.62		3.06		3.02	
Adjusted R^2	.34		.13		.19	
Number of stories (N)	191		177		108	

Table C.7 Candidate Exposure on Network News, by Network

Candidate	ABC	CBS	NBC	CNN	All Networks
A. Number (and percentage) of Stories Mentioning Candidates[a]					
Bush	742	729	707	831	3,014
	(71.6)	(77.7)	(79.9)	(77.7)	(76.5)
Clinton	566	538	494	587	2,190
	(54.6)	(57.4)	(55.8)	(54.9)	(55.5)
Perot	189	283	266	251	989
	(22.7)	(35.0)	(36.3)	(27.8)	(30.2)
Total stories	957	902	846	1,029	3,741
	(92.3)	(96.2)	(95.6)	(96.2)	(94.8)
B. Number (and percentage) of Stories in Which Candidates Are Seen[a]					
Bush	374	426	378	507	1,685
	(39.1)	(47.2)	(44.7)	(49.3)	(45.0)
Clinton	344	370	307	410	1,431
	(35.9)	(41.0)	(36.3)	(39.8)	(38.3)
Perot	98	172	141	168	579
	(12.5)	(22.0)	(20.0)	(19.2)	(18.4)
Total stories	642	683	576	776	2,677
	(67.1)	(75.7)	(68.1)	(75.4)	(71.6)

(*continued*)

Table C.7 *continued*

Candidate	ABC	CBS	NBC	CNN	All Networks
C. Number (and percentage) of Stories in Which Candidates Speak[a]					
Bush	288	207	246	263	944
	(23.8)	(22.9)	(29.1)	(25.6)	(25.2)
Clinton	210	192	225	179	806
	(21.9)	(21.3)	(26.6)	(17.4)	(21.5)
Perot	40	77	75	45	237
	(5.1)	(9.9)	(10.6)	(5.1)	(7.5)
Total stories	417	410	429	431	1,687
	(43.6)	(45.5)	(50.7)	(41.9)	(45.1)

[a]For February 1–November 8, 1992.

Appendix D
Focus Groups: Methods and Coding

Balance in demographic categories was achieved by using quotas in the selection process. Strong partisans and ideologues were screened out of the group. Undecided voters, or those who expressed that they had not determined their voting choice, were favored.

Focus groups were shown segments of political advertising, news, candidate interviews, and news analysis (ABC's "American Agenda").

After each message, voters were asked, "What's going on for you?" or "What are your feelings about the candidates?" Moderator questions were kept as general as possible to facilitate participant-generated discourse. Participants were asked to record their written impressions of candidates following the airing of each message segment, in order to ground discourse in their own point of view (see Kern and Just 1995).

Discussions following exposure to stimuli were divided into conversational exchanges. An "exchange" is a dialogue between two or more people about a subject. There may be either agreement or disagreement about the subject. Exchanges vary in length, but on the average there are six to eight exchanges, or topics of discussion, per exposure segment in a focus group discussion. Conversational exchanges in the focus group were coded for what voters brought to the discourse in three categories of resources used as part of arguments within the conversational exchanges: political knowledge, direct and indirect personal experiences (the latter based on the experience of the speaker, his or her family, or friends), and recalled media sources.

In addition, conversational exchanges were coded according to their relationship to the stimulus: ignoring, transforming, and following. Conversational exchanges were also coded for voter interpretations of visual and verbal information.

Visual: If only a visual aspect of the stimulus is mentioned, it is coded as "visual." Thus, a positive coding for visual information would occur, for example, when the men in the Boston primary focus group remark on the "solid, low-key, 'look the camera in the eye' look of Buchanan."

Audio-visual: If there is reference to a fact expressed in the stimulus both visually and through either spoken or written language, this is coded "audio-visual." Thus, for example, such a coding would occur for an ad stimulus when a focus group participant in a conversational exchange, or unit of conversation, comments on the fact that "Clinton was reelected five times," if this remark has been not only verbally stated but printed visually in a tagline that appears on the screen. Or it would occur for a news story in which the journalist mentions that Republican primary challenger Patrick Buchanan has been criticized by George Bush for driving a Mercedes automobile, if the Mercedes is in fact depicted visually on the screen.

Verbal: If only language from the stimulus is mentioned, this is coded "verbal." If, in a discussion about a talk show segment featuring Clinton speaking about his economic policy, a phrase from his talk is referred to, this is coded verbal only. If a phrase relating to the visual aspect of his speaking is mentioned—for example, "Clinton frowned as he said that the economy was in bad shape," the message is coded audio-visual.

It is important to note that the mere mention of a candidate's name in the discourse, even though it may have been mentioned in a stimulus or the candidate may have been depicted in the stimulus, is not coded in any of the categories, because the whole focus group discourse is about candidates.

References to visual or verbal information in the discourse must also be quite specific in order to be coded. Thus, for example, a general reference to Clinton's concern about health care, which is mentioned in a stimulus, without the use of some further verbal or visual cue to connect it to the stimulus was not coded.

Appendix E

Table E.1 Candidate Interview Program Grouping

Type	Category	Show	Network	Total
	News group			
1	Nightly news	Network Nightly News	NBC	2
		MacNeil/Lehrer	PBS	2
2	News interviews	Inside Politics '92	CNN	1
		Super Tuesday	NBC	1
		The Brokaw Report	NBC	1
3	News talk shows	Meet the Press	NBC	1
		This Week with David Brinkley	ABC	2
4	Town meetings	N/A	N/A	0
5	Late-night news	Nightline	ABC	1
				11
	Infotainment group			
6	Magazine shows	Primetime Live	ABC	3
		20/20	ABC	1
7	Morning shows	Today	NBC	5
		CBS This Morning	CBS	3
		Good Morning America	ABC	4
8	Interview shows	Larry King Live	CNN	3
		David Frost	PBS	1
				20
	Entertainment group			
9	Entertainment	Arsenio Hall	Synd.	1
		Donahue	Synd.	1
		Choose or Lose	MTV	2
				4
			Total	35

Table E.2 Questioner Categories for Candidate Interviews

Questioner	Network	Total
News reporters		
David Brinkley	ABC	2
Tom Brokaw	NBC	3
Sam Donaldson	ABC	3
Al Hunt	NBC	1
Ted Koppel	ABC	1
Jim Lehrer	PBS	2
Lisa Myers	NBC	1
Gene Randall	CNN	1
Tim Russert	NBC	2
Bernard Shaw	CNN	1
Nancy Snyderman	ABC	1
George Will	ABC	2
Judy Woodruff	PBS	1
Professional interviewers		
Katie Couric	NBC	4
Phil Donahue	Synd.	1
David Frost	PBS	1
Charlie Gibson	ABC	2
Arsenio Hall	Synd.	1
Larry King	CNN	3
Kurt Loder	MTV	1
Joan Lunden	ABC	2
Diane Sawyer	ABC	1
Harry Smith	CBS	2
Tabitha Soren	MTV	2
Barbara Walters	ABC	1
Paula Zahn	CBS	1
Audience		
Assembled audience	Various	3
Call-in audience	Various	5

Table E.3 Interview Programs Coded

No.	Date	Candidate[a]	Network	Program	Lines
1	Jan 27	CL	CNN	Inside Politics '92	136
2	Feb 20	PE	CNN	Larry King Live	1,270
3	Mar 3	CL	ABC	Nightline	221
4	Mar 4	CL	CBS	This Morning	111
5	Mar 10	QU	NBC	Super Tuesday	100
6	Mar 20	CL	PBS	MacNeil/Lehrer	385
7	Mar 26	PE	PBS	MacNeil/Lehrer	412
8	Apr 13	PE	NBC	Today	165
9	May 3	PE	NBC	Meet the Press	718
10	Jun 3	CL	Synd.	Arsenio Hall	769
11	Jul 1	BU	CBS	This Morning	1,166
12	Jul 12	GO	ABC	This Week with David Brinkley	496
13	Jul 13	GO	NBC	Today	132
14	Jul 22	QU	CNN	Larry King Live	1,233
15	Jul 30	GO	ABC	Primetime Live	477
16	Aug 14	QU	CBS	This Morning	361
17	Aug 24	CL	ABC	Good Morning America	132
18	Sep 6	CL	NBC	The Brokaw Report	310
19	Sep 9	GO	CNN	Larry King Live	1,155
20	Sep 13	QU	ABC	This Week with David Brinkley	832
21	Sep 28	CL	NBC	Today	257
22	Sep 30	CL	NBC	Today	208
23	Oct 2	PE	ABC	20/20	457
24	Oct 5	PE	NBC	Today	359
25	Oct 6	CL/GO	Synd.	Donahue	1,050
26	Oct 9	BU	ABC	Good Morning America	309
27	Oct 14	QU	ABC	Good Morning America	309
28	Oct 14	GO	ABC	Good Morning America	290
29	Oct 15	BU	NBC	Debate Coverage	27
30	Oct 21	GO	MTV	Choose or Lose	1,226
31	Oct 29	BU	ABC	Primetime Live	680
32	Oct 29	CL	ABC	Primetime Live	700
33	Oct 30	PE	PBS	David Frost	726
34	Nov 1	BU	MTV	Choose or Lose	277
35	Nov 2	CL	NBC	Nightly News	108

[a]BU = Bush, CL = Clinton, GO = Gore, PE = Perot, QU = Quayle.

Appendix F
Candidate Considerations: Coding in the In-Depth Interviews

A consideration as defined by Zaller is "any reason that might induce an individual to decide a political issue one way or the other. . . . [It is] a compound of cognition and affect—that is, a belief concerning an object and an evaluation of the belief" (1992, 40). This is close to Kelley's definition ("prima facie reasons for choosing in one way or another"; 1983, 10). We have expanded the definition somewhat to indicate any factors that a person takes into account when evaluating a particular political phenomenon and/or making a political decision (including answering questions on surveys and voting).

The coding categories for considerations generally follow the NES categories for "likes" and "dislikes":

1. party
2. ideology
3. policy (broadly defined to include "the economy," etc.)
4. group links (e.g., Duke with KKK, Bush in cahoots with the rich, etc.)
5. personal assessments (following Miller et al. 1986)
   a. integrity
   b. reliability
   c. competence (subdivided in order to ease our comparisons to the news, ads, etc.)
      i. ability as campaigner
      ii. ability as leader/professional experience
   d. charisma
      i. personal
      ii. interpersonal
   e. "personal"
6. additional mentions that are disconnected from any assessment according to the categories above. These categories were not used unless they were discrete *and* not linked to any of the above assessments.
   a. scandal (e.g., "Now they're saying Bush has a mistress too," but without any indication that this says something about Bush)
   b. horse race (e.g., focus on strategy without any indication that this says

something about the candidate; "Clinton will be going to the South for votes" would be horse race, but any discussion of his doing well or poorly should be categorized under ability as campaigner—e.g., "Buchanan is doing better than anyone expected")

c. other event ("event") (e.g., "I saw Clinton in a supermarket on the news")

These considerations were coded as positive, negative, or neutral. If the consideration was connected to something the interviewee evaluated positively or negatively, we used that as the basis. For example, if someone who has identified herself as "not well off" says that "Bush only associates with his kind—the rich", this is presumably a negative comment. Similarly, a black woman saying that the candidates are all "white men" is presumably not a simple demographic statement.

When the interviewee specifically indicated what the candidate has done prior to the campaign, we coded this as "retrospective"; when the interviewee specifically indicated what the candidate will/may do in the future, we coded this as "prospective." If there was no explicit or implicit time reference (or verb tense) that would reveal whether the consideration was retrospective or prospective, it was not coded on this dimension.

We broke down the interviewee's responses into the smallest possible units that indicated some discrete factor that the interviewee was taking into account in that context and at that time. Every sentence that referred to a candidate contained at least one consideration. If the subject repeated the consideration in another sentence, that was coded as an additional consideration of that type.

A sentence may contain more than one consideration. If, for instance, an interviewee criticized Bush for mudslinging when he talked about Clinton's trip to Moscow, that included two considerations, one about Bush's mudslinging and the other about Clinton's trip. If there were two separate considerations that fell into the same category, but separate subcategories, each was coded separately. For example an interviewee talking about the Richmond debate said:

> I feel Clinton gave the best answer [Clinton's ability as campaigner—positive]. Perot came in second [Perot's ability as campaigner—positive]. At least he talked about his grandchildren, you know, then you think, it could affect my grandchildren. It may not affect me, because I'm not a billionaire, but it could affect my grandchildren [Perot's personal background (grandfather)—neutral; Perot's personal background (billionaire)—negative].

Considerations were sometimes rebutted in the context of the overall interview but were coded even if the interviewee later said that they were false. The reason for doing this is that the considerations must have some salience and applicability to the interviewee to make that person respond to them—in other words, that they are willing to enunciate these as possible reasons to vote one way or the other. The interviewee often talked as though they were thinking out loud; for example:

> I guess a big thing back and forth is people changing their standing on issues. You know, that's what Bush is saying about Clinton—that he waffles and often changes his position [Bush, event; Clinton's integrity—negative]. But, everything to date that I've seen he's said the same thing [Clinton's integrity—positive]. So, I guess I'm starting to see him as consistent [Clinton's integrity—positive].

Notes

Chapter One

1. For a review of this literature, see Lewis-Beck and Rice (1992) and Campbell (1993).

2. The term "priming" gained currency from the experiments reported in Iyengar, Peters, and Kinder (1982). The most impressive recent work that confirms how campaigns can prime voters is Johnston et al.'s (1992) study of the 1988 Canadian general election; for electoral examples in the United States, see Aldrich, Sullivan, and Borgida (1989) and Jacobs and Shapiro (1994).

3. See the discussion of this point especially in Gaventa (1980).

4. Campbell et al.'s *The American Voter* speaks to partisanship, Nie et al.'s *The Changing American Voter* addresses issues, and Fiorina's *Retrospective Voting in American National Elections* focuses on evaluations of past performance.

5. It is not surprising that most of these studies have been based on predominantly qualitative small-N methodologies such as in-depth interviews (Lane 1962; Hochschild 1981) or focus groups (Gamson 1993). Quantitative work using Q-sorts (Brown 1980) or individual differences scaling (Marcus, Sullivan, and Tabb 1974) has also confirmed the often unique ways in which individuals make sense of their political worlds.

6. "How is it possible that given how little citizens know about politics, they nonetheless can frequently figure out what they are for and against politically?" (Sniderman et al. 1991, 18).

7. Three recent crucial works in political psychology that make this argument, albeit in slightly different ways, are Sniderman et al. (1991), Zaller (1992), and Page and Shapiro (1992).

8. The term derives, of course, from Kelley and Mirer (1974) and Zaller (1992). For more details, see chap. 2.

9. The term is borrowed from Page and Shapiro (1992).

Chapter Two

1. See, e.g., the classic demonstration in Nisbett and Wilson (1977).

2. See Lodge, McGraw, and Stroh (1989), McGraw, Lodge, and Stroh (1990),

and Lodge and Stroh (1993) for an overview of the Stony Brook experiments.

3. As Lodge and Stroh (1993) have admitted, on-line processing depends on the presumption that voters are primarily interested in using information to form an impression; however, much information about candidates is encountered haphazardly and may be kept around as interesting stories about celebrated people. We should also note that on-line processing is more available to and availed by more politically sophisticated citizens (McGraw et al. 1990). While having such running tallies might reduce processing time *once* they are constructed (Lodge and Stroh 1993), it takes resources to build them. The less sophisticated are "less adept at and less inclined to engage in, on-line processing and consequently more likely to retrieve specific information from memory before rendering an evaluation" (McGraw et al. 1990, 44).

4. The one exception, of course, is a referendum, but voters are volatile and late deciding, suggesting that they do not anticipate such votes at the start of a campaign.

5. See, for further insight on this point, Feldman and Conover (1983) or Rahn et al. (1990).

6. Only Rahn, Krosnick, and Breuning (1994) have provided nonexperimental evidence of on-line processing, by showing how, in successive waves of a panel study in an Ohio general election campaign, feeling thermometers influenced later likes and dislikes about that candidate, and not the other way around. However, it is unclear whether this demonstrates, as Rahn et al. claim it does, that voters provide reasons as rationalizations for voting decisions already made rather than as "derivations" for those decisions. For one, McGraw, Fischle, and Stenner (1994) have recently shown how the like/dislike questions of the NES may be unusually prone to rationalization, more so than alternative ways to ascertain political memory. Second, Rahn et al.'s study is limited once again to the fall campaign, neglecting earlier moments when the reverse causality might have been stronger.

7. In experimental research conducted since we completed our study, McGraw et al. (1994) compared different ways to measure memory about a fictitious candidate and about two presidents, George Bush and Bill Clinton. They conclude that the like/dislike question from the NES overestimates recall that is based on the politician's character and underestimates personal references such as the politician's home state, family, or hobbies. They do not find, however, a single best question, noting that "it is a mistake to conclude that any given memory test provides an accurate indication of what the individual knows," adding that tests "vary in the extent to which they suggest different strategies for providing acceptable responses." Our own question was not tested but seems to be midway between a free recall question ("Tell me what you know about Candidate X"), which they conclude best explores memory structure, and a "what comes to

mind" probe, which is useful for eliciting more intermediate inferences and statements of opinion.

8. Schuman and Presser (1979) have nicely demonstrated the potentially large differences between responses to open- and closed-ended questions. However, Foddy has cautioned: "The implied suggestion that open questions do not suggest answers to respondents is not necessarily valid. Indeed, the common practice of using 'probes' to clarify the meaning of responses to open questions comes close to turning them into closed ones" (1993, 129).

9. "The heart of the matter is that we must accept that *we do impose either our own view of reality, or our guesses about our respondents' views of reality, upon our respondents' answers* whether we admit it or not. The only issue is how self-conscious are we when we do this" (Foddy 1993, 192; emphasis in original).

10. These categories were derived from previous work on the like/dislike questions of the NES (Miller et al. 1986).

11. We did not conduct a survey in Moorhead in the spring or in September because we were offered the cooperation of the statewide Minnesota poll. For the last round, in late October, we conducted our own survey in Clay County, Minnesota, of which Moorhead is the seat.

12. The questionnaire asked about media usage, voter registration, past voting behavior, party and ideological leanings, and several indications of demographic background.

13. The Boston and Los Angeles surveys were conducted by the John Hazen White, Sr., Public Opinion Laboratory at Brown University. The Winston-Salem survey was conducted by Bellomy Research Associates. The margin of error in the Boston and Winston-Salem survey is ±4 percent, and in the Los Angeles survey ±4.5 percent.

14. All of the fall surveys had a margin of error of ±4 percent. The Boston surveys were conducted by the John Hazen White, Sr., Public Opinion Laboratory of Brown University. The Los Angeles surveys were conducted by Interviewing Service of America. The Winston-Salem surveys were conducted by Bellomy Research Associates. The Clay County (Moorhead) survey was conducted by the Bureau of Government Research, University of North Dakota.

To facilitate analysis, we pooled the surveys across locales from the respective waves. The pooled September survey from Boston, Winston-Salem, and Los Angeles had $N = 1,831$ and a margin of error of ±2.5 percent. The pooled October survey from Boston, Winston-Salem, Los Angeles, and Moorhead had $N = 2,436$ and a margin of error of ±2 percent. We checked our equations to see whether there was variation by site over and above the other variables, by incorporating dummy variables for individual sites.

15. To measure the extent to which citizens recognized the candidates vying for the nomination, we used a question developed by the *New York Times*/CBS

News polls: "Is your opinion of [candidate] favorable, not favorable, undecided, or haven't you heard enough about [candidate] yet to have an opinion?" Recognition is a two-category variable in which those saying their opinion was favorable or unfavorable were coded as recognizing the candidate, whereas the rest were classified as not so doing.

Electability refers to citizens' perceptions about a candidate's chances for winning the November election. We asked our subjects: "Regardless of which candidate you support, which of these candidates do you think would have the best chance of winning the election in November? [list of candidates]" In the spring waves, electability in Boston and Winston-Salem was asked only for competitors of the respective parties, and we reformulated the responses by candidate into dichotomous variables (1 if electable, 0 if not electable). In Los Angeles, this question was asked simultaneously of all the remaining active candidates: Brown, Clinton, Bush, Buchanan, and Perot.

16. See West (1993) for a discussion of self-reported media measures. We are aware that self-reports of media exposure may be prone to some overreporting (Price and Zaller 1993). We use these variables with caution, on the strength of Bartels's (1993) finding that the lower reliability of these measures tends to *under*estimate the impact of media exposure. We should note that the formats of the ads and news variables differ slightly, making it difficult to compare their contributions (cf. Zhao and Chaffee 1995).

17. Although there was a primary in each state, the turnout varied considerably (though never went above 50 percent). In particular, the Minnesota primary was a bit of a fiasco. It was a late entry into the campaign and was confused by the two parties treating the election differently: the Democrats presented the primary as a nonbinding "beauty contest" to precede a later round of caucuses and conventions, whereas Republicans were actually choosing delegates. Turnout in Minnesota for both parties was only 13 percent of registered voters; in Clay County (where Moorhead is located), turnout was even lower—1,627 of 27,426 registered voters bothered to show up at the polls. Massachusetts, despite (or because of) its early timing and home-state favorite, and with laws that enable independents to declare a party affiliation and vote in that party's primary on the day of the election, saw a turnout of 34 percent of registered voters (the congressional primary was not held until September). In North Carolina and California, the primaries were limited to those registered with the party but coincided with the choices for competitive U.S. Senate seats. Turnout of registered voters for the Republican primaries was 25 percent in North Carolina and 41 percent in California, and for the Democratic primaries was 32 percent in North Carolina and 44 percent in California.

18. See also Patterson and McClure (1976), Kaid, Nimmo, and Sanders (1986), Kern (1989), Pfau and Kenski (1990), and West (1993).

Chapter Three

1. To be sure, many studies have questioned or downplayed the citizens' role in this agenda-building process. Since McCombs and Shaw's (1972) demonstration that the amount of coverage that issues received in the news heavily predicted the priorities voters placed on those issues, the "agenda-setting" school has suggested that voters' issue concerns are largely a reflection of what the media emphasize. There is a good deal of evidence that confirms this relationship, whether by cross-sectional data such as McCombs and Shaw used, time-series data (e.g., MacKuen and Coombs 1981), or experimental studies (e.g., Iyengar and Kinder 1987). Yet there is also evidence that media agenda setting has its limits. In particular, when a policy problem is obtrusive—that is to say, when citizens may see the direct effects of the problem in their own immediate environments—the media's coverage has a considerably reduced impact (e.g., Erbring, Goldenberg, and Miller 1980).

2. Since we did not restrict our interviewees to a set number of problems, these questions give us a good insight into the full range of concerns. However, in examining the interviews, we were to find that new issue concerns often were mentioned later in the discussion, particularly when we asked, "What do you think the candidates should be emphasizing?" which tended to provoke issue-based responses. Rather than artificially restrict our inquiry to the "most important problem" question, then, we counted every time a political issue was mentioned somewhere in the course of an interview as something that the respondent both deemed to be an important public problem and saw political solutions as appropriate and necessary for. We excluded issues that citizens recognized as being talked about by the candidates which did not provoke their concern, as well as any personal or societal issues that they believed would best be handled outside of politics.

3. Throughout the year there were no consistent significant relationships between any of these variables and citing the economy as the most important problem. Indeed, our equations scarcely do better at predicting who would cite the economy as the most important issue than the percentage expected by chance alone.

4. The second wave combines interviews that took place at different times of the year, at the time of the primary in each state. In the fourth wave, we asked a slightly different question because we were concerned that the close proximity to the previous wave would be overly repetitive. Therefore, we asked: "In our last conversation, we talked about what you think is the most important problem facing the country today. Are there any new problems you would like to add?" This other question wording might have contributed to a decline in the willingness of interviewees to repeat prior answers; but this was at least partially mitigated by our examining the entire interview, and not merely the responses to the opening question.

5. We should note that this result is not inflated by general comments about "the economy" that could refer to other economic troubles, since we distinguished those people who talked about the economy in terms of inflation and prices, or in terms of tax burdens, and counted them separately.

6. Along these lines, we are reminded of the (by now well-established) finding in social psychology that vivid and personally salient evidence usually outweighs more abstract data in individuals' perceptions (see, in general, Nisbett and Ross 1980).

7. This point became more salient in the fall, when many of our respondents mentioned—with some astonishment—news stories about American companies receiving tax breaks to invest overseas and sometimes to take jobs "off-shore."

8. These concerns were already present but were magnified among our minority respondents by the Los Angeles riots. An illuminating example of this occurred in the Winston-Salem interviews, conducted right after the start of the riots. Intriguingly, while our white interviewees sometimes dismissed the riots as explicitly racial incidents, as Richard and J. D. each did, African Americans were more inclined to point to the riots as products of racism and the economy. Carlton said: "Right now, with all the other problems that we have, this is just a scratch on the surface of what's probably going to happen this summer when a lot of teenagers out of school with no jobs and nothing to do. It's going to spread across this country like wildfire." And Diane included the riots with her own experiences and the state of the economy as all pointing in a single direction:

> I'd say in light in of everything that's going on right now currently it would be racism and justice and unequality and employment and the list goes on and on. I'm a little preoccupied with all the things that are going on in L.A. . . . . I'm upset and frustrated because I'm experiencing some racism on my job so what's going on in L.A., I just feel angry and at this point we don't know what to do. I've taken action on my behalf but I don't know what they're going to do in L.A. to rectify what's going on out there.

Chapter Four

1. For description of the 1952 ads and the evolution in the nature of ads, see Diamond and Bates (1992) and Jamieson (1992a); for analysis of changes in how ads communicate, see Kern (1989); for systematic analysis of patterns in the content and uses of ads over that period, see West (1993).

2. See, e.g., Schwartz (1974), Jamieson (1988), Fisher (1989), and Pfau and Louden (1993).

3. See chap. 2 for a description of the methods used to analyze candidate communications.

4. For the nomination phase, we obtained and coded 9 ads for Bush, 11 ads

for Buchanan, 32 ads for Clinton, 4 ads for Brown, and 11 ads each for Harkin, Kerrey, and Tsongas; in the general election, we obtained and coded 23 ads for Bush, 25 for Clinton, and 18 for Perot. The ads were obtained from commercial vendors, from taping from broadcasts, and from Professor Patrick Devlin. For aggregating the data and for analysis of the data, we eliminated duplicates, ads run under party sponsorship that were the same as ads for the candidates, and ads in which there were no significant differences from the same ad in the series (using exacting criteria). Indeed, to include such ads in the aggregate data (as some have) would skew the totals.

The total number of ads, in some cases, is lower than the most comprehensive list available at the Political Commercial Archive, University of Oklahoma. There is, however, some duplication in the archive lists, and it is not established how many of the ads on that list were not actually aired. That the ad set for this project is a thorough representation of the number and types of ads aired in the 1992 presidential election has been confirmed by review of the ad buy data and by checking references in talks by campaign principals and articles written on the subject.

5. Clinton and Perot also aired some ads on the Fox network, but the ad buys were not large and the three major networks remain the prime source for ad exposure, so we focused on those.

6. Although a coding category was included for homelessness and poverty, there was almost no mention of such issues in any of the ads. Only 2 out 293 mentions of policy issues in all the nomination phase ads were on that topic; in the general election there were no such mentions in any ad.

7. Bush spent 99 seconds on economic matters, while Clinton spent 204 seconds. Bush spent 272 seconds on foreign affairs, while Clinton spent 52 seconds.

8. These included Perot's nonbiographical first, second, and seventh ads.

9. One other aspect of Perot's ad buys is interesting to note. Perot bought network time for 15-second promotional spots for his long-form ads, i.e., mini-advertisements to promote the coming attraction of his next long-form ad! He bought 48 such promotional ads on all three networks, from October 14 to November 2—the greatest number of which were for the second infomercial ("Solutions"). In this long-form ad (unlike his spot ads) he detailed actual solutions to the deficit problem and aspects of the economy. Perot also used the second debate—twice—to promote his upcoming infomercial, including citing the times and networks on which it could be seen. (This promotional effort was significant for gaining citizen viewers since the long ads did not air at any regular time.) It should also be noted that the long-form ads of Perot were a way to convey an image of a serious candidate ready to deal at length with policy issues—a notion he explicitly sought to reinforce.

10. The failure of dovetailing—and its apparent consequences for effective

candidate communication—are illustrated by an ad for Democratic candidate Bob Kerrey. A featured ad for Kerrey in the New Hampshire primary called "Net" (better known as the "hockey rink" ad) probably did not get the Kerrey message across because the visuals did not directly reinforce the verbal message. The message was about economics and Japanese trade, but the visual was of Kerrey standing on a hockey rink by the goal. It was intended to be a metaphor for defending America against unfair trading practices, but for the average viewer, the image of an unknown candidate standing in a hockey rink saying something about the Japanese and a little defense was unlikely to be remembered. Our in-depth interviews found people befuddled by this ad. Kerrey clearly failed to dovetail image and message in this ad.

11. Some spots did, however, attack an opponent's record and basic policy approach, the best example being the aptly titled "Trickle Down" ad; it did not specifically mention Bush, but there was little doubt about who was being criticized.

12. As Bush pollster and strategist Fred Steeper has noted: "The Republican party and the Bush/Quayle campaign probably got bluffed by the press into thinking that the first negative ad we ran, the press was going to pounce—'There they go again, they're doing the Willie Horton stuff.' We were very gun-shy about the timing of the first ad." Principal Quayle advisor Bill Kristol added, "There was just huge allergy at top levels throughout about being accused by the press of, quote, 'running a negative campaign'" (Royer 1994, 192). This makes the "stealth campaign" for the Bush ads even more interesting—was it a significant part of the Bush strategy to bypass the "ad police" (Milburn and Brown 1994) at the national level with a less intense attack while pulling out all the stops at the local level?

13. The "Trust" ad ran 15 times (at least 3 times on each network); two of the average citizen ads, in which they said "you can't trust Bill Clinton," "I wouldn't believe a word he says," and so on, ran 9 times; and an ad suggesting Clinton was two-faced ran once.

14. To shore up their position with the news media, the Clinton campaign constantly reminded journalists of the Bush record of attack politics and admonished them to watch out for similar attacks "this year" (see, e.g., Germond and Witcover 1993, 423–25).

Chapter Five

1. The best examples of this approach are Epstein's (1972) participant observation of NBC News, Altheide's (1976) study of network and local television news, Gans's (1979) comparison of NBC, CBS, Newsweek, and Time, and Tuchman's (1978) examination of metropolitan newspaper and television news.

2. The exceptions include Semetko et al.'s (1991, chap. 5) study of the 1984

fall campaign, which compared the three broadcast networks against each other and against British general election news coverage, and Kerbel's (1994) recent study of ABC and CNN.

3. Local television news represents a relatively neglected medium in political communication studies. The best comparison across levels of television news and across media remains Graber's (1980, 1984) examination of two Chicago television news broadcasts against network news and three Chicago newspapers.

4. Recently, good work has been done on local news operations by Kaniss (1991) and McManus (1994). Entman's (1992) comparison of 13 large-market local television news stations' coverage of Super Tuesday found that the principal variation was in attention to candidates presumed to be of interest to local audiences, usually the hometown boy. But it is interesting that the favorite-son angle was not important to the Los Angeles coverage of the primaries, even though Jerry Brown was a former California governor.

5. The Iowa caucuses were virtually uncontested in 1992 because the other candidates and the media conceded the state to one of the major contenders, Iowa Senator Tom Harkin.

6. Twenty-four percent of WDAY's stories were journalist initiated, compared to 16 percent at WCVB (Boston), 15 percent at WSTV (Winston-Salem), and 14 percent at KABC (Los Angeles).

7. The standard rule is that it takes about a half-hour to read aloud the front page of the *New York Times*. The conversion rule applied for the purposes of the graph was 200 inches per hour.

8. For similar approaches, see Sigal (1973), who distinguished between "enterprise" and "routine" stories, and Semetko et al. (1991, 28), who coded "the predominant subject" of American and British campaign coverage, classifying stories as either "media initiated" or "party/candidate initiated."

9. For further details, see Crigler et al. (1992, tables 3–5). The figures for the three major candidates for the entire election are given in appendix C.

10. The exceptions on the networks were Perot on ABC, CBS, and CNN and Tsongas on CNN.

11. Virtually all of our conclusions about the overall tone toward candidates of the coverage have been replicated in size and direction by other researchers (Noyes, Lichter, and Amundson 1993; Buchanan 1993; Kerbel 1994). Interestingly, Noyes, Lichter, and Amundson came to the same conclusions even though they analyze exclusively messages in a story that specifically refer to the candidate, while we dealt with the story as a whole. This ranking of candidates by verbal tone is not mirrored in the visual tone. Indeed, on television, visual tone was more similar across candidates than was verbal tone. Notably, the disadvantage that Bush faced on the verbal side on network and local television news was not found in the visual tone.

12. The summed variation of the differences from the neutral point was only 0.4 for CNN (as compared with 0.97 for NBC, 1.8 for ABC, and a whopping 2.4 for CBS).

13. Although for newspapers, wire service stories tended to be more positive toward the candidates than in-house stories, newspapers tended not to use campaign stories from the wire. For example, the *Fargo Forum* was the newspaper that relied *most* on wire stories, yet 69 percent of its campaign stories were written by a *Forum* staffer.

14. There were differences between local television news outlets in the verbal tone toward the candidates, between newspapers in both verbal and visual tone, and between networks in visual tone. Using Winston-Salem as the base for local television, we found that Fargo and Boston had significantly more negative verbal tone toward Bush over and above the predictor variables and that Los Angeles was significantly more negative in its verbal tone toward Perot, but that there were no site differences in visual tone. Again using Winston-Salem as the base for newspapers, we found Fargo and Los Angeles to be significantly more positive in verbal tone toward Bush and Perot, with Boston significantly more positive in verbal tone toward Clinton and Perot. Finally, although there were no network differences (using CNN as the base) in verbal tone, ABC was significantly more positive toward all three candidates and CBS was significantly more positive toward Bush in visual tone.

Chapter Six

1. Examples included the "Viewpoint" program of ABC's "Nightline" and a conference at Harvard's Institute of Politics.

2. Looking back, however, both campaign consultants and journalists agreed, following the 1992 election, on the oversight value of ad watches. According to Howard Kurtz of the *Washington Post,* 1992 was the year that journalists successfully made political consultants as well as the candidates "pay a price for stretching the truth" (Kurtz 1993, 258). Interestingly, consultants for the political candidates agreed that their feet were held to the fire in terms of producing documentation for their ads. This was true even of the losing Bush campaign. At least one of Bush's ad men noted that their side was constrained in articulating their claims by the fact that the ad watch format was in place (Annenberg School of Communication 1993).

3. Jamieson's answer was to develop a "visual grammar" for televised ad watches. She argued that journalists should critique ads for accuracy and developed techniques designed to help journalists do so without amplifying the ad's visual messages. Coverage of ads should be "previewed" through the use of a logo, "Ad Watch." It would clarify the fact that journalists are in charge of the message and are criticizing ads for accuracy, fairness, and whether claims are

taken out of context. She pressed journalists to reclaim the screen through the use of three devices: distancing, displacing, and disclaiming (Jamieson 1992a).

Distancing involves placing the ad content in a television screen and reducing its size.

Displacing involves *visual* effects such as "putting the universal warning sign over the ad's image;" *verbally* documenting the ad's inaccuracies; and turning down the sound of the ad and talking over it.

Disclaiming involves placing a label, e.g., "political advertisement" on the screen as ad visuals are aired.

4. Table 6.1 is based on an every-third-day sample of newspapers over the course of the election. Local and network television news was coded daily.

5. We shall see (chap. 7) that when ad visuals are critiqued by journalists in ad watches, even ones that involve the use of Jamieson's three "Ds," *if the visuals are salient to voters*, candidate messages will be amplified despite what the journalists say. This occurs because voters bring their own interpretations to the message.

6. See Crigler et al. (1992) for a report on the nominating campaign.

7. Edward R. Murrow interviewed politicians on "See It Now" and "Person to Person."

8. Of the 243 interviews with major candidates, 43 percent were from newscasts or news interview programs, 5 percent from magazine shows, 38 percent from weekday morning shows, and 15 percent from other kinds of talk shows (Stevens 1993).

9. Much of the analysis of candidate interview programs is indebted to Russell Stevens, who assisted in this research while writing his master's thesis on this topic. Stevens is completing a book with Marvin Kalb about the role of talk shows in American politics.

10. Reported by Dan Balz in the *Washington Post*, May 19, 1992.

11. King reported the incident on October 2, 1992 at the Shorenstein Center conference on Old Media/New Media at the National Press Club, Washington, D.C.

12. The campaign was not reticent about this approach, which was described by then–campaign manager James Squires. See Kurtz (*Washington Post*, May 3, 1992) and Goodman (*New York Times*, June 8, 1992).

13. Jerry Brown also appeared on "Donahue" and used the opportunity to draw graphs explaining his tax proposals.

14. Difference of means and χ^2 tests on various criteria including length were at the 95 percent confidence level or better. This sample was drawn from Legislate, which included 243 interviews (or 96 percent of the 254 confirmed interviews) because of the availability of transcripts for coding.

15. In the end, Clinton gained a significant increase in the youth vote over Dukakis's 1988 share.

16. Differences in level of confrontation for journalists, professional interviewers, and the audience were statistically significant ($F = 50$, $p < .05$).

17. Audience campaign process questions were significantly more confrontational than any other questions the audience asked, but were not significantly more confrontational than the questions about the campaign coming from journalists or professional interviewers.

18. Two newspapers, the *Wichita Eagle* and the *Charlotte Observer,* used public opinion surveys to establish a citizens' agenda prior to the candidate interview vogue. During the campaign, the newspapers geared their coverage of the campaign to the issues identified by the local citizenry. In 1994, National Public Radio and the Poynter Institute also launched a combined effort to involve communities in influencing campaign agendas. For a description of the project, see *Poynter Report* (1994).

19. Voter efficacy increased in 1992 and accounted for the largest part of the increase in voter turnout according to Rosenstone et al. (1993).

Chapter Seven

1. Similarly an ABC News/*Washington Post* poll taken in September found only 8 percent of respondents thought the news media "paid too much attention to" issues, as compared to 38 percent to opinion polls and 43 percent to media commentators.

2. The "Pipefitter" ads, the *Time* magazine ad, and the "Gray Dot" ad.

3. Figures 7.1 to 7.3 are based on a sample of 20 message segments, each of which totaled six to eight conversational exchanges, from the primary and general election phases of the focus groups. In the case of primary horse-race news and advertising, eight segments were randomly selected to represent all phases of the primary, an equal number of news stories about Democratic and Republican candidates, and an equal number of male and female focus groups. In the general election phase, segments of the October 5–6 focus groups in all four markets dealing with candidate interviews and "American Agenda" programming were included. Segments of the October 28–29 focus groups in all four sites dealing with ads and ad watches were also included.

4. Two of these concepts, "following" and "transforming" are related to the more familiar terms "(media) priming" and "(media) agenda setting." The new terms are used to emphasize that connections with media information depend on the audience interpretations.

5. This finding is reinforced by experimental evidence, showing how people are more inclined to attribute social rather than individual responsibility after watching analytic or "thematic" television as opposed to event-driven coverage (Iyengar 1991).

Chapter Eight

1. Clarity did not increase as the campaign moved to other states, even though several Democratic candidates dropped out of the race. Thus, by our May survey in Winston-Salem, when we asked questions only about Brown and Clinton, there was virtually no difference in the candidates' perceived stand on the balance between domestic needs and foreign policy, with Clinton being seen by 9 percent as more likely to fight unfair competition from Japanese imports and by 7 percent as more likely to favor middle-class tax breaks.

2. According to Fred Woods, a media advisor to the Tsongas campaign: "People reacted negatively. So his main ads did not have him [speaking] in them" (Interview with Montague Kern on April 2, 1992).

3. Ironically, this provided direct evidence of newspaper reading as the hair-combing statement came directly out of a Mike Barnicle column about Tsongas in the *Boston Globe* around the time of our focus group.

4. Both men and women in our focus groups, however, expressed concern about the manipulativeness of Clinton's ads, i.e., his tendency of "going to the strings of your heart."

5. Two types of regression analysis were used in this study. Depending on whether the object of study was categorical or continuous in measurement, the statistical analysis was based on either ordinary least squares regression (continuous dependent variables) or logistic regression (categorical dependent variables). The control variables were: party identification ("Regardless of how you vote, do you usually think of yourself as a Republican, a Democrat, an Independent, or something else?"), ideology ("How would you describe your views on most political matters? Generally, do you think of yourself as liberal, moderate, or conservative?"), age ("Which of the following age group are you in? 18–24, 25–34, 35–44, 45–54, 55–64, or 65 or older"), sex (coded 1 for male, 2 for female), race ("Are you white, black, Hispanic, Asian, or some other race"; recoded as 1 for white, 2 for nonwhite), education ("What is the last grade of school you completed? eighth grade or less, some high school, high school graduate, some college, college graduate, or postgraduate"), and political interest ("Some people seem to follow what's going on in government and public affairs most of the time, whether there's an election going on or not. Others aren't that interested. Would you say you follow what's going on in government and public affairs most of the time, some of the time, only now and then, or hardly at all?"). In the regressions a positive coefficient indicates an independent association between an information source and the candidate quality under consideration.

6. Content analysis shows that these impressions were not reinforced in the press, and respondents who relied on national television or newspapers were more likely to say that Perot made them worried.

7. Watching Perot ads was associated not only with positive views of the candidate but with negative views of his opponents. In our surveys, people who saw Perot ads were more likely to say that Bush did not care about people, that Clinton would make the economy worse, that Clinton also did not care about people, and that Clinton was not honest.

8. A dummy variable indicating either support (coded 1) or nonsupport (coded 0) was created for each campaigner.

Chapter Nine

1. Early studies of the NES data divided the likes and dislikes toward candidates into party, issue, and personal concerns. Later investigations have probed the personal category of assessments of candidates and found that voters focus on politically relevant questions of candidate competence and reliability and less on charisma, personal style, and individual background than was earlier supposed (e.g., Shabad and Andersen 1979).

2. The categories for the "kinds of consideration" are broadly based on the categories that Miller et al. (1986) derived from factor analysis of the NES data: competence, reliability, integrity, charisma, and personal traits.

3. We preserved their original categories of "integrity" and "reliability." We divided their other categories as follows. "Competence" was split into the candidate's ability as a campaigner and the candidate's ability as a leader or professional experience. "Charisma" was coded according to whether it referred to intrapersonal (e.g., sense of humor and strength) or interpersonal (e.g., empathy and ability to communicate) characteristics; we have then renamed those categories "personality traits" and "empathy." "Personal" was split into personal background (e.g., education and region) and visual appearance (e.g., tall, tired, and smiling). If the candidate was mentioned in a way that only evoked a verbally expressed emotional response (e.g., love, hate, and fear) or an evaluation (e.g., "I'm for him" and "I don't like Bush") separate from any indication of the basis of that emotional response or evaluation, we used the categories "emotional" and "evaluation." If candidates were simply mentioned, this was noted as a discrete mention, or if they were referred to in terms of what they were doing without any assessment thereof according to these categories, we coded this as an "event," with a separate subcategory for scandal. Horse-race considerations (e.g., the likelihood of winning, strategy, and tactics) were included with assessments of the candidate's ability as a campaigner. Each of these considerations were also coded as positive, negative, or neutral, basing it on an explicit statement by the interviewee. If and only if the interviewee made an explicit reference to distant past (i.e., prior to the campaign) or future behavior, we also labeled the consideration as "retrospective" or "prospective."

4. The increase over the baseline should be treated with caution since it may reflect either growing comfort with the interview or a sensitization effect.

5. Not surprisingly, the number of considerations an interviewee used at one wave was highly correlated with the number used in subsequent interviews; correlations between successive waves are in the range of .65 to .77. The Pearson's r for number of considerations used in waves one and two was .69, waves two and three .65, and waves three and four .77. However, the number of considerations used in January did not predict as well the number used in October, with a considerably lower correlation of .35 ($p = .008$).

6. We tested other equations including various demographics (gender, income, and education), self-reports of political behavior (media use and party strength), and dummies for two other sites (Winston-Salem and Los Angeles, using the least talkative Moorhead site as our base), in addition to these three independent variables. None of these variables reached statistical significance at the .10 level, and the resultant equations did not explain more variance than a simple three-variable model.

7. McGraw et al. (1994) have recently shown that the like/dislike questions that have been the focus of most scholarly inquiry tend to overestimate party, ideological, and group reference compared to alternative question wordings.

8. We constructed regression equations predicting the percentage of considerations used in each category for each wave of interviews by demographic variables (race, gender, education, and income) and political and media predispositions (partisanship, party strength, media use, attention to news, and political interest). Only 3 of 20 equations significantly explained the variance ($p < .05$) in the dependent variable. For further details, see Cook, Crigler, and Just (1995).

9. Nor could we argue that the use of ideological, partisan, or policy-based considerations is necessarily a sign of sophistication, given that these may be buzzwords, too.

10. A varimax factor analysis was undertaken on the five favorability indices at each wave. Each wave produced a two-factor solution at an eigenvalue of 1, but the second factor rarely explained much more than 20 percent of the variance, considerably behind the first factor.

11. This conclusion is based on correlation coefficients between the 7-point party identification scale and the favorability indices for each candidate and each consideration at each wave. The results were similar when we controlled for a variety of demographics (sex, income, race, and education) and political predispositions (party identification, media use, party strength, and political interest). For further details, see Cook et al. (1995).

12. Since these assessments are highly intercorrelated, they could not be entered into a single equation. Instead our strategy was to compare how well the

votes for and against Clinton, Bush, and Perot were predicted if we knew *only* the assessments made according to a particular type of consideration versus how well the equation predicts by looking at all assessments made regardless of consideration. The three-way race necessitated three dichotomous dependent variables: constructed as votes for or against Bush, votes for or against Clinton, and votes for or against Perot.

13. These percentages should not be regarded as absolute figures but should be compared against the percentages that would be correctly predicted solely by chance, which is determined by the underlying distribution (31 percent of our interviewees voted for Bush, 52 percent for Clinton, and 17 percent for Perot).

Chapter 10

1. Michael McGerr (1986), in a thought-provoking book, has argued that election campaigns in the nineteenth century were no less organized around spectacle and hoopla than their counterparts in the twentieth century. Instead, the rituals of the nineteenth century, such as torchlight parades and rallies, involved the voters as participants, whereas the rise of public relations and objective journalism distanced the spectacle from the electorate, which responded with declining interest and turnout.

2. Note that this description does not rely on the face-to-face contact that traveling home accomplished, which Fenno (1978) saw as perhaps the most important implication of presenting themselves. Fenno (1982), in later comparisons with the "home styles" of U.S. senators, noted the dilemma of moving from two-way "dialogue" to one-way "rhetoric" as states grew and senators depended more on the news media to reach out to constituents. In this context, we should also exercise caution, given the way in which television has transformed political speech, away from the abstract and the declamatory toward the intimate and personal, as Jamieson (1988) has brilliantly documented.

3. See, e.g., Hochschild (1981), Feldman and Zaller (1992), and Zaller (1992). For another attempt by a political theorist and an elections scholar to make theoretical sense of Converse, see Kinder and Herzog (1993).

4. Even if the reasons are mere rationalizations, we would point out that the first two definitions of "rationalize" listed in the *American Heritage Dictionary* are "to make conformable to reason; make rational" and "to interpret from a rational standpoint."

References

Abramson, Paul R., John H. Aldrich, and David Rohde. 1986. *Change and Continuity in the 1984 Elections.* Washington, D.C.: CQ Press.

Adams, William C. 1987. "As New Hampshire Goes . . ." In *Media and Momentum: The New Hampshire Primary and Nomination Politics,* edited by Nelson W. Polsby and Gary R. Orren, 42–59. Chatham, N.J.: Chatham House.

Adatto, Kiku. 1990. "Sound Bite Democracy." Research paper, Kennedy School Press Politics Center, Harvard University, June.

Aldrich, John H., John L. Sullivan, and Eugene Borgida. 1989. "Foreign Affairs and Issue Voting: Do Presidential Candidates 'Waltz before a Blind Audience'?" *American Political Science Review* 83:123–41.

Alger, Dean. 1995. *The Media and Politics,* 2d ed. Belmont, Calif.: Wadsworth.

———. 1996. "Constructing Campaign Messages and Public Understanding: The 1990 Wellstone-Boschwitz Senate Race in Minnesota." Forthcoming in *The Psychology of Political Communication,* edited by Ann N. Crigler. Ann Arbor: University of Michigan Press.

Alger, Dean, Montague Kern, and Darrell M. West. 1993. "Political Advertising, the Information Environment and the Voter in the 1992 Presidential Election." Paper presented at annual meeting of the International Communication Association, Washington, D. C., May 27–31.

Altheide, David L. 1976. *Creating Reality: How TV News Distorts Events.* Beverly Hills, Calif.: Sage.

Annenberg School of Communication. 1993. "Election Debriefing." Conference videotape, Annenberg School of Communication, University of Pennsylvania, December 12.

Arterton, F. Christopher. 1984. *Media Politics: The News Strategies of Presidential Campaigns.* Lexington, Mass.: Lexington Books.

———. 1993. "Campaign '92: Strategies and Tactics of the Candidates." In *The Election of 1992,* edited by Gerald M. Pomper, 74–109. Chatham, N.J.: Chatham House.

Bartels, Larry. 1988. *Presidential Primaries and the Dynamics of Public Choice.* Princeton, N.J.: Princeton University Press.

———. 1993. "Messages Received: The Political Impact of Media Exposure." *American Political Science Review* 87:267–86.

Beck, Paul Allen. 1991. "Voters' Intermediation Environments in the 1988 Presidential Contest." *Public Opinion Quarterly* 55:371–94.

Bennett, W. Lance. 1993. "Constructing Publics and Their Opinions." *Political Communication* 10:101–20.

Berelson, Bernard R., Paul F. Lazarsfeld, and William N. McPhee. 1952. *Voting*. Chicago: University of Chicago Press.

Boiney, John, and David L. Paletz. 1991. "In Search of the Model: Political Science versus Political Advertising Perspectives on Voter Decision Making." In *Television and Political Advertising*, vol. 1, edited by Frank Biocca, 3–27. Hillsdale, N.J.: Erlbaum.

Brace, Paul, and Barbara Hinckley. 1992. *Follow the Leader: Opinion Polls and the Modern Presidents*. New York: Basic.

Brady, Henry E., and Richard Johnston. 1987. "What's the Primary Message: Horserace or Issue Journalism?" In *Media and Momentum: The New Hampshire Primary and Nomination Politics*, edited by Gary Orren and Nelson Polsby, 127–86. Chatham, N.J.: Chatham House.

Broder, David. 1990. "Putting Sanity Back in Elections." *Washington Post*, January 14, D1.

Brody, Richard A., and Benjamin I. Page. 1972. "The Assessment of Policy Voting." *American Political Science Review* 66:450–58.

———. 1973. "Indifference, Alienation and Rational Decisions: The Effects of Candidate Evaluations on Turnout and the Vote." *Public Choice* 15:1–17.

Brown, Steven R. 1980. *Political Subjectivity: Applications of Q Methodology in Political Science*. New Haven, Conn.: Yale University Press.

Buchanan, Bruce. 1991. *Electing a President: The Markle Commission Research on Campaign '88*. Austin: University of Texas Press.

———. 1993. "A Tale of Two Campaigns, or Why '92's Voters Forced a Better Campaign Than '88's and How It Could Happen Again." Paper presented at annual meeting of the American Political Science Association, Washington, D. C., September 1–4.

Campbell, Angus, Philip E. Converse, Warren E. Miller, and Donald E. Stokes. 1960. *The American Voter*. New York: Wiley.

Campbell, Angus, Gerald Gurin, and Warren E. Miller. 1954. *The Voter Decides*. Evanston, Ill.: Row, Peterson.

Campbell, James. 1993. "Forecasting the Presidential Vote in the States." *American Journal of Political Science* 36:386–408.

Cappella, Joseph N., and Kathleen Hall Jamieson. 1994. "Broadcast Adwatch Effects." *Communication Research* 21:342–65.

Carroll, Raymond L. 1992. "Blurring Distinctions: Network and Local News." In *The Future of News,* edited by Philip S. Cook, Douglas Gomery, and Lawrence W. Lichty, 45–51. Washington, D.C.: Woodrow Wilson Center Press.

Castellanos, Alex. 1993. Talk given at Kennedy School of Government, Harvard University, March 17.

Conover, Pamela Johnston, and Stanley Feldman. 1989. "Candidate Perception in an Ambiguous World: Campaigns, Cues, and Inference Processes." *American Journal of Political Science* 33:912–39.

Converse, Philip E. 1964. "The Nature of Belief Systems in Mass Publics." In *Ideology and Discontent,* edited by David E. Apter, 206–61. New York: Free Press.

———. 1970. "Attitudes and Nonattitudes: Continuation of a Dialogue." In *The Quantitative Analysis of Social Problems,* edited by Edward R. Tufte, 168–89. Reading, Mass.: Addison-Wesley.

Cook, Timothy E., Ann N. Crigler, and Marion R. Just. 1995. "Considering the Candidates." Paper presented at annual meeting of the American Political Science Association, Chicago.

Cook, Timothy E., and Lyn Ragsdale. 1995. "The President and the Press: Negotiating Newsworthiness at the White House." In *The Presidency and the Political System,* 4th ed., edited by Michael Nelson, 297–330. Washington, D.C.: CQ Press.

Crigler, Ann N., Marion R. Just, and Timothy E. Cook. 1992. "Local News, National News and the 1992 Presidential Election." Paper presented at annual meeting of the American Political Science Association, Chicago.

Crigler, Ann N., Marion R. Just, and W. Russell Neuman. 1994. "Interpreting Visual versus Audio Messages in Television News." *Journal of Communication* 44:132–50.

Deaver, Michael. 1989. Interview by Bill Moyers, "Illusions of News." Videotape.

Delli Carpini, Michael X., and Bruce Williams. 1994. "The Method Is the Message: Focus Groups as a Method of Social, Psychological and Political Inquiry." *Research in Micropolitics* 4:57–85.

Diamond, Edwin, and Stephen Bates. 1992. *The Spot: The Rise of Political Advertising on Television.* Cambridge, Mass.: MIT Press.

Downs, Anthony. 1957. *An Economic Theory of Democracy.* New York: Harper & Row.

Entman, Robert M. 1989. *Democracy without Citizens: Media and the Decay of American Politics.* New York: Oxford University Press.

———. 1992. "Super Tuesday and the Future of Local News." In *The Future of News,* edited by Philip S. Cook, Douglas Gomery, and Lawrence W. Lichty, 53–68. Washington, D.C.: Woodrow Wilson Center Press.

Epstein, Edward Jay. 1972. *News from Nowhere: Television and the News.* New York: Vintage.

Erbring, Lutz, Edie M. Goldenberg, and Arthur H. Miller. 1980. "Front-Page News and Real-World Cues: A New Look at Agenda-Setting." *American Journal of Political Science* 24:16–49.

Feldman, Stanley, and Pamela Johnston Conover. 1983. "Candidates, Issues, and Voters: The Role of Inference in Political Perception." *Journal of Politics* 45:810–39.

Feldman, Stanley, and John Zaller. 1992. "The Political Culture of Ambivalence: Ideological Responses to the Welfare State." *American Journal of Political Science* 36:268–307.

Fenno, Richard F., Jr. 1978. *Home Style: U.S. House Members in Their Districts.* Boston: Little, Brown.

———. 1982. *The United States Senate: A Bicameral Perspective.* Washington, D.C.: American Enterprise Institute.

Festinger, Leon. 1957. *A Theory of Cognitive Dissonance.* Evanston, Ill: Row-Peterson.

Finkel, Steven E. 1993. "Reexamining the 'Minimal Effects' Model in Recent Presidential Campaigns." *Journal of Politics* 55: 1–21.

Fiorina, Morris P. 1981. *Retrospective Voting in American National Elections.* New Haven, Conn.: Yale University Press.

———. 1990. "Information and Rationality in Elections." In *Information and Democratic Processes,* edited by John A. Ferejohn and James H. Kuklinski, 329–42. Urbana: University of Illinois Press.

Fisher, Walter R. 1989. *Human Communication as Narration: Toward a Philosophy of Reason, Value and Action.* Columbia: University of South Carolina Press.

Foddy, William. 1993. *Constructing Questions for Interviews and Questionnaires: Theory and Practice in Social Research.* New York: Cambridge University Press.

Frankovic, Kathleen. 1985. "The 1984 Election: The Irrelevance of the Campaign." *PS: Political Science and Politics* 18:37–42.

———. 1993. "Public Opinion in the 1992 Campaign." In *The Election of 1992,* edited by Gerald M. Pomper, 110–31. Chatham, N.J.: Chatham House.

Fredin, Eric S., and Tracy Tabaczynski. 1994. "Media Schemata, Information Processing Strategies, and Audience Assessment of the Informational Value of Quotes and Background in Local News." *Journalism Quarterly* 70:801–14.

Friedenburg, Robert V. 1994. "The 1992 Presidential Debates." In *The 1992 Presidential Campaign: A Communication Perspective,* edited by Robert E. Denton, Jr., 89–111. Westport, Conn.: Praeger.

Gamson, William. 1988. "A Constructionist Approach to Mass Media and Public Opinion." *Symbolic Interaction* 11:161–74.

———. 1993. *Talking Politics*. New York: Cambridge University Press.

Gans, Herbert. 1979. *Deciding What's News*. New York: Pantheon.

Gaventa, John. 1980. *Power and Powerlessness: Quiescence and Rebellion in an Appalachian Valley*. Urbana: University of Illinois Press.

Gelman, Andrew, and Gary King. 1993. "Why Are American Presidential Election Campaign Polls So Variable When Votes Are So Predictable?" *British Journal of Political Science* 23:409–51.

Germond, Jack, and Jules Witcover. 1993. *Mad as Hell: Revolt at the Ballot Box, 1992*. New York: Warner.

Glass, David P. 1985. "Evaluating Presidential Candidates: Who Focuses on Their Personal Attributes?" *Public Opinion Quarterly* 49:517–34.

Graber, Doris A. 1984. *Processing the News: Taming the Information Tide*. New York: Longmans.

———. 1987. "Kind Words and Harsh Pictures: How Television Presents the Candidates." In *Elections in America*, edited by Kay Lehman Schlozman, 115–41. Boston: Allen & Unwin.

———, ed. 1994. *Media Power in Politics*. Washington, D.C.: CQ Press.

Greene, Jay P. 1993. "Forewarned before Forecast: Presidential Election Forecasting Models and the 1992 Election." *PS: Political Science & Politics* 26:17–22.

Greer, Frank. 1993. Talk given at preconference on Communication in the 1992 Presidential Campaign at annual meeting of the International Communication Association, Washington, D. C., May 27.

Hallin, Daniel C. 1992. "Sound Bite News: Television Coverage of Elections, 1968–1988 (Symposium: Television News and Its Dis-Contents)." *Journal of Communication* 42:5–25.

Hastie, Reid, and Bernadette Park. 1986. "The Relationship between Memory and Judgement Depends on Whether the Judgement Task Is Memory-based or On-line." *Psychological Review* 93:258–68.

Hastie, Reid, and Nancy Pennington. 1988. "Notes on the Distinction between Memory-based and On-line Judgements." In *On-line Cognition in Person Perception*, edited by John N. Bassili, 1–17. Hillsdale, N.J.: Erlbaum.

Hellweg, Susan A., Michael Pfau, and Steven R. Brydon. 1992. *Televised Presidential Debates*. New York: Praeger.

Hershey, Marjorie. 1989. "The Campaign and the Media." In *The Election of 1988*, edited by Gerald M. Pomper, 73–102. Chatham, N.J.: Chatham House.

Hertsgaard, Mark. 1988. *On Bended Knee: The Press and the Reagan Presidency*. New York: Schocken.

Hochschild, Jennifer L. 1981. *What's Fair? American Beliefs about Distributive Justice.* Cambridge, Mass.: Harvard University Press.

———. 1993. "Disjunction and Ambivalence in Citizens' Political Outlooks." In *Reconsidering the Democratic Public,* edited by George E. Marcus and Russell L. Hanson, 187–210. University Park: Pennsylvania State University Press.

Hofstetter, C. Richard. 1976. *Bias in the News: Network Television Coverage of the 1972 Election Campaign.* Columbus: Ohio State University Press.

Huckfeldt, Robert, and John Sprague. 1988. "Choice, Social Structure, and Political Information: The Informational Coercion of Minorities." *American Journal of Political Science* 32:467–82.

Iyengar, Shanto. 1991. *Is Anyone Responsible?* Chicago: University of Chicago Press.

Iyengar, Shanto, and Donald Kinder. 1987. *News That Matters.* Chicago: University of Chicago Press.

Iyengar, Shanto, Mark Peters, and Donald R. Kinder. 1982. "Experimental Demonstrations of the 'Not-So-Minimal' Consequences of Television News Programs." *American Political Science Review* 80:521–40.

Jacobs, Lawrence R., and Robert Y. Shapiro. 1994. "Issues, Candidate Image, and Priming: The Use of Private Polls in Kennedy's 1960 Presidential Campaign." *American Political Science Review* 88:527–40.

Jamieson, Kathleen Hall. 1988. *Eloquence in an Electronic Age: The Transformation of Political Speechmaking.* New York: Oxford University Press.

———. 1992a. *Dirty Politics.* New York: Oxford University Press.

———. 1992b. *Packaging the Presidency,* 2d ed. New York: Oxford University Press.

Jamieson, Kathleen Hall, and Karlyn Kohrs Campbell. 1983. *The Interplay of Influence: Mass Media and Their Publics in News, Advertising, Politics.* Belmont, Calif.: Wadsworth.

Janis, Irving. 1972. *Victims of Groupthink.* Boston: Houghton Mifflin.

Johnson-Carter, Karen, and Gary Copeland. 1991. *Negative Political Advertising.* Hillsdale, N.J.: Erlbaum.

Johnston, Richard, André Blais, Henry E. Brady, and Jean Crête. 1992. *Letting the People Decide: Dynamics of a Canadian Election.* Stanford, Calif: Stanford University Press.

Joslyn, Richard. 1986. "Political Advertising and the Meaning of Elections." In *New Perspectives on Political Advertising,* edited by Lynda Lee Kaid, Dan Nimmo, and Keith R. Sanders, 139–84. Carbondale: Southern Illinois Press.

Just, Marion, Ann Crigler, and Tami Buhr. 1995. "Discordant Discourse: News, Candidate Interviews, and Political Ads in the 1992 Presidential Campaign." Paper presented at annual meeting of the American Political Science Association, Chicago.

Just, Marion, Ann Crigler, and Lori Wallach. 1990. "Thirty Seconds or Thirty Minutes: What Viewers Learn from Spot Advertisements and Candidate Debates." *Journal of Communication* 40:120–55.

Kaid, Lynda Lee, Robert Gobetz, Jane Garner, Chris M. Leland, and David K. Scott. 1993. "Television News and Presidential Campaigns: The Legitimization of Televised Political Advertising." *Social Science Quarterly* 74:274–85.

Kaid, Lynda Lee, Dan Nimmo, and Keith Sanders, eds. 1986. *New Perspectives on Political Advertising.* Carbondale: Southern Illinois Press.

Kalb, Marvin. 1992. "From Sound Bite to a Mean." *New York Times,* July 3.

Kaniss, Phyllis. 1991. *Making Local News.* Chicago: University of Chicago Press.

Keeter, Scott, and Cliff Zukin. 1983. *Uninformed Choice.* New York: Praeger.

Kelley, Stanley. 1983. *Interpreting Elections.* Princeton, N.J.: Princeton University Press.

Kelley, Stanley, and Thad W. Mirer. 1974. "The Simple Act of Voting." *American Political Science Review* 68:572–91.

Kendall, Kathleen, ed. 1995. *Presidential Campaign Discourse: Strategic Communication Problems.* Albany: State University of New York Press.

Kerbel, Matthew. 1994. *Edited for Television: ABC, CNN and the 1992 Presidential Campaign.* Boulder, Colo.: Westview.

Kern, Montague. 1989. *Thirty-Second Politics: Political Advertising in the Eighties.* New York: Praeger.

———. 1993. "The Advertising-driven 'New' Mass Media Election and the Rhetoric of Policy Issues." In *Mass Media and Public Policy,* edited by Robert Spitzer, 133–52. Westport, Conn.: Praeger.

Kern, Montague, and Marion Just. 1994. "How Voters Construct Images of Political Advertising and Television News." Research Paper R–10, Joan Shorenstein Center on Press, Politics and Public Policy, John F. Kennedy School of Government, Harvard University.

———. 1995. "The Focus Group Method, Political Advertising, Campaign News and the Construction of Candidate Images." *Political Communication* 12:127–45.

Kern, Montague, and Robert Wicks. 1994. "Television News and the Advertising-driven 'New' Mass Media Election: A More Significant Local Role in 1992." In *The 1992 Presidential Campaign: A Communication Perspective,* edited by Robert E. Denton, Jr, 189–206. Westport, Conn.: Praeger.

Kinder, Donald R., and Don Herzog. 1993. "Democratic Discussion." In *Reconsidering the Democratic Public,* edited by George E. Marcus and Russell L. Hanson, 347–77. University Park: Pennsylvania State University Press.

Kosicki, Gerald M., and Jack M. McLeod. 1990. "Learning from Political News: Effects of Media Images and Information Processing Strategies." In *Mass Com-*

munication and Political Information Processing, edited by Sidney Kraus, 69–85. Hillsdale, N.J.: Erlbaum.

Krouse, Richard W., and George E. Marcus. 1984. "Electoral Studies and Democratic Theory Reconsidered." *Political Behavior* 6:23–39.

Kumar, Martha Joynt. 1995. "President Clinton Meets the Media: Communications Shaped by Predictable Patterns." In *The Clinton Presidency: Campaigning, Governing, and the Psychology of Leadership,* edited by Stanley A. Renshon, 167–93. Boulder, Colo.: Westview.

Kurtz, Howard. 1993. *Media Circus: The Trouble with America's Newspapers.* New York: Times Books.

Lane, Robert E. 1962. *Political Ideology: Why the American Common Man Believes What He Does.* New York: Free Press.

Lane, Robert E., and David Sears. 1964. *Public Opinion.* New York: Free Press.

Lanzetta, John T., Denis G. Sullivan, Roger D. Masters, and Gregory J. McHugo. 1985. "Emotional and Cognitive Responses to Televised Images of Political Leaders." In *Mass Media and Political Thought,* edited by Sidney Kraus and Richard M. Perloff. Beverly Hills, Calif.: Sage.

Lau, Richard R. 1989. "Construct Accessibility and Electoral Choice." *Political Behavior* 11:5–32.

Lazarsfeld, Paul F., Bernard R. Berelson, and Hazel Gaudet. 1944. *The People's Choice.* New York: Duell, Sloan, and Pierce.

Lederman, Linda Costigan. 1990. "Assessing Education Effectiveness: The Focus Group Interview as a Technique for Data Collection." *Communication Education* 38:117–27.

Lewis-Beck, Michael S., and Tom W. Rice. 1992. *Forecasting Elections.* Washington, D.C.: CQ Press.

Lodge, Milton, and Kathleen McGraw, eds. 1995. *Political Judgment.* Ann Arbor: University of Michigan Press.

Lodge, Milton, Kathleen M. McGraw, and Patrick Stroh. 1989. "An Impression-driven Model of Candidate Evaluation." *American Political Science Review* 83:399–420.

Lodge, Milton, and Patrick Stroh. 1993. "Inside the Mental Voting Booth: An Impression-driven Process Model of Candidate Evaluation." In *Explorations in Political Psychology,* edited by Shanto Iyengar and William J. McGuire, 225–63. Durham, N.C.: Duke University Press.

Louden, Allen. 1991. "A Narrative Approach to the Examination of Political Advertising: Perspectives on the 1990 Gantt-Helms Senate Campaign." Paper prepared for presentation at annual meeting of the International Communication Association, Chicago, May.

———. 1994. 'Special Issue: Condensed Mediated Argument." *Argumentation and Advocacy* 31(3):51–53.

Lupia, Arthur. 1994. "Shortcuts versus Encyclopedias: Information and Voting Behavior in California Insurance Reform Elections." *American Political Science Review* 88:63–76.

MacKuen, Michael, and Steven Coombs. 1981. *More than News: Media Power in Public Affairs.* Beverly Hills, Calif.: Sage.

MacKuen, Michael, and George E. Marcus. 1994. "Emotional Intelligence." Paper prepared for the American Political Science Association, Washington, D.C.

Marcus, George E. 1988. "Democratic Theories and the Study of Public Opinion." *Polity* 21:25–44.

Marcus, George E., and Michael MacKuen. 1994. "Anxiety, Enthusiasm, and the Vote: The Emotional Underpinnings of Learning and Involvement during Presidential Campaigns." *American Political Science Review* 87:672–85.

Marcus, George E., John L. Sullivan, and David Tabb. 1974. "The Application of Individual Differences Scaling to the Measurement of Political Ideologies." *American Journal of Political Science* 18:405–20.

Mayer, William G. 1994. "Trends: The Rise of the New Media." *Public Opinion Quarterly* 58:124–46.

McCombs, Maxwell E., and Donald L. Shaw. 1972. "The Agenda Setting Function of the Mass Media." *Public Opinion Quarterly* 36:176–87.

McCracken, Grant David. 1988. *The Long Interview.* Newbury Park, Calif.: Sage.

McGerr, Michael. 1986. *The Decline of Popular Politics: The American North, 1865– . . .* New York: Oxford University Press.

McGraw, Kathleen, Mark Fischle, and Karen Stenner. 1994. "Probing Political Memory: A Comparison of Measures." Revised version of paper presented at annual meeting of the Midwest Political Science Association, Chicago, April.

McGraw, Kathleen, Milton Lodge, and Patrick Stroh. 1990. "On-line Processing in Candidate Evaluation: The Effects of Issue Order, Issue Importance and Sophistication." *Political Behavior* 12:41–58.

McManus, John. 1994. *Market-driven Journalism: Let the Citizen Beware?* Thousand Oaks, Calif.: Sage.

Meadow, Robert, and Lee Sigelman. 1982. "Some Effects and Noneffects of Campaign Commercials." *Political Behavior* 4(2):163–77.

Milburn, Michael A., and Justin Brown. 1994. "Busted by the Ad Police: Journalists' Coverage of Political Campaign Ads in the 1992 Presidential Campaign." Research Paper R–15, Joan Shorenstein Center on Press, Politics and Public Policy, John F. Kennedy School of Government, Harvard University.

Miller, Arthur H., Martin P. Wattenberg, and Oksana Malanchuk. 1986. "Schematic Assessments of Presidential Candidates." *American Political Science Review* 80:521–40.

Mishler, Elliot G. 1986. *Research Interviewing: Context and Narrative.* Cambridge, Mass.: Harvard University Press.

Neuman, W. Russell, Marion Just, and Ann Crigler. 1992. *Common Knowledge: News and the Construction of Political Meaning.* Chicago: University of Chicago Press.

Newhagen, John E., and Byron Reeves. 1991. "Emotion and Memory Responses for Negative Political Advertising: A Study of Television Commercials Used in the 1988 Presidential Election." In *Television and Political Advertising,* vol. 1, edited by Frank Biocca, 197–221. Hillsdale, N.J.: Erlbaum.

Nie, Norman H., Sidney Verba, and John R. Petrocik. 1976. *The Changing American Voter.* Cambridge, Mass.: Harvard University Press.

Nimmo, Dan. 1994. "The Electronic Town Hall in Campaign '92: Interactive Forum or Carnival of Buncombe?" In *The 1992 Presidential Campaign: A Communication Perspective,* edited by Robert E. Denton, Jr., 207–227. Westport, Conn.: Praeger.

Nisbett, Richard E., and Lee Ross. 1980. *Human Inference: Strategies and Shortcomings of Social Judgment.* Englewood Cliffs, N.J.: Prentice-Hall.

Nisbett, Richard, and Timothy Wilson. 1977. "Telling More Than We Know: Verbal Reports on Mental Processes." *Psychological Review* 84:231–59.

Noelle-Neumann, Elisabeth. 1993. *Spiral of Silence,* 2d ed. Chicago: University of Chicago Press.

Noyes, Richard E., S. Robert Lichter, and Daniel R. Amundson. 1993. "Was TV Election News Better This Time? A Content Analysis of 1988 and 1992 Campaign Coverage." *Journal of Political Science* 21:3–25.

Page, Benjamin I. 1978. *Choices and Echoes in Presidential Elections.* Chicago: University of Chicago Press.

Page, Benjamin I., and Richard A. Brody. 1972. "Policy Voting and the Electoral Process: The Vietnam War Issue." *American Political Science Review* 66:979–95.

Page, Benjamin I., and Robert Y. Shapiro. 1992. *The Rational Public: Fifty Years of Trends in Americans' Policy Preferences.* Chicago: University of Chicago Press.

Paivio, Allan. 1991. *Images in Mind: The Evolution of a Theory.* New York: Harvester Wheatsheaf.

Patterson, Thomas E. 1980. *The Mass Media Election: How Americans Choose Their President.* New York: Praeger.

———. 1993. *Out of Order.* New York: Knopf.

Patterson, Thomas E., and Robert D. McClure. 1976. *The Unseeing Eye: The Myth of Television Power in National Elections.* New York: Putnam.

Perloff, Richard M. 1993. "Third-Person Effect Research 1983–1992: A Review and Synthesis." *International Journal of Public Opinion Research* 5:167–84.

Pfau, Michael, and Henry Kenski. 1990. *Attack Politics.* New York: Praeger.

Pfau, Michael, and Allan Louden. 1993. "Effectiveness of Adwatch Formats in Deflecting Political Attack Ads." *Communication Research* 21:325–41.

Pitkin, Hanna Fenichel. 1967. *The Concept of Representation.* Berkeley: University of California Press.

Pomper, Gerald, ed. 1993. *The 1992 Elections.* Chatham, N.J.: Chatham House.

Popkin, Samuel L. 1991. *The Reasoning Voter: Communication and Persuasion in Presidential Campaigns.* Chicago: University of Chicago Press.

Poynter Report. 1994. St. Petersberg, Fla.: Poynter Institute, Spring.

Price, Vincent, and John Zaller. 1993. "Who Gets the News? Alternative Measures of News Reception and Their Implications for Research." *Public Opinion Quarterly* 57:133–65.

Rahn, Wendy M., John H. Aldrich, Eugene Borgida, and John L. Sullivan. 1990. "A Social-Cognitive Model of Candidate Appraisal." In *Information and Democratic Processes,* edited by John A. Ferejohn and James H. Kuklinski, 136–59. Urbana: University of Illinois Press.

Rahn, Wendy M., Jon A. Krosnick, and Marijke Breuning. 1994. "Rationalization and Derivation Processes in Survey Studies of Political Candidate Evaluation." *American Journal of Political Science* 38:582–601.

Roberts, Marilyn, and Maxwell McCombs. 1994. "Agenda Setting and Political Advertising: Origins of the News Agenda." *Political Communication* 11:249–62.

Robinson, Michael J., and Margaret A. Sheehan. 1983. *Over the Wire and on TV: CBS and UPI in Campaign '80.* New York: Russell Sage Foundation.

Rosenstiel, Tom. 1994. *Strange Bedfellows: How Television and the Presidential Candidates Changed American Politics, 1992.* New York: Hyperion.

Rosenstone, Steven J., John Mark Hansen, Paul Freedman, and Marguerite Grabanek. 1993. "Voter Turnout: Myth and Reality in the 1992 Election." Paper prepared for presentation at annual meeting of the American Political Science Association, Washington, D.C.

Rothenberg, Randall. 1990a. "Newspaper Notes What People Watch in the Television Campaign." *National Journal,* October 27, 2595.

———. 1990b. "The Press Plays Referee on Campaign Ads." *New York Times,* November 4, A1.

Royer, Charles T., ed. 1994. *Campaign for President: The Managers Look at '92.* Hollis, N.H.: Hollis Publishing.

Sabato, Larry. 1991. *Feeding Frenzy: How Attack Journalism Has Transformed American Politics.* New York: Free Press.

Schattschneider, E. E. 1960. *The Semi-Sovereign People.* New York: Holt, Rinehart & Winston.

Schor, Juliet. 1991. *The Overworked American: The Unexpected Decline of Leisure.* New York: Basic.

Schneider, William. 1992. "When Issues, Not Personalities, Rule." *National Journal,* December 5.

Schuman, Howard, and Stanley Presser. 1981. "The Open and Closed Question." *American Sociological Review* 44:692–712.

Schwartz, Tony. 1974. *The Responsive Chord.* Garden City, N.Y.: Anchor.

Semetko, Holli A., Jay G. Blumler, Michael Gurevitch, and David H. Weaver. 1991. *The Formation of Campaign Agendas: A Comparative Analysis of Party and Media Roles in Recent American and British Elections.* Hillsdale, N.J.: Erlbaum.

Shabad, Goldie, and Kristi Andersen. 1979. "Candidate Evaluations by Men and Women." *Public Opinion Quarterly* 43:18–35.

Shepsle, Kenneth A. 1986. "Institutional Equilibrium and Equilibrium Institutions." In *Political Science: The Science of Politics,* edited by Herbert F. Weisberg, 51–81. New York: Agathon.

Sigal, Leon V. 1973. *Reporters and Officials: The Organization and Politics of Newsmaking.* Lexington, Mass.: Heath.

Sigelman, Lee, and David Bullock. 1991. "Candidates, Issues, Horse Races, and Hoopla." *American Politics Quarterly* 19:5–32.

Smith, Eric R. A. N. 1989. *The Unchanging American Voter.* Berkeley and Los Angeles: University of California Press.

Sniderman, Paul M. 1993. "The New Look in Public Opinion Research." In *Political Science: The State of the Discipline,* vol. 2, edited by Ada W. Finifter, 219–45. Washington, D.C.: American Political Science Association.

Sniderman, Paul, Richard Brody, and Philip Tetlock. 1991. *Reasoning and Choice.* New York: Cambridge University Press.

Stevens, Russell. 1993. "Talk Show Democracy: The Effect of Televised Talk Shows on the 1992 Presidential Election Campaign." Policy analysis exercise, John F. Kennedy School of Government.

Tuchman, Gaye. 1973. "Making News by Doing Work: Routinizing the Unexpected." *American Journal of Sociology,* 110–31.

———. 1978. *Making News: A Study in the Construction of Reality.* New York: Free Press.

Wattenberg, Martin. 1990. *The Decline of American Political Parties: 1952–1988.* Cambridge, Mass.: Harvard University Press.

———. 1991. *The Rise of Candidate-centered Politics.* Cambridge, Mass.: Harvard University Press.

West, Darrell M. 1993. *Air Wars: Television Advertising in Election Campaigns, 1952–1992.* Washington, D.C.: Congressional Quarterly Press.

West, Darrell, Montague Kern, and Dean Alger. 1992. "Political Advertising and Ad Watches in the 1992 Presidential Nominating Contests." Paper prepared for presentation at annual meeting of the American Political Science Association, Chicago.

West, Darrell M., Montague Kern, Dean Alger, and Janice M. Goggin. 1994. "Ad Buys in Presidential Campaigns: The Strategies of Electoral Persuasion." Paper prepared for presentation at annual meeting of the Midwest Political Science Association, Chicago.

Wicks, Robert H., and Montague Kern. 1993. "Cautious Optimism: A New Proactive Role for Local Television Departments in Local Election Coverage?" *American Behavioral Scientist* 37:2.

Zaller, John. 1992. *The Nature and Origins of Mass Opinion.* New York: Cambridge University Press.

Zhao, Xinshu, and Steven Chaffee. "Campaign Advertisements versus Television News as Sources of Political Issue Information." *Public Opinion Quarterly* 59:41–65.

Author Index

Abramson, Paul, 44
Adams, William, 94
Adatto, Kiku, 120, 135, 161
Aldrich, John H., 44, 261
Alger, Dean, 63–64, 78, 182, 201
Altheide, David, 89–90
Andersen, Kristi, 210
Annenberg School of Communication, 86, 122
Arterton, Chrisopher, 7, 78

Bartels, Larry, 89
Bates, Stephen, 63
Beck, Paul, 23
Bennett, W. Lance, 280
Berelson, Bernard, 5, 20, 89
Blais, André, 261
Boiney, John, 37
Borgida, Eugene, 261
Brace, Paul, 76
Brady, Henry E., 99, 261
Breuning, Marijke, 262
Broder, David, 38, 121–22
Brody, Richard, 8, 11, 20, 23, 89
Brown, Steven, 261
Brydon, Steven, 65
Buchanan, Bruce, 142
Buhr, Tami, 96
Bullock, David, 99

Campbell, Angus, 7, 24, 89, 216, 241–42
Campbell, James, 5, 261
Campbell, Karlyn, 64
Cappella, Joseph N., 134
Carroll, Raymond, 95
Castellanos, Alex, 80
Chaffee, Steven, 30
Conover, Pamela Johnston, 21–22, 262
Converse, Philip, 7, 21, 24, 89, 241–42, 261
Cook, Timothy, 113, 183, 241
Coombs, Steven, 43
Copeland, Gary, 64, 81, 86
Crête, Jean, 261
Crigler, Ann, 36, 96, 113, 172, 173, 183

Deaver, Michael, 12, 135
Delli Carpini, Michael, 28
Diamond, Edwin, 63
Downs, Anthony, 148

Entman, Robert, 13, 91
Epstein, Edward, 90
Erbring, Lutz, 43

Feldman, Stanley, 21–22, 242, 262
Fenno, Richard, 8, 237–38

293

General Index

233; Democratic, 66, 94, 136, 178–85, 192, 193, 217, 270; evaluations, 9, 66, 99, 109, 188; image, 8, 62, 66, 78, 118, 180–203, *184, 188;* independent, 76, 80, 201 (*see also* Perot, Ross); interviews, 33, 121, 135–48, 167, 176, 236; messages/positions, 65–68, 88, 89, 99, 106, 162–63, 210; personality, 8, 13, 78, 99, *101–3,* 143, 146, *184, 188, 189,* 209–30, *225–28;* Republican, 66, 179–85; strategy, 65, 155 (*see also* campaign, strategy; *candidates by name*)

CBS, 33, 91, 124, 130, 132, 141, 147, *257–59, 270–72*

changes over time: candidate strategy, 177–203; character, 16–19, 26, 44, 56–57, 106, 193–99, 206–15; citizen issue agenda, 171–72, 235; considerations, 9, 18–19, 26, 44, 56–57, 106, 192–99, 206–15, 221–30; use of prior knowledge, 163–67; media coverage, 157, 240–43; public interest, 152; relevance of study, 18–19

Changing American Voter, The, (Nie et al.), 263

character: candidates and, 6, 8, 17, 38, 58, 62, *82,* 99, 102, *102–3, 209,* 220, *225–28,* 243; changes over the campaign, 16–19, 26, 44, 56–57, 106, 193–99, 206–15; citizens' assessment of, 13, 88, 92, *184–89,* 209–30, *225–28;* considerations, 13, 209–30, 276; definition, 210; media coverage of, 13, 57–58, 99. *See also candidates by name*

citizen(s): and access to information, 89–119, 128, 151, 176, 206; agenda, 14, 43–61, 148, 233; candidate preferences, 88, 147; capacity to participate, 43–44, 89–95, 135–47, 151–52, 176, 230, 234, 242–43; considerations, 9, 10, 20–21, *225–28;* information processing and, 10–14, 22–23, 39, 88–120, 128, 133, 151–76, 206–43; issue priorities, 15, 88, 237–43

citizen assessments: of ad watch, 16, 125–33, 236; of advertising, 59–60, 159–67; of campaign, 159–67; of candidates, 99, 119, 169, 177–203, *184, 188, 189, 202,* 215–30, 234, 243; of character, 13, 88, 92, *184–89,* 209–30, *225–28;* of horse-race coverage, 13, 169, 171–72, 176, 179, 236, 240; of image, 187–93; of issues, 43–55, 61, 70–72, 116, 237; of media, 43–44, 151–76; of coverage of campaign, 152–59; of morality, 219, 215–21; personal considerations, 215–30

Clinton, Bill: ads, 36, 39, 67, 69, 88, 126, 127, 131–34, 160, 161, 182–86, 192–94, 201–3, 269; attack ads, 77, 128, 146, 161, 171, 175, 197; campaign abilities, 15, 80, 101, 137–38, 201–3, 226–27, 234, 243; character, 58–59, 78, 86, 113, 182–203, 222–24, 227, 234; considerations, 164, 221–30; conventions, 67, 87; coverage of, 58, 101–15, 131–48, 157–58, 170; debates, 67, 71, 87, 234; emotions and, 78–79; general election coverage, 70; horse-race coverage, 110; image, 19, 67, 75, 78–79, 86, 126, 143, 173, 175, 180, 203, 213–16, 221–23, 234, 243; interviewees on, 59, 79, 130, 189, 191–93, 213–15; and issues, 57, 58, 69–67, 76, 78,